Islamic Veiling in Legal Discourse

Islamic Veiling in Legal Discourse looks at relevant law and related discourses in order to examine the assumptions and limits of the debates around the issue of Islamic veiling, which has become so topical in recent years. For some, Islamic veiling indicates a lack of autonomy, the oppression of women and the threat of Islamic radicalism to western secular values. For others, it suggests a positive autonomous choice, a new kind of gender equality and a legitimate exercise of one's freedom of religion – a treasured right in democratic societies. This book finds that, across seemingly diverse legal and political traditions, a set of discursive frameworks – the preoccupation with autonomy and choice; the imperative of gender equality; and a particular western understanding of religion and religious subjectivity – shapes the positions of both proponents and opponents of various restrictions on Islamic veiling. Rather than take a position on one or the other side of the debate, the book focuses on the frameworks themselves, highlighting their limitations.

Anastasia Vakulenko is a lecturer in law at the University of Birmingham.

Islamic Veiling in Legal Discourse

Anastasia Vakulenko

Routledge
Taylor & Francis Group
a GlassHouse Book

First published 2012
by Routledge
2 Park Square, Milton Park, Abingdon, Oxon OX14 4RN

Simultaneously published in the USA and Canada
by Routledge
711 Third Avenue, New York, NY 10017

Routledge is an imprint of the Taylor & Francis Group, an informa business

A GlassHouse book

British Library Cataloguing in Publication Data
A catalogue record for this book is available from the British Library

Library of Congress Cataloging in Publication Data
Vakulenko, Anastasia.
Islamic veiling in legal discourse / Anastasia Vakulenko.
p. cm.
Includes bibliographical references and index.
1. Hijab (Islamic clothing) 2. Purdah. 3. Veils–Religious aspects–Islam. 4. Muslim women–Clothing. 5. Muslim women–Conduct of life. 6. Clothing and dress–Religious aspects–Islam. 7. Sex discrimination. I. Title.
KBP528.H54V35 2012
346.01'34–dc23

2011052590

ISBN: 978-0-415-53336-2 (pbk)
ISBN: 978-0-415-56550-9 (hbk)
ISBN: 978-0-203-11759-0 (ebk)

Typeset in Baskerville
by Wearset Ltd, Boldon, Tyne and Wear

First issued in paperback in 2013

Contents

Preface vii

1 **Islamic veiling in legal discourse: an introduction** 1
1 'Islamic veiling' 2
2 The approach of the book 6
3 The book's critical method 7
4 Islamic veiling and 'legal discourse' 10
5 Structure of the book 12

2 **Islamic veiling restrictions: an overview** 15
1 France 16
2 United Kingdom 22
3 Germany 33
4 The Netherlands 36
5 Norway 40
6 European Court of Human Rights 42
7 United Nations 51
8 Concluding remarks 55

3 **Autonomy and choice** 56
1 Islamic veiling as a lack of autonomy and choice 56
2 Islamic veiling as a positive choice 64
3 What is wrong with autonomy and choice? 69
4 Towards a different view of religious agency 73
5 Concluding remarks 78

4 **Gender equality** 80
1 Islamic veiling as subordination of women 81
2 Islamic veiling as emancipation of women 90
3 What is wrong with the gender equality argument? 95

4 Why gender equality at all? 105
5 Concluding remarks 111

5 Religion and secularism 112
1 Islamic veiling as dangerous Islamic radicalism 113
2 Islamic veiling as a legitimate exercise of freedom of religion 123
3 How is freedom of religion understood in law? 126
4 What is wrong with the secular view(s) of religion? 132
5 Concluding remarks 141

Bibliography 142
Table of legislation and international instruments 155
Table of cases 157
Index 161

Preface

This book evolved considerably over the time that it took to complete. Originally it was envisaged as a more or less straightforward case-study on gender, religion and human rights. As Islamic veiling was beginning to become quite a prominent issue in news reports across Europe, it seemed a prime candidate for a critical feminist analysis, with the gender aspect being both obvious and neglected. Much has changed since then. On the one hand, the controversy surrounding the issue shows no signs of subsiding – quite the contrary – with yet more restrictive legal measures being passed in several countries, generating more public discontent and debate. On the other hand, there is no longer a shortage of feminist voices analysing and commenting on Islamic veiling from within different feminist traditions. Still, it is an inexhaustible issue that constantly challenges our familiar ways of seeing the world. As my own thinking has evolved, interestingly I have found myself less driven by a feminist agenda (although by no means could this be said to be exhausted), and more by a certain sense of inadequacy when it comes to theorising anything to do with religion – a sense heightened by both scholarly explorations and personal experience.

The result is a book written from a particular critical perspective purporting to complicate the critiques that preceded it. Admittedly, the problem with calling something 'critical' is that it could mean almost anything, yet nothing in particular. Although I go to some length in Chapter 1 elaborating on what I mean by critique, it is perhaps more accurate, and simpler, to say that the book is written from *a* perspective. As any other, my perspective is limited by its own assumptions, as well as constraints of time and format. Inevitably, one adjusts one's views and agendas with the passage of time – a process that always tends to be ahead of the time it takes to produce a book. Still, it is hoped that the book's arguments will be seen as offering new, if not exactly revolutionary, ways of reflecting on the seemingly familiar.

Small parts of Chapters 2, 3 and 5 may have previously appeared in the following articles: 'Gender Equality as an Essential French Value: The Case of *Mme M*' (2009), *Human Rights Law Review*, 9(1): 143; 'Liberalism,

Civilisation and the (Non-)Oxymoronic Limits of Tolerance' (2008), *International Journal of Law in Context*, 3: 323; 'Islamic Dress in Human Rights Jurisprudence: A Critique of Current Trends' (2007), *Human Rights Law Review*, 7: 717; and '"Islamic Headscarves" and the European Convention on Human Rights: An Intersectional Perspective' (2007), *Social & Legal Studies*, 16: 183. I am grateful to the publishers for their permissions to use these in the current text.

I have been very fortunate to benefit from the kind help, understanding and encouragement of many people while writing this book. Sadly, my Grandfather did not live to see it in print, but he will always be an inspiration. My family and friends have given me unconditional support, which is much appreciated. I am indebted to Professor Thérèse Murphy for her advice and guidance during my time at the University of Nottingham where the book was conceived. The book was completed at the University of Birmingham and has benefited from numerous academic interactions with colleagues there and elsewhere. I particularly thank Stewart Motha for enriching exchanges that helped to develop some of the book's ideas. Tawhida Ahmed and Mark Flear read drafts and provided career encouragement and enduring friendship, in their very different ways. Thank you to Gulara Guliyeva for words of wisdom and to Judith Prais for wonderful support and academic spirit at the time when it was most needed. Benjamin Nash created the specially commissioned artwork that made the cover of the book, which is a rare privilege. Thanks to Melanie Fortmann-Brown for her efficient and patient editorial support. I am also thankful to the Fehler family for their generous hospitality and kindness (and the occasional ideological challenge) during the crucial final stages of writing the book. And finally very special thanks to Raphael Prais who has been the best critic of the manuscript I could have wished for. The book would have been much better had I taken on board all of his comments.

London, May 2012

Chapter 1

Islamic veiling in legal discourse

An introduction

A curious story was reported in 2010. A group of women belonging to the ultra-orthodox Jewish community of Edah Haredit in Ramat Beit Shemesh, Israel took it upon themselves to advance the standards of modesty by wearing what had come to be known as the 'Jewish burka'. They believed that this attire, consisting of many layers of fabric to conceal the shape of the body and a veil to cover the face completely, would help bring holiness into this world and accelerate the coming of the Messiah. The women received a hostile reaction from almost everyone, including their own community, mainstream press and the Israeli state. A few got arrested trying to board buses as they were mistaken for Muslim suicide bombers. Their own husbands asked the rabbinical court of Edah Haredit to interfere and ban the practice. The court ruled against the burka in no uncertain terms, declaring that this novel practice had no basis in Jewish law and teaching.[1] According to the rabbis, the women were seriously misguided in their belief that their extreme modesty was bringing redemption to the world. Rather, their attire was declared to be extremely immodest as they attracted much unwanted attention to themselves and thus achieved the opposite of their aim, committing 'severe transgressions in sexual matters' (Blomfield, 30 July 2010; Jeffay, 29 July 2010).

Despite its extremity and uniqueness, this odd episode is in many ways a mini mirror image of the contemporary debate on the accepta-

1 Covering the face is not unprecedented in Jewish history as the matriarchs Rebecca, Leah and Rachel veiled themselves at certain junctures of the biblical narrative. Yet this tends to be attributed to the pre-Jewish Semitic customs prevailing at the time, rather than a precept of Judaism. The face has special importance in the Jewish tradition, being considered a crucial medium connecting one's inner self to the world, and hence the normative argument against concealing it. Although face-covering was also practised among pre-Islamic Arabs, it has a much stronger normative basis in Islam proper. Still, there is no universal consensus within Islam as to whether the face *must* be covered, and hence there is much greater variation in Muslim women's veiling practices.

bility of various forms of *Islamic* veiling. The reaction of 'progressive' Jewish press to the Beit Shemesh affair was that the orthodox obsession with modesty had gone mad and the rabbinic preoccupation with suppressing female sexuality was to blame (e.g. Shaviv, 18 April 2011; Sztokman, 7 April 2010). Yet, the radicals who adopted the 'Jewish burka' clearly went too far even by the standards of their own, ultra-orthodox community, whose ways of dress would already be considered very strict by most. Far from being coerced by men, they appeared to be following a certain Beruria Keren nicknamed 'Taliban Mother' by Israeli press (e.g. Edelman, 19 July 2009), donning the burka in defiance of their husbands and rabbinic authorities. Furthermore, the trend was clearly new.

One finds much more variation in Islam than in Judaism as to what exactly is necessary or desirable when it comes to female modesty, and thus the Edah Haredit religious reasoning might not apply in an Islamic context. But theological differences aside, the Beit Shemesh scenario has much in common with various Islamic veiling controversies as they have played out in Europe and elsewhere. In most of these, the women seem to go, in one form or another, against the grain of feminism, acceptable forms of religiosity and modernity itself. Many engage in this seemingly anti-feminist behaviour in spite of, and even against, the wishes of their often more moderate husbands and community leaders, highlighting the radical nature of their 'false consciousness'. This book aims to explore these contradictions. It tries to make sense of underlying assumptions and forces that shape the debate around Islamic veiling, which has captured popular imagination in the West over the last decade or so.

I 'Islamic veiling'

The amount of attention the issue of veiling has received recently may seem puzzling and disproportionate. At first sight, this is merely a mode of dress adopted by some Muslim women, who themselves may be a minority within their minority cultural religious group. Yet it soon becomes clear to anyone who has ever read or seen a news item reporting yet another legal measure restricting Islamic veiling that the issue is at the crossing of two important dimensions of human identity: gender and religion. Veiling is an obviously gendered practice as it particularly affects women. There are religious requirements of modesty for both men and women in most religious and cultural traditions, but it is safe to say that women are invariably subject to more extensive standards of what exactly needs to be covered and how. Veiling is also an issue that is largely associated with Islam today. That is not to say that the ideal of modesty is not important in other religions. An orthodox Jewish woman is expected to be covered from neck to knees and to cover her hair if married (although the Beit Shemesh practice of concealing the face was clearly considered excessive). Rather, the point of describing veiling practices as *Islamic* is that it is specifically Muslim dress codes that have provided abundant material for legal intervention, news reportage and academic commentary. This is not surprising as all things Muslim have become an intense site of antagonism and incomprehension in the post-9/11 era. At the same time, veiling practices have burgeoned among Muslim women living in the West.

The Islamic practice of veiling is sometimes referred to in modern English as *hijab*, which is a recent borrowing from Arabic to denote specifically Muslim dress codes. Hijab (ħijāb) is a term from classical Arabic, meaning covering, veiling, screening or sheltering. The original meaning of the word did not necessarily refer to a sartorial practice, rather denoting the idea of 'a spatial curtain that divides or provides privacy' (Martin 2003: 721). The Koran instructed that male believers should speak to the Prophet's wives behind a hijab (Sura 33:53). It is thought that later Muslim societies generalised this injunction and extended it to all Muslim women, rather than just the wives of the Prophet. Thus, the hijab has become linked with modesty, encompassing 'both men's and women's gaze, gait, garments, and genitalia' (Martin 2003: 721).

The Koranic verse that instructs Muslim women to observe modesty in their dress is Sura (chapter) 24 (*An-Noor*) (The Light) āya (verse) 31, which reads:

> And speak to the believing women that they refrain their eyes, and observe continence; and that they display not their ornaments, except those which are external; and that they throw their veils over their bosoms, and display not their ornaments, except to their husbands or their fathers, or their husbands' fathers, or their sons, or their husbands' sons, or their brothers, or their brothers' sons, or their sisters' sons, or their women, or their slaves, or male domestics who have no natural force, or to children who note not women's nakedness. And let them not strike their feet together, so as to discover their hidden ornaments. And be ye all turned to God, O ye Believers! that it may be well with you.

Sura 33 (*Al-Ahzab*) (The Confederates) āya 59 suggests that a veil should be worn by Muslim women to distinguish them from non-believing women:

> O Prophet! speak to thy wives and to thy daughters, and to the wives of the Faithful, that they let their veils fall low. Thus will they more

> easily be known, and they will not be affronted. God is Indulgent, Merciful![2]

It is believed that guidance for covering the entire body, except for the hands, feet and face, is found in the Hadith, which were developed over some three centuries after the death of the Prophet Mohammed. The Hadith are traditions concerning the practices of the early Muslim community, accepted as canonical by Sunni Muslims. Despite some several indications in the Hadith as to what dress standard is considered to be acceptable for women, there is no universal agreement on this among Muslims. In this spectrum, covering the entire body and face is the most extensive standard.

At present, different types of Islamic veiling are practised by Muslim women, which varies according to the individual's religious persuasion as well as ethnic and cultural background. The word hijab is most often used today to refer to the Koranic injunction that women should dress modestly. And thus, it is at times used interchangeably with 'Islamic veiling' in the book.

The different types of the hijab merit a brief explanation. One of the most popular contemporary forms of the hijab is the *Islamic headscarf*, which is a piece of cloth covering a woman's hair and neck, usually clasped or tied tightly at the back. Although the headscarf has been referred to as a *hijab* in some of the English language literature, the book tries to avoid this usage as the primary meaning of the word is closer to 'veiling'. There are different types of headscarves, with some fitting less closely than others. The Arabic word for headscarf is *khimār (khumūr)*, which usually denotes a circular type of headscarf, which comes down to the waist. The *shayla* and the *dupatta*, popular in the Gulf and South Asia respectively, are loosely wrapped over the head. The *chador*, common in Iran, is a larger version of the *khimār*, wrapped around the head and whole body in a semicircular way. *Jilbāb* is the Arabic word for a cloak, or an outer garment covering the whole body except for the hands. The *abaya*, worn in Saudi Arabia and other Gulf countries, is a large square of fabric draped from the shoulders or head, or a long caftan covering the entire body. The *niqab (nikaab)* is a veil that covers the entire head and face, with an open slit for the eyes. The word *niqab* primarily refers to face covering; however, it is also often used to denote a type of veil covering both the entire face and the body. The *burka (burqa)* is considered to be the most extreme form of the hijab as it was rigidly enforced in Afghanistan throughout the Taliban rule. It is a single garment covering the entire body from top to toe, with a grille over the eyes to allow the woman to see through.

2 The Arabic word translated as 'veils' in this verse is *jilbāb*. See the discussion below.

This selection suggests that there is considerable variety in Muslim women's sartorial practices. The book refers to particular types of Islamic dress where necessary, but at most times it uses the general terms 'Islamic veiling', 'hijab' or 'Islamic dress' more or less interchangeably. It purports to do so in a purely descriptive way. It is possible to perceive 'veiling' as a loaded term as currently it is associated, rightly or wrongly, with specifically Islamic ways of dressing, as opposed to generic modest dress. But the usage is still appropriate in the context of this book: it explores the reactions that Islamic veiling has provoked in western law and surrounding discourses, rather than providing a normative assessment of the practice itself. It thus uses the term 'veiling' simply to refer, in as neutral a way as possible, to various practices and ways of covering some or most of a woman's body, hair and/or face.

This is not to erase the differences between the different forms of dress, but rather to emphasise the commonality of issues raised in the contemporary legal, political and popular debate around them. As the book hopes to show, legal (as well as journalistic, academic and popular) responses to various forms of Islamic veiling across various places have much in common, regardless of the precise type of dress at issue. This is so even if different jurisdictions 'draw the line' at different points on the spectrum of covering. France and Turkey have been known as Europe's most intolerant of veiling practices, with legal restrictions in place even for headscarves. Britain, on the other hand, has been much more 'moderate', traditionally tolerating headscarves, but full face or body coverings became a legal issue recently. Although there is something to be said for these differences, the book concentrates on commonalities of reasoning underlying the legal measures.

Such legal developments, in domestic jurisdictions as well as international human rights regimes, have made an increasingly frequent appearance in western media. The growing worldwide popularity of veiling practices has provoked abundant academic, including legal, commentary (recent books include Ahmed 2011; Bowen 2006; Bullock 2007; Howard 2011; Joppke 2009; Mahmood 2005; McGoldrick 2006; Scott 2007; Tarlo 2010). There are several significant strands in this literature. There is a bulk of doctrinal commentary exploring the compatibility of Islamic veiling restrictions with international human rights standards (e.g. Howard 2011; McGoldrick 2006; Ssenyonjo 2007). On the other hand, there are discernible voices criticising veiling as a misogynist practice perpetuated by male-dominated religious ideology (e.g. Mernissi 1991; Fourest 2005). Others have enthusiastically defended Islamic veiling (e.g. Bullock 2007; Tarlo 2010). Further, there is critique of Islamic veiling restrictions as a symptom of liberalism's failure to resolve the challenge of Muslim difference, written from both liberal and legal pluralist perspectives (e.g. Bowen 2006; Joppke 2009).

2 The approach of the book

To some extent, this book draws on and adds to that literature. Yet more significantly, it pursues a different line of enquiry. It does not provide a comprehensive doctrinal analysis of legal developments concerning Islamic veiling and is not interested in the question of whether or not Islamic veiling restrictions are actually compatible with human rights standards. It does not side with either proponents or opponents of Islamic veiling or associated legal restrictions. Rather, it explores, first, what these opposing sides of the debate have in common. Second – and both more tentatively and more ambitiously – it examines the underlying assumptions made and attempts to point towards a possible different way of looking at matters.

In sum, the debate goes like this. Those who oppose the right of Muslim women to cover themselves consider that Islamic veiling practices indicate a lack of autonomy, the oppression of women and the threat of Islamic radicalism to western secular values. Those who support it argue, in contrast, that veiling is a positive autonomous choice, a new kind of gender equality and a legitimate exercise of one's freedom of religion – a treasured right in democratic societies. This book hopes to make it clear that, across seemingly diverse legal and political traditions, a set of discursive frameworks – the preoccupation with autonomy and choice; the imperative of gender equality; and a particular western understanding of religion and religious subjectivity – shapes the positions of both proponents and opponents of various restrictions on Islamic veiling. Thus, the book focuses on these frameworks themselves, highlighting their indispensability, limitations and possible repressive tendencies.

At first sight, it may seem like a good thing that both sides agree on the terms of the debate. Surely that makes reasoned argument possible, just like two mathematicians might agree on the rules of maths, but come to a different conclusion on the substance of their dispute, disagreeing until one overcomes the other with logic and reason. But what if the shared assumptions are not exactly incorrect, but somewhat limiting and repressive? What if they are really dictated by one side and the other has no alternative but to build its whole argument to fit in with them? If it did not, its point would not get across or even be comprehensible to its more powerful interlocutor that sets the assumptions. Such a situation is constraining for both sides and perpetuates continuous missing of each other. It occludes the possibility of a 'third option', which would be more attuned to the richness of human experience and ideas. It is the option that may remain forever slightly beyond our grasp, but we know it is there.

In concentrating on these three frameworks of autonomy, gender equality and secularism, the book does not claim that this is the only or the best way to see the debate. Indeed, there are many collisions between them, and it is perfectly possible to see, for example, autonomy as the main analytical framework, subsuming gender equality and freedom of religion. However, the book offers its own perspective. Acknowledging the interconnectedness of its three frameworks, it perceives all three as meriting attention in their own right. It is through this perspective that it contributes to broader critical theory that engages with underlying questions of human rights, gender, culture, religion and secularism.

Essentially, the book asks: *what has Islamic veiling come to represent in legal and surrounding discourses in the current historical-political moment?* The book is predominantly concerned with the effects and implications of debating Islamic veiling within a contemporary liberal, secular, human rights context. It is mainly about the debate as it is conducted in the West, mainly Europe, as that is where the issue has been most topical and legal responses most illuminating. As such, its analysis may be somewhat western-centric, but that is an unavoidable consequence of such a focus.

3 The book's critical method

The book is a kind of critical analysis that implies engagement with the very parameters of the debate, rather than advocating straightforward legal change. Its method was initially inspired by the work of Wendy Brown, and in particular *States of Injury* (1995). As explained below, the book builds on some of Brown's seminal concepts and ideas, but it also departs from them, finding further inspiration elsewhere. Ultimately, the book aims to provide its own perspective on the Islamic veiling debate and its own take on the issues at heart.

Engaging with the parameters of the debate is not the same as claiming somehow to transcend these parameters. Rather, the method adopted in the book can be described as guided by the idea of counterpoint. This has been described as:

> a deliberate practice of multiplicity that exceeds simple opposition and does not carry the mythological or methodological valence of dialectics or contradiction. At once open-ended and tactical, counterpoint emanates from and promotes an anti-hegemonic sensibility and requires a modest and carefully styled embrace of multiplicity in which contrasting elements, featured simultaneously, do not simply war, harmonize, blend or compete but rather bring out the complexity that cannot emerge through a monolithic or single melody. This complexity does not add up to a whole but, rather, sets off a theme by providing an elsewhere to it; indeed, it can even highlight and thus contest dominance through its work of juxtaposition.
>
> (Brown 2003: 367)

Thus, counterpoint provides a technique for a critical analysis, which does not insist on the correctness of its approach. Rather, it presents a set of observations *in counterpoint* to other arguments advanced on the subject. It thus offers perspective, rather than objectivity or comprehensiveness. The book chooses to explore certain angles and advance certain arguments and perspectives in counterpoint to some currently prevailing positions or approaches. This does not necessarily imply disagreement with those; rather, it complicates them by 'providing an elsewhere' to them. Certain perspectives are ultimately advanced in the book as they are believed to be either under-represented in the current debate or strategically desirable from a 'critical' point of view.

Of course, there is only so much that can be said on an issue as topical as Islamic veiling, without repeating others. Yet critical scholarship is best seen as developing incrementally and in a spiral fashion, rather than as a circular or linear movement. It is thus hoped that the book makes an original contribution to the Islamic veiling debate, as well as critical and feminist scholarship more generally, as it purports to emphasise angles which have not been explored sufficiently in the debate or merit further elaboration in different contexts. The book's analysis certainly shows that issues salient in the Islamic veiling debate are of broader relevance.

In this connection, it is relevant to say a few words on the value of critique in general. Critique has been 'variously charged with being academic, impractical, merely critical, unattuned to the political exigencies at hand, intellectually indulgent, easier than fixing things or saying what is to be done' (Brown and Halley 2002: 25). This is not a vision shared in this book. For a more positive vision of critique, it is useful briefly to highlight its genealogy in western thought. Critique has its origins in the ancient Greek *krisis*, which was 'a jurisprudential term identified with the art of making distinctions, an art considered essential to judging and rectifying an alleged disorder in or of the democracy' (Brown 2005: 5). Although the modernist usages of 'critique' and 'criticism' in Western European languages have etymologically travelled away from the ancient Greek usage, '[the] quality of urgency, [the] depiction of critique as nonoptional in the restoration of the organism's or a polity's health' is still salient in the work of the great 19th century European philosophers (ibid.: 7).

Although much of the critical (in particular, Hegelian–Marxist) tradition has presumed the revelation of *truth* as critique's ultimate object, it is crucial that this is not an indispensable or even a necessary attribute of critique. Rather, the aim is 'to reveal subterranean structures or aspects of a particular discourse' (Brown and Halley 2002: 26). In this way, the promise of critique is 'not objectivity but perspective' (ibid.). This is exactly what this book aims to do.

The implication is that critique does not guarantee outcomes or resolutions, an aspect well worth affirming. This is in contrast with assertions such as 'deconstructive analyses can be of no use *unless the deconstructive arguments assume the existence of an alternative: one that is more just than the one being deconstructed*' (Marshall 2006a: 33, citing Balkin 1994). To take a prominent example, Marx's early work indicates that he did not know in advance that he would arrive at dialectical materialism and political economy as the alternative to left Hegelianism. Rather, he found his way to these '*through* the process of subjecting political and philosophical idealism to critique' (Brown and Halley 2002: 27). Critique is thus in a certain sense disorienting, which does not necessarily mean suspension of political and intellectual values or normative judgment. At times, though, there is indeed much to be said for 'taking a break', for suspending judgment and resisting the impulse to subject everything to analysis immediately. This is what the book tries to do at junctures where critical judgment seems premature, advocating critical distance instead.

Crucially, critique gives one an opportunity to *examine positions*, rather than be trapped in compulsive position-taking. As Brown and Halley put it, 'critique affords us something to do besides voting for "neither of the above"' (ibid.: 29). This 'something to do' can be conducive to reworking current political and intellectual constraints through their articulation, through the very act of bringing them to light. Critique is thus a process – not of rejection, but of thorough scrutiny and reengagement: for it is precisely the importance and omnipresence of the object of critique that does not allow us to reject or discard it as insignificant (Brown 2005: 16). Rather, critique is a practice of continued revaluation and renewal of the object, which is ultimately connected with the object's transformation. In this way, the book's engagement with the three frames of the Islamic veiling debate – autonomy and choice; gender equality; and secularism – does not reject them. Rather, its scrutiny means reassessment and reaffirmation of their importance.

Finally, there is the problem of 'untimely' critique – that is, critique that is perceived as strategically undesirable at a given political historical moment. Tarlo (2005), for example, has described the difficulty of engaging in a critique of Muslim radicalisation in the post-9/11 era, when any criticism of Islam may be perceived as counterproductive. There is a possibility that certain arguments in this book, such as the issue taken with Islamic feminist approaches in Chapter 4, may be seen as conducive to reactionary co-optation, in a climate when anything to do with Islam is expected to be approached with great sensitivity. Similarly, some might perceive the book's reexamining of the normative pursuit of gender equality more generally as anti-feminist. It is hoped that the book works with enough nuance to deflect such possibilities. More to the point, it is believed that the existence of any such danger ought not to outweigh the importance of reassessing and reengaging with difficult subject matters. Any other position would effectively remove such uncomfortable issues from scrutiny. According to Brown, 'untimely critique' can itself be 'an effective intellectual and political strategy', 'a bid to reset time', 'to breathe new possibility into the age' (Brown 2005: 4–5). Indeed, critique is 'the art of not being governed quite so much' (Foucault 2001: 193).

4 Islamic veiling and 'legal discourse'

The point of examining Islamic veiling in *legal discourse* is that it is legal restrictions on this practice that have sparked controversy. The wearing of Islamic dress has been subjected to increasing legal regulation in Europe over recent years. The book takes the repressive power of law as a given. It does not engage with law in a black letter way – that is, it does not seek to establish whether certain laws are compatible with others. It is, however, interested in the question of how legal reasoning concerning Islamic veiling restrictions is constituted. In other words, what underlying assumptions inform the legislators and judges who make and interpret the law concerning Islamic veiling? To answer that question, the book looks at surrounding academic and popular commentary, as well as law. In doing so, it does not necessarily assume that legislators, judges and lawyers making arguments on behalf of their clients are always conscious makers of the discursive outcomes their words produce. Rather, it treats them as agents who operate in broader contexts of western liberalism, secularism, legal formalism and human rights culture.

As to the law itself, a great chunk of the examined material is human rights case-law, including that under the European Convention of Human Rights (ECHR). Indeed, human rights play a crucial part in the Islamic veiling debate, both rhetorically and practically. Legal challenges to various Islamic veiling restrictions have primarily been articulated through human rights provisions, both in national legal systems and within international human rights regimes. Human rights can be assumed to form the core of the legal discourse in which the debate unfolds. It thus merits some special attention to foreground the book's analysis.

The paradox of human rights is well known. On the one hand, universal rights operate on the assumption of the autonomous, rational, 'relentlessly self-interested subject of liberalism' (Brown 1995: 25), which naturalises differences between people and discursively erases the disadvantage hinging on those differences. On the other, rights refashioned for and by the *particular* subject, as pertaining to a specific identity (be it rights for women, blacks or gays, or, in the case of this book, Muslim women), further entrench what Brown calls the identity's constitutive injury, as well as the discourses that frame it. Human rights thus become linked with the anti-emancipatory function of identity, reminiscent of Nietzsche's slave morality (1969), in which the subject feels morally right and politically righteous *because* s/he is disadvantaged. According to Nietzsche, *ressenti-*

ment channels the subject's otherwise unendurable suffering into 'a negative form of action', deploring the nature's 'true reaction', 'that of deeds', as well as denouncing power and action themselves as morally wrong. Thus, Brown characterises identity politics as 'the moralizing revenge of the powerless, "the triumph of the weak as weak"', which 'is as likely to seek generalized political paralysis … as it is to seek its own or collective liberation through empowerment' (1995: 70, 66–67, 71).

Human rights action can never adequately address historical disadvantages befalling minorities, although it can be rhetorically empowering and pragmatically useful. It is noteworthy, however, that human rights has become the unconditional ideology of (purportedly universal) western modernity, indeed the quintessence of its project, alongside other hegemonic discourses such as secularism (Asad 2003, 2000). A recent collection on the anthropology of human rights summarises that 'human rights is to modernity what culture is to tradition', explaining that '[a]s a language of social transformation and even emancipation, rights interventions are teleologically focused on the transformation of tradition to modernity, and of culture to rights' (Rajagopal 2007: 274). According to Kennedy, '[e]ven within the liberal West, other useful emancipatory vocabularies (including the solidarities of socialism, Christianity, the labor movement, and so forth) are diminished by the consolidation of human rights as the international expression of *the* Western liberal tradition' (2002: 114).

The contemporary ascendancy of human rights also involves a certain conflation between local and international discourses of human rights. This conflation has been theorised as the 'global diffusion of norms' (Knop 1999; Moran 2004, 2006; Kumm 2006), which implies growing interpenetration of the different systems of legal norms and related discourses. Domestic rights frameworks increasingly embrace 'international standards', which is achieved not just through classic incorporation, but also through a range of innovative ways, such as judges using international human rights law as a 'persuasive' authority (Moran 2004). On the other hand, it has become common for international adjudicating bodies to refer to the practice of other international bodies and/or domestic courts.

The upshot is that a rigid distinction between the 'domestic' and 'international' jurisdictions becomes somewhat artificial in the discussion of human rights. As the burgeoning literature on law and globalisation and on the interaction between the local and global dimensions of human rights demonstrates, the interplay between the universal language of human rights and local belonging often proves key to the success of 'new' social movements (see, for example, Stychin 2003, 2004). International law has firmly become 'the official language of human rights, quite distinct from customary or even constitutional rights regimes' (Rajagopal 2007: 275), to the point of 'this language [being] the only, sole, legitimate discourse of resistance recognised by law' (ibid.). Accordingly, this book adopts a methodology that does not make rigid distinctions between the domestic and international dimensions of human rights in its analysis of the Islamic veiling debate. It does, however, provide an account (in Chapter 2) of how Islamic veiling cases have been treated in different jurisdictions and international human rights regimes, emphasising distinctive features of such systems, where appropriate.

Rather than simply a system of legal norms, the book mobilises a vision of law and human rights as an important 'site of conversation', infused with other discursive dimensions, such as political and popular culture. Hence, in its overview of Islamic veiling developments, Chapter 2 not only provides a bare account of relevant laws and cases, but also puts them in context, by highlighting some historical background as well as media and public reactions. Thus, the analysis laid out in Chapters 3, 4 and 5 ought to be read with such a broader understanding of law and human rights in mind.

5 Structure of the book

The book has a fairly straightforward structure. Chapter 2 gives an overview of recent developments concerning Islamic veiling in both law and the surrounding public debates. This includes developments in France, the United Kingdom, Germany, the Netherlands and Norway, as well as those within the system of the European Convention on Human Rights (ECHR) and United Nations human rights treaties systems. This largely descriptive account does not cover all relevant developments or jurisdictions in which the Islamic veiling issue has arisen. Rather, it intends to give a good sense of such developments, which then provides ground for their actual analysis, pursued in Chapters 3, 4 and 5. By its very nature, such an account is in constant need of updating as new Islamic veiling restrictions are being introduced with increasing frequency across Europe. However, this stream of developments shows a steady continuation, and even strengthening, of the trends highlighted in Chapters 3, 4 and 5. Thus, any developments that have been missed out are not likely to invalidate the ensuing analysis.

Chapters 3, 4 and 5 are the most important chapters of the book, as it is there that the analysis of the Islamic veiling debate is actually carried out. Each of these three chapters takes up one aspect salient in the debate and explores it in some detail. Chapter 3 is thus concerned with the rhetoric of autonomy and choice, while Chapter 4 looks at the general gender equality argument, as it is deployed in the debate. Chapter 5 is concerned with religion and secularism as the background to the Islamic veiling debate. All three chapters are guided by the idea of counterpoint in both their structure and substance, as described earlier. The three chapters' analysis draws on the material set out in Chapter 2, engaging with it in some detail.

Chapter 3, which examines the rhetoric of autonomy and choice, first considers the arguments of those who consider Islamic veiling to signify a blatant lack of autonomy and thus to merit discouragement, if not prohibition. This argument tends to prevail in the debate. The chapter then proceeds to consider the opposite argument – namely, that Islamic veiling is a positive choice and, as such, ought to be celebrated. This kind of argument provides an obvious counterpoint to the first, prevailing position. Having discussed both sides of the debate, the chapter then employs a different strategy by highlighting commonalities and problems with arguments on both sides of the debate and, in particular, with the very frames of autonomy and choice which currently configure the Islamic veiling issue. It suggests that obsessive scrutiny of Muslim women's autonomy is unhelpful as it assumes a belief in absolute free choice, which hinders one's ability to live out one's agency meaningfully and relate to the world around. Finally, it advances some alternatives to conceptualising agency, which do not necessarily revolve around the classic liberal notion of autonomy.

Chapter 4 adopts an analogous approach, but concentrates on a different aspect: the deployment, as well as normative value, of gender equality. First, it outlines the currently prevailing position that Islamic veiling is incompatible with the principle of gender equality as such (as opposed to the autonomy of an individual Muslim woman). Second, it sketches out the opposite, if minority, view – namely, that Islamic veiling signifies women's empowerment and emancipation, and thus is pro- rather than anti-equality. Third, the chapter goes into some length to bring out commonalities and problems with both these arguments. It explores the extent to which mainstream western feminism has been successful in making (a certain understanding of) gender equality an unconditional normative value against which all gender practices, including Islamic veiling, are to be assessed. That is linked to the longstanding western habit of utilising feminist rhetoric in racist and imperialist ways. On the other hand, and in contrast with what is claimed by many Islamic feminists, the values of women who veil may not square perfectly with feminist ideas. Importantly, the chapter engages with broader implications of the normative status that feminism has – at least rhetorically – achieved in mainstream legal and political discourse, suggesting that this may be problematic and in some ways limiting.

Chapter 5 explores the nature of contemporary secularism and its treatment of religion as these are vividly played out in the Islamic veiling debate. First, it sketches out the argument in support of legal intervention as Islamic veiling is perceived as a symptom of unacceptable religious fundamentalism. The chapter proceeds by outlining the arguments of those who defend Islamic veiling as a legitimate exercise of freedom of religion, which is an important human right. It then explores common assumptions behind both these arguments and why they are problematic. The chapter's point is that the currently dominant model of secularism, far from being universal, represents a rather particular historical formation and political rationality. It finds that contemporary secularism, by and large, encourages a certain 'compartmentalisation' and transformation of religion, rather than its total eradication. Refusal to downgrade religion from an encompassing way of life to a mere human right is associated with backwardness, irrationality, religious fundamentalism and even terrorism. Accordingly, Islamic religious practices, such as veiling, are being 'reinterpreted', with various degrees of persuasiveness, in order to repudiate the charge of fundamentalism and be made compatible with the dominant understanding of religion and secularism. Although Islam certainly enjoys a special status in the current political moment, the chapter considers contemporary secular understanding of religion more generally as such more illuminating. Theoretical critique is enhanced by more pragmatic criticisms of the currently prevalent, legalistic treatment of freedom of religion as a human right like any other. A survey of relevant case-law (not limited to Islamic veiling) shows how the courts systematically miss the point of religion, artificially subdividing religious freedom into a right to have a religion and a right to 'manifest' it, the latter being subject to 'legitimate' restrictions.

As said before, the book purports to avoid taking positions on one or the other side of the debate. It is more interested in highlighting, engaging with and interrogating the frames within which the debate is conducted. It is, of course, sometimes hard to avoid agreeing or disagreeing with a certain legal measure: the reader may detect that the book considers many of the veiling restrictions unnecessary. That is, however, not the point or the impetus of the book. Rather, its objective is to stimulate reflection on the very way the issue is approached in legal discourse and the surrounding debate. The book critiques the frameworks of autonomy, gender equality and secularism, but it does not reject them altogether. Instead, it hopes to promote their more nuanced and reflective operation, as well as point tentatively towards a different way of looking at matters.

Chapter 2

Islamic veiling restrictions

An overview

This chapter provides a core context for the book's exploration. It contains an overview of recent legal developments restricting Islamic veiling. The chapter is intended to give a general sense of the debate as it is conducted at present, thus preparing ground for the analysis carried out in the rest of the book. This is done through an overview of law and cases, but some brief historical-political background is also given, as well as an impression of public, activist and media reactions as these surrounding discourses constitute an integral part of the debate. The account presented in the chapter is mostly descriptive and chronological, organised by jurisdiction.

A research project, sponsored by the European Union, classifies the current approaches of European states to regulating Islamic dress into three main categories, namely: 'established restrictive bans'; 'soft, selective regulations'; and 'no restrictive regulations' (Sauer and Rosenberger 2005). Albania, Azerbaijan, France and Turkey are the four countries that fall within the 'established restrictive ban' category. The 'soft, selective regulation' approach, meaning a line being drawn between headscarves and 'stricter' forms of dress, such as full-face veils and fully covering clothing, currently applies in the Netherlands, Finland and Sweden. The 'no regulation' category covers the United Kingdom, Austria, Germany, Spain, Switzerland, the Czech Republic, Greece, Hungary, Poland and Slovakia (Skjeie 2007: 138). Thus, the majority of European states do not formally regulate the wearing of Islamic dress in schools or elsewhere. Yet controversy has arisen across most of these countries, as well as at the level of the European Convention on Human Rights (ECHR) supervisory system, in recent years. Islamic dress has been the subject of controversy in other parts of the world also (Brown and Lombardi 2005; Deeb 2006; Mahabir 2004; Ong 1990, 2006; Ssenyonjo 2007), which is however outside the scope of this book.

The chapter proceeds by presenting an overview of such developments, without aiming to provide a fully comprehensive comparative analysis. Rather, the objective is to give a sense of the debate across a number of jurisdictions and international human rights regimes, which provide the most fertile ground for reflection. Thus, Part 1 of this chapter gives a general account of the veiling controversy which has been unfolding in France over the last few years. Part 2 is a summary of the recent Islamic dress litigation in the United Kingdom. Part 3 is concerned with the developments in Germany, while Parts 4 and 5 overview the situation in the Netherlands and Norway, respectively. Part 6 deals with the case-law of the (now superseded) European Commission on Human Rights (ECmHR) and European Court of Human Rights (ECtHR) under the European Convention on Human Rights. Part 7 considers the approach of the United Nations' (UN) quasi-judicial bodies, established under international human rights treaties.

1 France

The French veiling controversy has been the stuff of international news for some years now. Its distinctive feature is the ideology of *laïcité*, a foundational principle of the French Republic.[1] While this principle will be explored more relevantly in Chapter 5, at this stage it is useful to have an essential summary. *Laïcité* is only roughly equivalent to the more generic term 'secularism'. It denotes a much stronger normative aspiration of the total banishing of religion from the public sphere, completely relegating it to the realm of private, individually held, beliefs. At the same time, *laïcité* is supposed to provide 'a system of public order (*l'ordre public*) under which religious freedom can flourish' (McGoldrick 2006: 39), notably by providing protection from religious pressure and proselytism.

The origins of *laïcité* go back to the Great French Revolution of 1789, in which atheist ideology and anti-clericalism played a prominent part. The most important legal source is considered to be the Law of Separation, which was adopted in 1905 as a reaction to what was perceived as excessive powers of the Catholic Church, including its control of schools. It was as a result of that law that crucifixes were taken down in classrooms. Although the 1905 law was historically motivated by the troubled relationship between the French state and the Catholic Church, it purports to apply to all religions alike. At present, Muslims constitute the largest religious minority in France, amounting to approximately 10 per cent of the population. For the most part, Muslim presence in contemporary France is a historic consequence of the French colonisation of North Africa, with its largely Arab and Muslim populations.

1 Article 1 of the Constitution of the current Fifth Republic refers to France as a *laïque* republic: 'La France est une République indivisible, laïque, démocratique et sociale. Elle assure l'égalité devant la loi de tous les citoyens sans distinction d'origine, de race ou de religion. Elle respecte toutes les croyances. Son organisation est décentralisée.'

France takes pride in its tradition of respect for human rights and individual liberty, which is reflected in the French Republic's motto, *Liberté, Égalité, Fraternité* ('Liberty, Equality, Fraternity'). This tradition dates back to the 1789 Declaration of the Rights of Man and Citizen (which is part of the current, 1958 Constitution). The key values of individualism and equality underlie the French model of rights and citizenship. France is notorious, however, for not recognising the possibility that individual situations may be shaped by historic injustices resulting from group affiliations. The concept of group rights is 'alien on the surface to French legal and political traditions' (Berthou 2005: 315). Accordingly, France, although a party to the United Nations International Covenant on Civil and Political Rights (ICCPR), does not consider itself bound by Article 27 ICCPR, which deals with guaranteeing minority rights. Although the Human Rights Committee (HRC), the ICCPR monitoring body, has accepted France's declaration to this effect as a valid reservation under international law (*TK* v. *France; SG* v. *France*), it has expressed disagreement with the official French position that there are no ethnic, religious or linguistic minorities in France (Concluding Observations 1997: para 24; HRC General Comment 23, 1994).

An earlier instantiation of the current veiling controversy was the 1989 *affaire du foulard* (affair of the headscarf), when the Conseil d'État, the highest administrative quasi-judicial body in France, gave an advisory opinion, upon a request of the Minister for National Education, Youth and Sport, on the legality of banning headscarves in schools (Conseil d'État 1989). This was prompted by the actions of a school in Creil, a town outside Paris, which had expelled some female students for refusing to comply with such a ban that was introduced by the school. The Conseil d'État advised that the wearing of religious symbols is not by itself incompatible with the principle of *laïcité*, unless such symbols are flaunted in a way that would constitute pressure, proselytism or propaganda. A few years later, the Conseil d'État struck down several complete bans, having clarified that a ban would only be justified in extreme cases (Conseil d'État 1992). The Board of Experts of the International Religious Liberty Association (IRLA) notes that, between 1989 and 2004, the Conseil d'État had issued approximately fifty decisions and judgments in which it determined that 'Muslim school girls had a right to wear headscarves in state schools provided that they did not display the headscarves in a proselytizing manner and that they did not disrupt schools' (2005: Background, para 9).

This relatively benign stance on headscarves, which some commentators characterise as 'open neutrality' (e.g. Ssenyonjo 2007: 684), had, however, changed by 2003 when the Commission for the Reflection on the Application of the Principle of *Laïcité* in the Republic (*La Commission de Reflexion sur l'application du principe de la laïcité dans la République*) (the Stasi

Commission) was formed by the then President Jacques Chirac. The Commission's report, released in December 2003, recommended, among other measures, a ban in state schools on clothing and signs that manifest religious affiliations. One of the justifications for such a ban was that Muslim girls were coerced into wearing headscarves by their families and communities, which aggravated 'religious polarization and sexual discrimination', and thus a ban was necessary in order to safeguard 'public order'. Peer pressure and the need to protect girls who did not wish to wear the hijab were also cited as important factors for the introduction of such a ban.

These recommendations were followed, and on 10 February 2004 the French Parliament enacted a law which banned ostentatious (*ostensible*) religious signs and dress in public primary and secondary schools.[2] Although the law was phrased in neutral terms, it is clear that it has had a disproportionate impact on Islamic dress. In a televised speech prior to the introduction of the new law, the then President Chirac openly asserted that it was designed to particularly target the 'Islamist veil', 'an aggressive, ostentatious sign of religious proselytism' (BBC Online News, 17 December 2003).

The law caused a strong reaction among French Muslims. However, the Muslim community as a whole was divided on the issue as Muslims in France by no means present a coherent group. The French Council of the Muslim Faith (*Conseil Français du Culte Musulman*) (CFCM), established in 2003 with the sponsorship of the French Government, appeared to support the ban as 'Muslims must embrace a modern form of Islam in the name of the Republic' (Smith, 1 February 2004). In contrast, some organisations, members of the Union of the Islamic Organisations of France (*Union des Organisations Islamiques de France*) (UOIF), were strongly opposed to the ban. The Collective of Muslims in France (*Collectif des Musulmans de France*) has been cited as one of the most 'radical' opponents of the law, as they believed that 'both the CFCM and UOIF had been compromised and lost their legitimacy among young Muslims' (McGoldrick 2006: 96). The largest-scale protest against the law took place on 17 January 2004, when thousands of Muslims demonstrated in France and foreign cities, including London, Berlin, Brussels, Cairo and Bethlehem (ibid.: 97).

Two books by Muslim women were published in France in the aftermath of the law banning Islamic dress in schools. The first one, *One Veiled,*

2 Loi n° 2004–228 du 18 mars 2004 encadrant, en application du principe de laïcité, le port de signes ou de tenues manifestant une appartenance religieuse dans les écoles, collèges et lycées publics. The Stasi Commission made twenty-five recommendations altogether, not all of which were followed (for example, the recommendation to recognise 'the most important Jewish and Islamic holy days as national holidays in the school and workplace calendars').

the Other Not (*L'une voilée, l'autre pas*), is an exchange, in a spirit of mutual engagement and dialogue, on the topic of veiling between two Muslim women who differ in their personal approaches to religiously mandated dress (Bouzar and Kada 2003). The veiled author, Saïda Kada, is the founder of the organisation entitled French Muslim Women in Action (*Femmes françaises et musulmanes engagées*). The other book, *Ordinary Girls* (*Des filles comme les autres*), is a series of interviews with sisters Alma and Lila Lévy, teenage girls born to an atheist Jewish father and a non-practising Catholic mother of Berber origin (Lévy and Lévy 2004). The girls had converted to Islam, much to their family's disapproval. As they were expelled from their school in Aubervilliers outside Paris for wearing headscarves, they also took part in what were heated televised debates around the time of the introduction of the law. These books will be explored in more detail in Chapter 3.

Wider public opinion was also deeply divided on the issue. According to *Le Figaro* (8 November 2003), a leading French newspaper, the ban was supported by 70 per cent of the French population (including a small majority of Muslims). It is noteworthy that the introduction of the law was staunchly supported by French feminist groups, such as *Ni Putes Ni Soumises* ('Neither Whores Nor Submissives'). The international reaction appears to have been mostly negative, with figures such as the Pope, the Archbishop of Canterbury, the Mayor of London and the Vice-President of the World Jewish Congress criticising the ban (McGoldrick 2006: 98). A number of leading international human rights NGOs opposed the ban on the grounds that it violated international human rights law (Human Rights Watch, 27 February 2004; Human Rights Without Frontiers International, 17 December 2003; Minority Rights Group, 28 January 2004).

As to the official position of international human rights bodies, Jean-Paul Costa, Vice-President of the European Court of Human Rights, was reported to indicate, during the public hearings of the Stasi Commission, that 'a law banning religious signs in schools would not in itself be contrary to the European Convention on Human Rights' (McGoldrick 2006: 98). By contrast, the United Nations human rights bodies have expressed opinions that the application of the law may present a problem in view of international human rights standards. In its 2004 concluding observations regarding France, the UN Committee on the Rights of the Child (CRC) noted that the law 'may be counterproductive, by neglecting the principle of the best interests of the child and the right of the child to access to education, and not achieve the expected results' (Concluding Observations on France, 30 June 2004: para 25). The 2005 concluding observations of the UN Committee on the Elimination of Racial Discrimination (CERD) recommended that France should ensure that the law 'has no discriminatory effects and that the procedures followed in its implementation always place emphasis on dialogue, to prevent it from denying any pupil the right to education and to ensure that everyone can always exercise that right' (Concluding Observations on France, 18 April 2005: para 18). However, it has been observed that these recommendations are of limited significance as they are concerned with monitoring the law's application, rather than 'extend to consider a review of the relevant legislation' (Ssenyonjo 2007: 687). Indeed, the ideology of *laïcité* itself does not tend to be challenged in the debate; rather, differences arise as to its interpretation and application.

In September 2005, France was visited by Asma Jahangir, UN Human Rights Commission's Special Rapporteur on Freedom of Religion, who expressed concern at 'the selective interpretation and rigid application of the law' and 'the indirect consequences of the law in the longer term', such as 'abuses that provoked feelings of humiliation, in particular amongst young Muslim women [leading to radicalisation and stigmatisation]' (UN Press Release, 30 September 2005). However, the Special Rapporteur also commended the law's 'positive element' – that is, that 'it takes into account the autonomy of a female child who may be subjected to gender discrimination at a stage when she is unable to realize the consequences of being lured or forced into wearing a headscarf' (ibid.).

In June 2004, Hanifa Chérifi, an Inspector General and Mediator, appointed by the French Ministry of National Education, submitted a report to the Ministry, according to which the application of the law in the 2003/2004 academic year had been a success. The report indicated that there had been 639 attempts to wear 'religious signs', which constituted a 50 per cent decrease from the previous year. Out of these, 626 cases concerned Islamic dress (eleven were Sikh turbans and two large Christian crosses) (McGoldrick 2006: 100). Out of forty-seven students who were excluded for refusing to comply with the law, forty-four were Muslim girls. Ninety-six students altogether went for alternative educational provision. It was also suggested in the report that some schoolgirls and their parents 'had found the new law liberating' (ibid. See also EUMC 2006: 41). Other reports note that many students who removed their headscarves when at school would put them back on after school hours.

Various types of unofficial discrimination have been noted, including being barred from naturalisation ceremonies, getting married in a civil ceremony, serving as witnesses at trials, being served at a bank and persistent employment discrimination (Scott 2007: 178–179). In 2006, the French National Assembly awarded its annual prize for the best book about politics to Caroline Fourest's (2005) *The Obscurantist Temptation (La tentation obscurantiste)*, which fiercely opposes 'religious fundamentalism' and defends *laïcité*. Fourest is a high-profile feminist who is known for her support for the Islamic dress ban.

More recent developments take the *official* French stance on veiling even further. The case of Mme M, considered by the Conseil d'État in

June 2008, purports to inculcate the values of *laïcité* and sex equality well beyond the public sphere. The case concerned a Moroccan woman, Faiza Silmi, who in 2000 married a French national and moved to live with him in a suburb of Paris, where their several children were born. In France, she adopted a dress style typical of 'women of the Arabian Peninsula' (Conclusions de Mme Prada Bordenave, Commissaire du Gouvernement, *Mme M* case: 3) – that is, a long cloak and a niqab (full-face covering with a slit for the eyes). In an interview to the *New York Times* given in July 2008, she explained that this was because 'her traditional Moroccan djelaba – a long flowing garment with a head scarf – was not modest enough' (Bennhold, 19 July 2008). In 2004, Mme M applied to acquire French nationality, which the French Government opposed by means of a special decree on the grounds of 'insufficient assimilation, other than linguistic competence', in accordance with Article 21(4) of the Civil Code. Mme M was informed that the reason for the Government's opposition was the fact that she had 'preserved very strong ties with [her] culture of origin' and that her dress and daily conduct was indicative of 'a radical religious practice incompatible with the essential values of French society', in particular equality of the sexes (Conclusions: 2). Notably, the Conseil d'État examined Mme M's internalisation of the French values of *laïcité* and sex equality, as well as her outward compliance with them. The ruling thus heralds a potentially more far-reaching approach to Islamic veiling on the part of the French Republic, having received wide support in France. For example, Fadela Amara, the ex-leader of *Ni Putes Ni Soumises* and Minister for Urban Affairs at the time, hailed the decision in Mme M's case, calling the niqab a 'prison' and a 'straightjacket', 'not a religious insignia but the insignia of a totalitarian political project that promotes inequality between the sexes and is totally lacking in democracy' (*Parisien*, as cited in BBC Online News, 16 July 2008).

In February 2010, a somewhat similar case was reported, in which a Moroccan man was denied French citizenship as his behaviour towards his (French) wife was not compatible with the principles of *laïcité* and sex equality. According to a statement issued by Eric Besson, the then Minister of Immigration, Integration, National Identity and Mutually-Supportive Development, 'Monsieur X' 'forced his wife to wear the full veil, deprived her of freedom of movement with her face exposed and rejected the principles of secularism and equality between men and women' (Davies, 2 February 2010). In addition, 'Monsieur X display[ed] in an everyday manner a discriminatory attitude towards women, going as far as refusing to shake their hands and advocating the separation of boys and girls including, at home, of brothers and sisters' (ibid.).

The most restrictive French measure so far is the Law of 11 October 2010 'prohibiting the concealment of the face in public space'. This legislative development was initiated in June 2009, when the President of

France, Nicolas Sarkozy, announced that the burka was 'not welcome on the territory of the Republic' as it was incompatible with the French ideas of individualism and women's dignity. The law was passed by both chambers of the French Parliament with overwhelming majority, with only one member of the National Assembly and Senate voting against. This was despite the Conseil d'État's opinion that a general ban of this nature would be legally questionable. The law provides that 'no one can, in the public space, wear clothing intended to conceal one's face'. There is a broad definition of 'public space', including streets, markets, open spaces, public transport and 'places affected by a public service'. The most notable exception from the prohibition concerns clothes worn 'in the context of festivities (disguise for a carnival or as Father Christmas) ... or traditional expression (processions, particularly religious)'. The latter clearly refers to traditional Catholic processions, an interesting contrast with the recent ban on Muslim street prayers in Paris (BBC Online News, 16 September 2011). According to Claude Guéant, the French Minister of the Interior, the ban was enacted as '[p]raying in the street is not dignified for religious practice and violates the principles of secularism' (Samuel, 15 September 2011).

The 2010 burka law prescribes a fine of up to €150 for 'concealing the face in public' and more serious penalties, including a €30,000 fine and up to a year in prison, for a related offence of a male forcing a female relative to cover her face. The law entered into force in April 2011. First sentences were passed by an administrative tribunal in September 2011, with two women being fined €120 and €80, respectively. The fines were settled by Rachid Nekkaz, a French businessman who in July 2011 set a fund of €1,000,000 for this purpose. One of the women announced her intention to challenge her penalty at the European Court of Human Rights (*Le Monde*, 22 September 2011).

2 United Kingdom

In contrast with France, the United Kingdom takes pride in its tradition of multiculturalism, respect for cultural diversity and tolerance. Until at least recently, individuals from immigrant communities have not been expected to give up their cultural loyalties in order to become proper British citizens. According to a 2005 Home Office Paper:

> Our respect for freedom means that no one set of cultural values should be privileged more than another. With the exception of the values of respect for others and the rule of law, including tolerance and mutual obligations between citizens, which we consider as essential elements of Britishness, differences in values and customs need to be resolved through negotiation.
>
> (Chapter 4: para 42)

The Church of England is the official established church in England, with the Monarch remaining its Supreme Governor, a position to which the UK Government 'remains committed' ('The Governance of Britain', July 2007: para 57). Unlike in France, there is no prohibition of state funding for denominational schools. Indeed, it is estimated that the state finances a high proportion of the cost of religious schools in the United Kingdom (McGoldrick 2006: 173–174). Religious education, as well as multiculturalism, is part of the national curriculum.

Muslims constitute approximately 2.7 per cent of the UK population, which amounts to about 1.6 million. Although Muslims in the UK represent a wide variety of ethnic backgrounds, most are the descendants of immigrants from Pakistan, India and Bangladesh, which used to be part of the British Empire. Although there has been some notable accommodation of Muslim religious requirements (such as in relation to prayer, food and burials), it has been estimated that Muslims are the most discriminated group in the United Kingdom (ibid.: chapter 6).

It is relevant to recall that the publication of Salman Rushdie's *Satanic Verses* in 1988 caused strong protests among the Muslim population, causing considerable civil unrest. An attempt was made to rely on the English blasphemy law in force at the time (repealed in 2008) to ban the book. This was unsuccessful as the law protected Christian beliefs only (*ex parte Choudhury* 1991). The case eventually reached the (now superseded) European Commission on Human Rights, which considered that it did not raise any issues under Article 9 ECHR, which protects freedom of religion (*Choudhury* v. *UK* 1991). That was in contrast with cases such as *Otto-Preminger-Institut* v. *Austria* (1994) and *Wingrove* v. *UK* (1997), in which restrictions on the freedom of artistic speech motivated by Christian sensibilities were considered not to violate Article 10 ECHR. Neither was the *Choudhury* case considered to involve an Article 14 issue, despite the clearly discriminatory nature of the law, as the ECHR does not include a right to be free from blasphemy (which would be necessary as Article 14 could only be used in conjunction with other, 'substantive' articles of the ECHR).

After the 9/11 events in the United States and the London underground bombings on 7 July 2005, public animosity towards Muslims has increased, raising renewed concerns over integration. In 2004, a 'special ambassador' for Muslim communities was appointed by the UK Commission for Racial Equality. In September 2005, the Chair of the latter, Trevor Phillips, said in a speech at the Manchester Council for Community Relations that the UK was 'sleepwalking to segregation' as '[a]longside hard, spatial segregation, we increasingly inhabit separate social and cultural worlds' (Phillips, 22 September 2005). About the same time, an advisory Commission on Integration and Cohesion for British Muslims was established, with the task of reporting on practical ways of overcoming obstacles to integration (Travis, 22 September 2005). Interestingly, on the international stage, the United Kingdom has been a leading proponent of Turkey's membership of the European Union.[3]

It is noteworthy that, until recently, Islamic dress codes did not present a legal or social problem in the United Kingdom. Schools are generally permitted to adopt their own policies on uniform, 'sensitive to the needs of different cultures, races and religions' (Department for Children, Schools and Families, School Uniform Guidance, June 2004, cited in Ssenyonjo 2007: 676). Accordingly, most schools have been, to an extent, accommodating of Muslim students, so that Islamic headscarves, by and large, are not considered incompatible with school uniforms (see Poulter 1997).[4] More recently, however, controversies have arisen as regards some forms of Islamic dress, the timing of which broadly coincides with the pursuit of the 'war on terror'.

In 2003, Icknield High School in Luton, Bedfordshire, turned down a request from a student's parents that their daughter be allowed to wear a headscarf, as this was against the school uniform policy prohibiting headgear. The case, which was understood to be the first express headscarf ban in the UK, received much media coverage and provoked a strong reaction among some Islamic groups (see McGoldrick 2006: 179). Despite the lack of an express prohibition of religious discrimination in English law at the time,[5] the Commission for Racial Equality advised that a headscarf ban could breach the Race Relations Act 1976 and threatened legal action against the school (Docherty 2004, cited in McGoldrick 2006: 179).[6] The school governing body subsequently revised its policy on uniform, allowing the student to wear the headscarf (provided it was in school colours).

3 McGoldrick (2006: 176) points out that this is in contrast with France, which opposes Turkey's membership.

4 McGoldrick (2006: 177), however, notes a few cases in the 1960s when shalwar kameeze (form of dress consisting of trousers and a tunic, traditional to South Asian Muslims) was not considered acceptable in British schools. In 1990, the Headteacher of Altrincham Grammar Schools for Girls sent home two schoolgirls who wore headscarves; however, this was overturned by the school governors, provided the headscarves were in the colour of the school uniform: see Poulter (1997: 45).

5 A prohibition of religious discrimination became operative in December 2003, when Employment Equality (Religion and Belief) Regulations, implementing EU Framework Directive 2000/78/EC of 27 November 2000, were introduced. Being limited to employment, this prohibition does not cover discrimination in the provision of education. The Equality Act 2006 introduced a more general prohibition of religious discrimination, now replaced by the Equality Act 2010.

6 Under English law, some religious minorities could also qualify as ethnic ones, which would bring them within the scope of prohibited race discrimination (see, for example, *Mandla* v. *Dowell Lee* in respect of Sikhs). However, Muslims have not traditionally qualified as an ethnic minority under the Race Relations Act 1976 as British Muslims have a rather diverse ethnic cultural composition.

It is another Luton school, Denbigh High, which is mostly associated with reigniting the debate, when the case of Shabina Begum was considered in the High Court in June 2004 (*R* v. *The Headteacher and Governors of Denbigh High School*). Denbigh High School provided secondary education for students from diverse communities (it is estimated that twenty-one ethnic groups were represented). The overwhelming majority (79 per cent) of students were Muslim and about 71 per cent identified with 'Pakistani or Bangladeshi heritage'. Denbigh HS was considered to be a multicultural success story, as it had been transformed from an underachieving school into one of the best in the region within years. The school has also been praised, by judges as well as the press, for its 'thoughtful' and 'inclusive' uniform policy. Muslim (as well as Hindu and Sikh) girls were permitted to wear shalwar kameeze, so long as it was combined with elements of more traditional uniform (such as a shirt and jumper). Islamic headscarves were also permitted since 1993, when this modification to the uniform was made in response to requests. Local mosques had been consulted in devising this uniform policy, which was believed to satisfy most pupils and their parents.

Shabina Begum was born in 1988 to parents who had immigrated from Bangladesh. She joined Denbigh HS in September 2000, and wore the shalwar kameeze for two years. In September 2002, she and her brother, Shuweb Rahman, informed the school that she wanted to wear a stricter form of Islamic dress, the jilbab. This is a long plain dress, or a cloak, which is believed to conceal most of a woman's body. The jilbab is not common among the Bangladeshi community. According to Shabina, this was necessary in view of her religious beliefs as she understood Islam to require a woman, who had reached puberty, to cover herself in this thorough way. In her view, the shalwar kameeze did not satisfy the requirements of modesty for a girl of her age. She was informed that she would not be permitted to enter the school unless she wore the approved uniform. Shabina refused to comply and instituted judicial review proceedings against the school, with her brother acting as her litigation friend.

In the High Court, Shabina Begum sought a declaration that: (i) she had been unlawfully excluded from the school since September 2002, contrary to sections 64–68 of the School Standards and Framework Act 1998 and/or section 52 of the Education Act 2002; (ii) she had been unlawfully denied access to education in breach of Article 2 of Protocol 1 to the ECHR and section 6(1) of the Human Rights Act (HRA) 1998;[7] and (iii) she had been unlawfully denied the right to manifest her religion in

7 Section 6(1) of the HRA 1998 reads: 'It is unlawful for a public authority to act in a way which is incompatible with a Convention right.'

breach of Article 9 ECHR and section 6(1) HRA. She also sought damages from the school and Luton Borough Council. All these claims were dismissed. In respect of her allegation that her freedom of religion rights had been violated, Bennett J stated that she was not excluded for reasons of her religious beliefs as such; rather, the exclusion was based on her failure to comply with school uniform (Bennett J: para 74). He then considered that, if Shabina's right to freedom of religion had been limited, the limitation satisfied the requirements of Article 9(2) ECHR. That is, the limitation was 'prescribed by law' (i.e. school uniform policy was publicly available) (ibid.: paras 78–79); pursued a 'legitimate aim' ('protection of the rights and freedoms of others' as the uniform policy 'promoted a positive ethos and a sense of communal identity' (McGoldrick 2006:183), whereby the wearing of the shalwar kameeze allowed to avoid distinctions between Muslims and Sikhs and Hindus, as well as among Muslim girls themselves); and was proportionate (satisfied the majority of Muslims) (Bennett J: paras 90–91).

Shabina Begum appealed against this decision. In the Court of Appeal, she sought the same three declarations, but dropped her claim for damages. Her appeal was successful in March 2005, when the High Court judgment was overturned (*R* v. *Headteacher and Governors of Denbigh High School* [2005]).[8] The Court of Appeal did not, however, rule on whether the school uniform policy was lawful as such; rather, Denbigh HS lost due to what has been described as a 'technicality'.

The Court of Appeal accepted the sincerity of Shabina's religious belief and that it had been limited by the school. The importance of context was emphasised: unlike in France or Turkey, secularism is not a constitutional value in the United Kingdom. Indeed, religion could already be manifested in Denbigh HS, insofar as headscarf-wearers could be easily identified as Muslim. The question thus was whether it was necessary, in view of the absence of general considerations against manifesting religious affiliation in British schools, particularly to single out those Muslim girls whose Islamic belief required them to cover themselves more thoroughly than the majority of Muslims (ibid.: para 74). Scott Baker LJ noted the importance of individual belief in deciding whether Article 9(1) is engaged: 'it is not for school authorities to pick and choose between religious beliefs or shades of religious belief' (ibid.: para 93).

With these background considerations in mind, a six-stage test was proposed, which the school should have adopted in its handling of Shabina's request. According to Brooke LJ (ibid.: para 75), the school's decision-making should have proceeded as follows:

8 The court consisted of Lord Justices Brooke, Mummery and Scott Baker.

1. Had the claimant established that she had a relevant Convention right which qualified for protection under Article 9(1)?
2. Subject to any justification that was established under Article 9(2), had that Convention right been violated?
3. Was the interference with her Convention right prescribed by law in the Convention sense of that expression?
4. Did the interference have a legitimate aim?
5. What were the considerations that need to be balanced against each other when determining whether the interference was necessary in a democratic society for the purpose of achieving that aim?
6. Was the interference justified under Article 9(2)?

The school lost because it had not approached the matter in this, pro-HRA, way. Its starting premise was that the uniform policy was there to be complied with, rather than that Shabina Begum had a right to freedom of religion under Article 9 ECHR, which had been interfered with due to uniform restrictions (ibid.: para 76). This does not mean that such a restriction could never be justified, but, in attempting to justify such restrictions, schools should apply the test outlined by Brooke LJ. The following questions were advanced as the sorts of questions schools would need to address in similar cases (ibid.: para 81):

1. Whether the members of any further religious groups (other than very strict Muslims) might wish to be free to manifest their religion or beliefs by wearing clothing not currently permitted by the school's uniform policy, and the effect that a larger variety of different clothes being worn by students for religious reasons would have on the school's policy of inclusiveness;
2. Whether it is appropriate to override the beliefs of very strict Muslims given that liberal Muslims have been permitted the dress code of their choice and the school's uniform policy is not entirely secular;
3. Whether it is appropriate to take into account any, and if so which, of the concerns expressed by the school's three witnesses as good reasons for depriving a student like the claimant of her right to manifest her beliefs by the clothing she wears at school, and the weight which should be accorded to each of these concerns;
4. Whether there is any way in which the school can do more to reconcile its wish to retain something resembling its current uniform policy with the beliefs of those like the claimant who consider that it exposes more of their bodies than they are permitted by their beliefs to show.

Brooke LJ also suggested that the Department for Education and Skills (DfES) consider issuing further guidance for schools in light of this judgment, as 'one is bound to sympathise with the teachers and governors of this school when they have had to try and understand quite complex and novel considerations of human rights law' (ibid.: para 82).

This rather unusual approach of the Court of Appeal has been criticised, on the one hand, for not going far enough as it found the school in breach of the Human Rights Act due to procedural reasons, rather than because of the substance of its uniform policy. Davies has commented that 'retreat to procedure is of course a way of avoiding difficult questions' (Davies 2005: 517). On the other hand, the Court of Appeal judgment has been criticised for introducing 'a new formalism' to an already burgeoning, post-HRA, culture of rights fetishism and 'a recipe for judicialisation on an unprecedented scale' (Poole 2005: 695).

The latter criticisms were shared by the House of Lords, which in March 2006 overturned the Court of Appeal judgment, on the school's appeal (*R* v. *Headteacher and Governors of Denbigh High School (Appellants) 2006*). The majority of the House of Lords decided that there was no violation of Article 9 as Shabina Begum was aware of the school uniform policy when she chose to attend the school. Furthermore, all of the Law Lords agreed that, even if her right to freedom of religion in Article 9(1) had been interfered with, Article 9(2) nonetheless justified the interference. The school uniform rules were praised for their inclusiveness and promoting 'multicultural social cohesion' (to borrow the phrase from Motha 2007: 143).

The House of Lords reinforced the message that 'people sometimes have to suffer some inconvenience for their beliefs' because of the choices they make (Lord Hoffman: para 50), a position derived from the 'expectation of accommodation, compromise and sacrifice' in relevant ECHR jurisprudence (ibid.: para 54). It was elaborated that there were other schools in the area in which the wearing of a jilbab was permitted or would not be a religious requirement (i.e. female-only schools). The majority of the House of Lords thus found no interference with Shabina Begum's Article 9 rights as there was 'no evidence to show that there was any real difficulty in her attending one or other of these schools' (ibid.: para 25).

Of particular interest is the concurring opinion of Baroness Hale, the only female judge in the House of Lords. Unlike the other Law Lords, she acknowledged such complex considerations as consent, autonomy, gender equality and cultural diversity, which underpinned the dispute. Her speech expresses concerns over the 'free will' of Muslim schoolgirls who adopt such radical attire as the jilbab. She states: 'If a Sikh man wears a turban or a Jewish man a yamoulka, we can readily assume that it was his free choice to adopt the dress dictated by the teaching of his religion' (ibid.: para 94). She is also prepared to 'make the same assumption about an adult Muslim woman who chooses to wear the Islamic headscarf' (ibid.). She would not, however, extend this assumption to a Muslim schoolgirl like Shabina Begum, because 'genuine individual consent to a discriminatory practice or dissent from it may not be feasible where these girls are not yet adult' (ibid.: para 98, citing Raday 2003: 709). On the contrary, the role of the school is to teach equality of men and women (ibid.: para 97).

Baroness Hale also speaks of the balancing of the 'conflicting priorities' of gender equality and cultural diversity. She quotes an article by Frances Raday, an ex-member of the UN Committee on the Elimination of Discrimination Against Women, according to which a 'mandatory policy that rejects veiling in state educational institutions may provide a crucial opportunity for girls to choose the *feminist freedom* of state education over the patriarchal dominance of their families' (ibid.: para 98, citing Raday 2003: 709; emphasis added). However, both Raday and Hale appear to agree that such a prohibition risks offending 'cultural and religious diversity'. Thus, the two 'conflicting policy priorities' of gender equality and cultural diversity are to be balanced 'in a specific social environment' (which was, according to Baroness Hale, 'exactly what [Denbigh High School] was trying to do when it devised the school uniform policy') (ibid.: para 98).

The House of Lords' opinion in *Denbigh High School* remains, so far, the most significant legal authority on Islamic dress in the United Kingdom. It has provoked a substantial amount of academic commentary as well as media coverage. Apart from implications for the development of Article 9 jurisprudence, the most commented issues have concerned the UK's multicultural policies, calls for 'secular' schooling, Islamic radicalism and repercussions for the 'war on terror'.

The High Court case of *X* v. *Y School* (2007), decided by Silber J, follows the House of Lords' approach in *Denbigh High School* quite closely. The case concerned a schoolgirl who wanted to wear yet a stricter form of Islamic dress – 'the niqab veil, which is a veil which covers her entire face and head save for her eyes' (ibid.: para 1). The claimant was a twelve-year-old girl who was a pupil at Y School, a selective all-girls grammar school. Having reached puberty, she wished to wear the niqab 'when she attended the school and while she was being taught by male teachers or likely to be seen by men' (ibid.: para 3), which was in line with her genuinely held religious beliefs. She had three older sisters, who had previously attended the school wearing the niqab (all of them left the school before she joined in 2005). The girl and her parents were told that she could not wear the niqab to school, so that she stopped attending in October 2006. The school arranged to provide her with alternative tuition (although considerably less than what she would have received at school). She was offered a place at another selective entry girls' grammar school where she would be permitted to wear the niqab, and the local authority was prepared to provide transport. This offer was not accepted, although the reasons for this were not explained. A meeting was planned between the headteacher, the parents and an Islamic scholar the parents wished to consult, in order to discuss the issues involved.

On the morning before the meeting, the headteacher received a letter from solicitors, who had been instructed on behalf of the claimant, stating that 'legal action would ensue if a satisfactory arrangement was not reached at the meeting' (ibid.: para 19). The High Court judgment records that the headteacher thought it was 'regrettable that the claimant's family had taken this step' (ibid.: para 20). At the meeting, she stated that she was unwilling to discuss the issues as originally planned, until she had obtained legal advice. In December 2006, judicial review proceedings were commenced by the claimant who claimed that: (a) the school's refusal to allow her to wear the niqab was against Article 9 ECHR; (b) she had a legitimate expectation that she would be allowed to wear it, and there was no proportionate or objective justification for changing the school's uniform policy; and (c) as her three older sisters had been allowed to wear the niqab, there was no good reason for changing the policy, which amounted to treating the claimant differently from her sisters (ibid.: para 23).

Of greatest interest is the first of these claims, 'the Article 9 claim'. According to Silber J, the difference between this case and *Denbigh High School* was that 'there ha[d] not been a well-known practice at the claimant's school of prohibiting the wearing of the article in question' (ibid.: para 30). Thus, his task was to ascertain whether there could still be an interference with Article 9 ECHR, given that there was an alternative school available. It was decided that there was not; and, even if there had been an interference, it could still be justified under Article 9(2). Having cited *Denbigh High School* and relevant Strasbourg jurisprudence quite extensively, Silber J concluded that the availability of an alternative was key as 'Article 9 does not require that one should be allowed to manifest one's religion at any time of one's own choosing' (*Denbigh High School*, Hoffmann LJ: para 50, cited in *X* v. *Y School*: para 33).[9] As regards the Article 9(2) issues, the *Denbigh High School* approach was likewise followed, as the limitation was 'prescribed by law', pursued a legitimate aim and was proportionate. The judge agreed with the school's arguments that the uniform restriction was necessary in view of educational factors; the importance of promoting 'uniformity and an ethos of equality and cohesion'; security; and 'avoiding applying pressure on girls to wear a niqab' (*X* v. *Y School*: para 65).

The *X* v. *Y School* case can be contrasted with *Watkins-Singh* (2008), in which Silber J found in favour of a Sikh schoolgirl who was prevented from wearing the kara, a metal bangle which represents one of the five symbols of faith worn by Sikhs. This case was decided on a rather different legal

9 Silber J also cited *Jewish Liturgical Association Cha'are Shalom ve Tsedek* v. *France* (2000), *Konttinen* v. *Finland* (1996), *Valsamis* v. *Greece* (1996) and *Stedman* v. *UK* (1997).

basis though: the school's actions were found to amount to indirect discrimination on grounds of race under the Race Relations Act 1976 (as Sikhs and Jews qualified as 'ethnic groups' according to *Mandla* v. *Lee* (1983), but not Muslims) and on grounds of religion under the Equality Act 2006. The relevant test was whether the kara was of *exceptional importance* to the girl's religion or race, even if it was not a mandatory requirement of the religion. The distinction was also drawn between the five-millimetre-thick kara and items such as jilbabs and niqabs, which are much more visible.

In October 2006, the then Leader of the House of Commons, Jack Straw, caused much controversy around the issue of veiling. He published a column in a local newspaper, *Lancashire Telegraph*, which recounted his experience as a Member of Parliament (MP) of meeting with members of his constituency who wore full-face veils. Jack Straw commented that he 'felt uncomfortable talking to someone "face-to-face" who [he] could not see', describing the veil as 'such a visible sign of separation and of difference'. He was also troubled by 'the apparent incongruity between the signals which indicate common bonds' (such as a woman's 'entirely English accent' and education in the UK) and 'the fact of the veil'. The column concluded as follows: 'I thought a lot before raising this matter a year ago, and still more before writing this. But if not me, who? My concerns could be misplaced. But I think there is an issue here.'[10] Despite this rather cautious tone, Jack Straw's comments sparked a heated public debate, with strong opinions being voiced by both proponents and opponents of veil-wearing.

The timing of this controversy coincided with the news of an employment tribunal's finding of no religious discrimination in the case of *Aishah Azmi* v. *Headfield School and Kirklees Metropolitan Borough Council* (2006), which concerned a school teaching assistant from West Yorkshire who had been suspended and subsequently dismissed from her job for wearing the niqab. Mrs Azmi's face covering was considered to hinder the communicative process between her and her pupils, thus interfering with the quality of the teaching (BBC Online News, 19 October 2006a). Unlike *Denbigh High School*, this case was not decided on HRA grounds, but religion was still central to the case as the Employment Equality (Religion and Belief) Regulations 2003 provided the legal basis. The regulations were enacted in order to implement EU Council Directive 2000/78/EC. They prohibit both direct and indirect discrimination, as well as victimisation or harassment in the workplace by reason of 'any religion, religious belief or similar philosophical belief' (Regulations 2–5).

10 The text of Jack Straw's column, originally published in *Lancashire Telegraph*, is available at: http://politics.guardian.co.uk/homeaffairs/story/0,,1889231,00.html.

Aishah Azmi claimed direct discrimination (her comparator was a Muslim woman who covered her head but not her face); indirect discrimination (arguing that the school's policy against covering faces was driven by their 'intention to target the veil' and was not proportionate); and that the way the school dealt with her religious discrimination complaint amounted to harassment and victimisation. Out of these three claims, only the last one was successful before an employment tribunal.[11]

In March 2007, Aishah Azmi lost her appeal in the Employment Appeal Tribunal (EAT), which endorsed the reasoning of the employment tribunal (judgment of 30 March 2007). The EAT considered that the correct comparator for her direct discrimination claim was 'a woman who, whether Muslim or not, for a reason other than religious belief wears a face covering' (ibid.: para 55). The 'potential' indirect discrimination was justified on the facts of the case, as the school's action was proportionate in pursuance of the legitimate aim of upholding educational standards. This was because wearing the full-face veil impeded her communication with the children.

Aishah Azmi's case provoked a strong public response, so that she chose not to attend the EAT hearing in London. Of some relevance to this book was the media's speculation around her decision to wear the veil in the classroom (which she announced to the school after her employment had commenced) and around the reasons for not wearing it to her job interview. The tribunal recorded that she was not veiled at the interview because 'her husband had suggested to her that she should go unveiled' (ibid.: para 8), while in a BBC interview she said that she did not realise that she was going to be interviewed by a male (see, for example, BBC Online News, 19 October 2006b). The *Sunday Times* reported that Azmi decided to wear the veil in the presence of male colleagues as she was obeying a fatwa from her local cleric, Mufti Yusuf Sacha (who apparently 'follows the teachings of the Tablighi Jamaat, a hardline Muslim group, elements of which are suspected by western intelligence agencies of having links with terrorism') (Taher, 29 October 2006). These aspects will be explored in more depth in the subsequent chapters.

Another unusual feature of the case was that it provoked a number of comments from British politicians when it was still *sub judice*. For example, the then Community Cohesion Minister, Phil Woolas, was reported to demand that Azmi be sacked, accusing her of 'denying the right of children to a full education'. He also insisted that barring men from working in the same classroom with her (so that she could teach unveiled) would amount to 'sexual discrimination' (see Herbert, 20 October 2006, cited in

11 This was welcomed by the Islamic Human Rights Commission (IHRC). See IHRC (19 October 2006).

Ssenyonjo 2007: 699; see also Stokes, 20 October 2006). The then Prime Minister, Tony Blair, also made negative comments in respect of veiling as Azmi's case was pending.

About the same time, it was also reported that schools in the UK would be 'able to ban pupils from wearing full-face veils on security, safety or learning grounds under new uniforms guidance' (BBC Online News, 20 March 2007). It appears that Imperial College London is so far the only higher educational institution in the UK that has banned, on security grounds, full-face veils on its campus, prompting student union leaders to voice concerns over civil liberties (Garner, 23 November 2005).

3 Germany

In Germany, Islam is estimated to be the third largest religion; there are about 3.5 million Muslims living in the country, which amounts to approximately 4 per cent of the population. It is noteworthy that the majority of German Muslims are of Turkish descent and have, until at least recently, been seen as *Gastarbeiter* ('guest workers'), invited in the aftermath of the Second World War to help rebuild the West German economy, who would eventually leave. Thus, (the lack of) integration with mainstream society was not regarded as a problem in German politics. It may be for this reason that women in headscarves had not, until recently, been cause for concern.

The official position regarding religion in Germany is quite different from both France and the United Kingdom. According to the 1949 German Constitution (*Grundgesetz*), there is no established church.[12] The German state follows the principles of neutrality, non-discrimination and tolerance in religious matters. Neutrality is quite different from secularism (or *laïcité*) as it is to be interpreted as 'open, encompassing: The idea is to open the sphere of the state for religions in principle though within certain limits, to give them room without endorsing any of them' (Mahlmann 2003: 1114). Therefore, there is a strong tradition of religiosity in German schools, which are regarded by the state as 'the place where the cultural heritage, including the religious heritage, of the German society is transmitted to the young generation, and renewed' (Häußler 2001, cited in McGoldrick 2006: 108). Article 7 of the German Constitution guarantees religious instruction in schools. This is confined to special 'religion classes', and 'any religious instruction must be done with a minimum of forced persuasion' (Eberle 2005). Recognised churches in Germany receive the status of a 'public corporation', and the state collects taxes

12 Article 140 of the *Grundgesetz* provides that certain provisions of the earlier German Constitution (1919), including Article 137 which states that 'there is no state church', are now part of this Constitution.

from the members on their behalf. There are currently no Muslim organisations in Germany that have achieved this status.

A number of cases involving Islamic headscarves have come up before German courts in recent years. In 2003, the Federal Labour Court (*Bundesarbeitsgericht*) heard a case involving an employee at a department store who was dismissed because of wearing a headscarf. The employer argued that it would incur losses as a result of the employee's unusual appearance. The Court ruled in the employee's favour as no evidence for the economic losses had been produced; there was no discussion of freedom of religion or other fundamental rights. This line of reasoning was endorsed by the Federal Constitutional Court (*Bundesverfassungsgericht*; '*Verkäuferin mit Kopftuch*', 30 July 2003). However, in a similar case decided later in the same year, the Federal Labour Court held that a shop assistant wearing a headscarf had been unfairly dismissed as she was still capable of performing her duties and her appearance was motivated by a religious conviction, which was protected as a fundamental right according to the German Constitution ('*Verkäuferin mit Kopftuch*', 10 October 2003; for a commentary, see Seifert 2003).

The most significant German case on the issue of Islamic dress so far is that of *Fereshta Ludin* v. *Land Baden-Württemberg* ('*Lehrerin mit Kopftuch*'), which was decided by the Federal Constitutional Court in September 2003.[13] Fereshta Ludin was born in Afghanistan in 1972 and acquired German citizenship in 1995. She wore a headscarf during her teacher training without causing concerns. In 1998, she was refused a permanent position as a teacher in a primary school in Baden-Württemberg, which qualified as a permanent civil service post. It was the position of the Stuttgart School Supervisory Authority that young children would be negatively influenced by her wearing a headscarf. Ludin relied on Article 4(1) and (2) of the Constitution, which protects freedom of religion, as well as Article 33(3), which guarantees equal eligibility of all German citizens for employment in the civil service. Thus, the case was framed as a clash between the rights of the teacher and those of pupils and their parents. The Federal Constitutional Court emphasised that an appropriate balance had to be struck between the rights of German Muslims and neutrality in schools.

Interestingly, the Court also addressed the issue of what the headscarf actually symbolised (providing a list of possible meanings – such as adherence to tradition, refusal to westernise, women's sexual purity and religious or cultural identity), but considered that this could only be

13 The case reached the Federal Constitutional Court after being considered before administrative trial and appellate courts in Baden-Württemberg and before the Federal Administrative Court (*Bundesverwaltungsgericht*). For commentary on the Federal Constitutional Court's judgment (and other cases), see von Campenhausen (2004); Gerstenberg (2005); Fogel (2007); Schiek (2004); and Skach (2006).

determined with reference to the person wearing it (*Ludin*: para 52). However, the subjective intentions of the wearer were not decisive. It was a 'neutral observer' (*objektiver Empfängerhorizont*) whose 'objective understanding' provided the test (ibid.). The Court concluded that the headscarf could not simply be construed as a sign of the oppression of women, and that it did not, in principle, necessarily contradict the values of the German Constitution that teachers are expected to inculcate.[14]

Thus, the Federal Constitutional Court found that there was no concrete evidence to suggest that wearing a headscarf by a school teacher would endanger the constitutional principle of neutrality or would encroach upon the fundamental rights of her pupils and their parents. Furthermore, Baden-Württemberg's Civil Service Law did not contain a provision that could justify a prohibition such as that imposed by the school in this case. Thus, the Court ruled (by five votes to three) that the school authority had acted illegally.

As to the minority judgment, it stated that the case involved no issue of freedom of religion as the teacher voluntarily chooses to limit her freedoms by entering into civil service employment. The three judges considered that public sector employment did not raise a freedom of religion issue as religion was a private matter. They also considered that the headscarf symbolised political Islamism and the oppression of women, which went beyond an acceptable level (compared to other religions). Because of this, the headscarf could be prohibited without empirical evidence of its impact upon education and without a specific legal basis.

It is crucial that the majority's finding of a violation of Ludin's constitutional rights was based on the absence of an explicit legal basis for prohibiting headscarves in the civil service. The Court also said that the regional legislator was free to enact such a prohibition. As a result of the ruling, eight German *Länder* (Baden-Württemberg, Bavaria, Berlin, Bremen, Hessen, Lower Saxony, North Rhine-Westphalia and Saarland) have adopted laws prohibiting religious or political manifestations in schools. Brandenburg and Rhineland-Pfalz have drafted bills. The remaining *Länder* (Hamburg, Mecklenburg-Lower Pomerania, Saxony, Saxony-Anhalt, Schleswig-Holstein and Thuringia) have decided to abstain from such legislation.[15]

It is noteworthy that a number of the enacted laws, including that in Baden-Württemberg, introduce an exception concerning 'exhibition of

14 McGoldrick (2006: 113) points out that this echoes the approach of the French Conseil d'État in the 1989 *affaire du foulard*.

15 For an overview, see Institut für europäisches Verfassungsrecht (IEVR), Arbeitsmaterialen zum Staatskirchenrecht: Kopftuchverbot für Lehrkräfte in Deutschland, available at: www.uni-trier.de/index.php?id=7524&L=0 (German) and www.uni-trier.de/index.php?id=7524&L=2 (English).

Christian and occidental educational and cultural values or traditions'.[16] The Baden-Württemberg law was further challenged by Fereshta Ludin before the Federal Administrative Court (*Bundesverwaltungsgericht*), which considered her case on remand from the Federal Constitutional Court (*Ludin* v. *Baden-Württemberg*, 24 June 2004). Ludin's claims were unsuccessful, which has prompted commentators to call her previous victory 'largely pyrrhic' (e.g. McGoldrick 2006: 115). The Federal Administrative Court ruled that the new law provided the necessary legal basis, the absence of which had previously justified the finding of a violation by the Federal Constitutional Court. It was also reasoned that the 'Christian and occidental values', referred to in the law, are divorced from their religious underpinnings and as such fundamentally underlie the German Constitution, including rights such as inviolable human dignity (Article 1), the equality of all humans and the sexes (Article 3) and religious freedom (Article 4) (*Ludin* 2004: 14, cited in Fogel 2007: 639–640). The Court considered that demonstration of such values is not the same as manifesting individual religious faith (ibid.: 10). Thus, all public servants should be able to agree on 'Christian' values, regardless of their religious persuasion (ibid.: 14). The Islamic community was not considered to be 'excessively affected' by this law as the 'prohibition is limited to teachers in public schools' (ibid.: 15, cited in Fogel 2007: 640).

4 The Netherlands

The Netherlands has often been regarded as the model liberal multicultural state, with the state approach to religion and minorities being based on the values of tolerance and neutrality (rather than secularism). It is estimated that approximately 6 per cent (just under a million people) of the Dutch population are Muslim, representing a variety of ethnic backgrounds. Recently, however, there has been a somewhat radical shift in state policy and attitudes towards minorities, with anti-Muslim sentiments becoming more and more prominent.

In May 2002, a populist right-wing politician, Pim Fortuyn, whose policies were openly anti-Muslim and anti-immigrant, was assassinated by an animal rights activist a few days before the election for the Lower House of Parliament, for which Fortuyn's recently created party (*Lijst Pim Fortuyn*) was running. Fortuyn became a posthumous candidate and his party won 17 per cent of the seats, which was an exceptional outcome for a newly created party.[17] In 2004, a parliamentary report was published, according

16 'die ... Darstellung christlicher und abendländischer Bildungs- und Kulturwerte oder Traditionen', amendment of §38 of the Baden-Württemberg School Act 2004, available at: www.uni-trier.de/index.php?id=7524&L=2#c8460.

17 By 2006, however, *Lijst Pim Fortuyn* was left with no seats.

to which Dutch society was becoming increasingly segregated along cultural and religious lines. Concerns were also raised over the activities of radical mosques (see BBC Online News, 21 January 2004).

In November 2004, an author and filmmaker, Theo van Gogh, who was known for his radical libertarian as well as strong, cynical anti-Muslim views, was murdered by a twenty-six-year-old Dutch-born Muslim who was reported to have links with terrorist organisations. During the month following the murder, the Dutch Monitoring Centre on Racism and Xenophobia recorded 106 violent incidents against Muslims. The murder itself followed the release of van Gogh's ten-minute film entitled *Submission* (the English translation of the Arabic word 'Islam'), which featured four fictional characters played by the same actress. The film begins with the actress praying in Arabic, followed by her four stories of brutal violence and abuse against women, over which she challenges Allah (the stories are told in American-accented English). The actress wears a full body covering made of a transparent fabric, with Koranic verses being inscribed over her bruised naked body. She also recites the Koranic verses on menstruation, disobedient wives and adultery, in English.[18] The film provoked a strong public and political reaction, but did not receive much critical acclaim for its artistic value (and has even attracted plagiarism claims). One reviewer noted:

> Artists from Abbas Kiarostami to Shirin Neshat to Ousmane Sembene have confronted the misogyny of conservative Islam in ways that are at once more damning and less willfully [*sic*] profane. Van Gogh's film, which aired on Dutch TV in August, plainly hopes to inspire not argument but anger. *Submission* and its dire aftermath are symptomatic of a contradictory culture where the official myth of multiculturalism has finally collapsed under the weight of street-level racism and long-simmering hatreds on the part of both the white and non-white populations. As a cycle of retaliatory attacks on mosques and churches rages on in the Netherlands, American neocons, smugly gleeful at the so-called war on terror's decisive entrenchment on European soil, are clamoring to install van Gogh as a martyr.
>
> (Lim, 9 November 2004)

Submission was based on a script by Ayaan Hirsi Ali, a well-known Dutch feminist and politician of Somali origin. In 2002, Hirsi Ali denounced her Islamic faith and announced that she had become an atheist. She was elected to the Dutch Parliament as a member of the centre-right People's

18 An unauthorised recording of *Submission* is available at: http://video.google.com/video play?docid=-7106648073888697427. The film is unlikely to be officially released, in view of the controversy it has provoked.

Party for Freedom and Democracy, but resigned in 2006 following an admission that she had made certain false statements to obtain her refugee status in 1992. After an investigation into her naturalisation process, the Minister for Integration and Immigration annulled her Dutch citizenship, which was however restored on the Parliament's urging. Hirsi Ali received numerous death threats after the release of *Submission* and has been working from a secret location since van Gogh's assassination. She then moved to the United States and worked as a fellow at the American Enterprise Institute for Public Policy Research, which is associated with neoconservative domestic and foreign policy views. Hirsi Ali has written several books in which she attacks Islam for its absolutism and argues that it needs to undergo a drastic reformation, along the lines of the western Enlightenment.

In 2008, another short film was made by a populist Dutch parliamentarian, Geert Wilders. The film, entitled *Fitna* (which means 'disagreement' or 'division' in Arabic), provoked controversy for its single-minded, uncompromising portrayal of Islam as an inherently anti-secular, radical and fundamentalist threat about to swamp the Netherlands and western values. The film deploys techniques not dissimilar to those used in *Der Ewige Jude,* a notorious piece of Nazi anti-semitic propaganda, in both its selective, decontextualised quotation from the scriptures and its crude exploitation of populist fears of being contaminated by an unpalatable alien minority. It juxtaposes verses from the Koran with footage of the New York, Madrid and London terrorist attacks, as well as some anonymous imams' inflammatory speeches, implying an undisputable equation between Islamic doctrine, on the one hand, and terrorism and incitement to hatred, on the other. The film ends with a hand tearing out a page from the Koran and a call to defeat 'Islamic ideology', which is likened to 'Communism' and 'Nazism'. In December 2008, *Fitna* was shown at a conference entitled 'Facing Jihad' at the Begin Centre in Jerusalem, after which Wilders planned to take it to several European capitals. In February 2009, he was invited by Lord Pearson of the UK Independence Party to present his film in the House of Lords, but was denied entry to the UK on public policy grounds. The film was nevertheless shown in the House of Lords.

As to Islamic dress, the European Court of Human Rights has observed that this question is 'considered [in the Netherlands] from the standpoint of discrimination rather than of freedom of religion' (*Şahin* v. *Turkey* 2007: para 64). Headscarves are generally permitted, except if worn by members of the judiciary, who are expected to prioritise their identification with the Dutch state over their religious convictions (see Maris 2007). The Dutch Equal Treatment Commission (*Commissie Gelijke Behandeling*) has delivered a number of opinions in cases involving various restrictions on Islamic dress. Although the Commission examines cases for their compliance with the General Equal Treatment Act (*Algemeen Wet Gelijke Behandeling*) 1994,[19] its opinions have persuasive rather than binding legal force. However, they enjoy a high standing and are often referred to in public debates.

In 1996, the Equal Treatment Commission gave an opinion in the case of a Muslim woman of Moroccan origin who was registered with an employment agency (Commissie Gelijke Behandeling, Opinion 1996–109). In this case, the agency would not give the applicant work as a data typist or a production helper due to her allegedly insufficient typing speed and body height. The applicant, however, suspected that the real reason was her wearing a headscarf as she had been previously advised by the agency that placements might be difficult to secure unless she considered removing the headscarf. The Commission found indirect discrimination on the grounds of religion. Schiek (2007: 429) criticises this approach, arguing that this sort of case should be seen as a certain one of direct discrimination.

There have also been attempts by some local authorities to introduce Islamic dress bans in schools. In 1999, the Equal Treatment Commission issued an opinion in the case of a Muslim intern in a public primary school in Haarlem, which requested both pupils and teachers not to wear headscarves (Commissie Gelijke Behandeling, Opinion, 1999–18, cited in Werdmölder 2007; see also Duits and van Zoonen 2006). The school emphasised its neutral position and open attitude. The Commission decided in favour of the intern, stressing that the school could not presume a lack of a neutral and open attitude on the basis of someone's attire and religious affiliation. Such a presumption constituted a violation of the principle of equality.

In 2003, the Commission gave another opinion concerning Islamic dress, this time in a case involving the wearing of the niqab by school pupils (Commissie Gelijke Behandeling, Opinion 2003–40, cited in Werdmölder 2007: 161). The Commission decided that the niqab could be seen as a religious manifestation, and could be forbidden. It was stressed, however, that the prohibition was for practical, rather than religious, reasons. The niqab could be prohibited as it hindered open and non-verbal communication. This approach is reminiscent of that of the British Employment Appeals Tribunal in the *Azmi* case (see Part 2 of this chapter).

In 2005, the Equal Treatment Commission considered the case of Samira Haddad, who was not able to get a job as an Arabic teacher at the Islamic College in Amsterdam because she did not want to wear a headscarf (see

19 The Netherlands enacted the General Equal Treatment Act, which prohibits discrimination on a number of grounds, including religion, in 1994, which was well in advance of EU Council Directive 2000/78 EC, which requires Member States to take action to prohibit religious discrimination in employment.

BBC Online News, 17 October 2005). She claimed that the College rule that Muslim teachers wear the headscarf was discriminatory as it did not apply to non-Muslims. The Commission found that this was indeed contrary to Dutch law, which requires that employees must be treated equally. The Islamic College in Amsterdam subsequently announced that it was not going to comply with the Commission's opinion.

In late 2005, following the assassination of Theo van Gogh, the Dutch Government considered imposing a national ban on the burka (full body covering) in public places such as schools, shops, public buildings, cinemas, train and bus stations, and airports, as well as on trains and buses (see Browne, 13 October 2005). This was framed as a safety measure. The Utrecht City Council was reported to be planning to stop paying social security benefits to women who wore burkas or headscarves to job interviews (BBC Online News, 17 October 2005). In late 2011, a national ban was back on the legislative agenda, as Geert Wilders' Freedom Party became the third largest political party in power after the 2010 elections. The proposal is expected to become law shortly, making the Netherlands the third European country to ban full-face veils, after France and Belgium. Exceptions will be granted for religious buildings and foreign women in airport transit zones.

It is noteworthy that bans on burkas and niqabs in public places had been in place in some parts of Belgium since 2003. By 2004, more than twenty Belgian communes had such bans. In August 2005, a Moroccan woman refused to obey a municipal injunction to stop wearing the burka in the Flemish town of Maaseik, which triggered a national debate. She was reported to refuse to pay the €150 fine or even to co-operate with the authorities. A police inspector in Maaseik was reported to say that '[y]ou cannot identify or recognise someone when they're wearing a *burqa*, especially at night. It's not normal, we don't have that in our culture' (Rennie, 30 August 2005). Apparently the woman's husband was named in a Brussels court as one of thirteen men accused of aiding and abetting terrorists linked to the Madrid train bombings on 11 March 2004 (McGoldrick 2006: 212). In 2010, the Belgian Parliament passed a general law prohibiting wearing clothes 'obscuring identity' in public. Much like the analogous French law, it was passed almost unanimously.

5 Norway

There are about 70,500 Muslims in Norway, which amounts to 1.5 per cent of the population. Norwegian Muslims are mainly of Albanian, Arab, Pakistani, Somali and Turkish origin. The legal approach to Islamic dress in Norway is rather unusual. Skjeie comments that 'the use of headscarves in workplaces is generally viewed to be protected by the new Act which forbids ethnic and religious discrimination' (Skjeie 2007: 140).[20] Headscarf prohibitions have also been seen as instances of indirect discrimination prohibited in the Gender Equality Act 1978, as amended in 2003 (ibid.).

Of particular interest are the cases decided by the Norwegian Equality and Anti-Discrimination Ombud (*Likestillings- og discrimineringsombudet*). One case involved a large hotel in Oslo that practised a uniform code for employees, which they would not reconcile with head covering. The Ombud considered that such a prohibition would have a particular impact on women who wore the hijab. Thus, the gender-neutral wording of the uniform code could produce a discriminatory result. The Ombud also reasoned that the hijab was part of the wearer's personal integrity, so that many women would not work without head covering, and thus a prohibition would lead to significant disadvantages for them (ibid.: 140–141, citing Craig 2012).

Another case concerned a furniture store, *A-møbler*, which in January 2004 fired a Muslim employee who refused to remove her headscarf. The store alleged that the headscarf was incompatible with its dress code, which was motivated by a 'desire to secure value neutrality' (ibid.: 141). The Ombud decided that, although the promotion of a common profile was a legitimate aim, the measure was disproportionate as the headscarf is part of a person's personal integrity. The Ombud stated that sometimes hijab bans could be justified by considerations of value neutrality, but this would have to be shown with reference to a specific workplace having a special need for such neutrality. This was not the case with the furniture store, and thus the prohibition amounted to indirect gender discrimination. *A-møbler* accepted the Ombud's decision and the employee was reinstalled in her job. As to the question of whether the hijab as such is oppressive to women, the Ombud was reported to say in an interview to a Norwegian newspaper, *Aftenposten*:

> That is maybe something the Muslim environment has to discuss, but to forbid the use of the headgear is something completely different.... That means that we would shut women out of the work life and it would then be twice as oppressing.
>
> (UNHCR, 3 February 2004)

In 2007, the Equality and Anti-Discrimination Ombud heard another case in which a woman was fired from her job as a shop assistant for refusing to remove her headscarf.[21] On this occasion, the Ombud split its assessment into two parts: first, gender and, second, religious equality. She concluded

20 The law in question is the Act relating to prohibition of discrimination on the basis of ethnicity, national origin, ancestry, skin colour, language, religious and ethical orientation (Discrimination Act) 2006.

21 Likestillings- og diskrimineringsombudet (2007) 'Oppsigelse på grunn av hijab er multi-diskriminerende' (no longer available online), as cited in Skjeie (2009: 304).

that the shop's hijab ban amounted to both indirect gender and direct religious discrimination. This case is now presented by the Ombud agency as a 'case example of multiple discrimination' (Skjeie 2009: 304).

The wearing of the niqab, however, has proved to be more controversial. In 2005, two girls came to an Oslo secondary school wearing niqabs. The school's rector approached municipal authorities on this matter, which was perceived to create educational problems as well as general tension, and was advised that the school could impose a ban on the niqab. However, the school took a cautious approach and would not impose a ban on its own as it feared it might lead to students' exclusion (for a more detailed account, see Skjeie 2007: 142). After about a year of negotiations, the municipality received guidance from the State Educational Directorate enabling a ban on face veils in municipal schools. There is no nationwide ban.

The Islamic Council of Norway (*Islamsk Råd Norge*), which is an umbrella organisation for major mosques and Islamic centres, expressed its willingness to be part of the negotiations about the ban and issued a press release stating that the 'use of the niqab is not obligatory in Islam', which was accompanied by a picture of girls wearing the headscarf and the niqab, with the text reading 'obligatory' and 'voluntary' under the headscarf and the niqab respectively. The Council insisted that religious leaders were the relevant authority on such matters. It also deplored the fact that it was not consulted in the negotiations, and expressed a view that such issues had to be solved by 'dialogue not prohibition'.[22]

6 European Court of Human Rights

The issue of Islamic dress has been the subject of human rights litigation within the Council of Europe system for some years now. A number of complaints involving various prohibitions on the wearing of Islamic headscarves, mainly in state educational establishments, have been introduced as part of the Council of Europe, ECHR-based individual complaint procedures. Most cases originate from France and Turkey as the secular ideologies of those countries are most intolerant of veiling.

Turkey has, since the change of regime in 1923 under the leadership of Mustafa Kemal Atatürk, embraced western-style democratic secular values. Islamic caliphate was abolished in Turkey in 1923 and the principle of secularism received constitutional recognition in 1937. Atatürk also introduced the Latin alphabet in place of the previously used Arabic one, as well as a number of legal provisions safeguarding equal rights for women. According to Article 2 of the current, 1982 Constitution, '[t]he Republic

22 The press release is available at the Islamic Council of Norway's website at: www.irn.no. See Skjeie (2007: 142).

of Turkey is a democratic, secular (*laik*) and social state governed by the rule of law; bearing in mind the concepts of public peace, national solidarity and justice; respecting human rights; loyal to the nationalism of Atatürk…'. The wearing of Islamic headscarves is considered to be antithetical to these values, and has been legally restricted since the 1930s,[23] as part of Turkey's thorough secularisation. This is despite Turkey's population being almost entirely Muslim (99 per cent).

In the early 1980s, the Higher Educational Authority in Turkey specifically banned the wearing of the hijab in lecture theatres. Following a constitutional controversy, amendments were made to the Higher Education Act, as a result of which Islamic dress is not allowed in higher educational institutions.[24] According to Human Rights Watch (HRW), bans on the wearing of Islamic headscarves had been sporadically enforced since as early as the 1960s. In 1997, stricter implementation became the norm, following pressure from the Turkish Army, which by that time had become an influential force in Turkish politics (see Human Rights Watch, 24 June 2004 and 16 November 2006). According to HRW, this has resulted in thousands of women being barred from higher education each year (ibid.). Officers whose wives wore headscarves have also been dismissed from the Turkish Army. In February 2008, the Turkish Parliament finally voted to lift the ban on Islamic dress at universities. This provoked strong public protests and was eventually declared unconstitutional by the Turkish Constitutional Court (CNN, 9 February 2008). The following selection of cases is representative of the way the Strasbourg authorities have approached the issue.

Senay Karaduman v. *Turkey* was one of the earlier cases, decided by the (now superseded) European Commission on Human Rights in 1993 (see also *Bulut* v. *Turkey*). In this case, a university graduate could not obtain a provisional certificate confirming her qualifications because the university rules required her to submit a photograph with an uncovered head in order for such a certificate to be issued. She alleged breaches of Article 9 (freedom to manifest one's religion, 'in public or private', in 'worship, teaching, practice and observance') and Article 14 ECHR, which prohibits discrimination in the exercise of other ECHR rights on a number of grounds. The Article 14 complaint was based on nationality; sex discrimination was not pleaded. The case did not pass the admissibility stage. Although not much can be surmised from this short decision, it contains some preliminary indications of the ECtHR's subsequently developed approach to the issue of headscarves.

As regards the Article 9 complaint, the ECmHR was of the opinion that the article in question 'does not always guarantee the right to behave in public ["dans le domaine public" in the French original] in a way dictated

23 See the Dress Regulations Act of 3 December 1934, Law No 2596.
24 Higher Education Act 1988/1990, Law No 2547.

by this conviction', and that 'the term "practice", in the sense of paragraph 1 of Article 9..., does not denote any act motivated or inspired by a religion or a conviction' (p. 100).[25] Furthermore, the ECmHR referred to the applicant's 'choice' to study at a secular university, and noted that such a status 'naturally' implied submission to certain rules (i.e. not to wear a headscarf) established in order 'to ensure respect for the rights and freedoms of others' (p. 101).[26] The ECmHR also explained that such protection was justified in view of 'certain religious fundamentalist currents' (ibid.).[27] The complaint, therefore, was declared 'manifestly ill-founded', according to Article 27(2) (now Article 35(3)) ECHR.

The ECmHR's reasoning, albeit rather underdeveloped, contains several basic points of reference. First, a strong public/private division underlies its approach to the issue, reinforcing the perception of headscarves as an essentially political, publicly oriented religious statement (note the reference to 'certain religious fundamentalist currents'). Second, the ECmHR did not appear to believe that headscarf-wearing as such fell within the scope of Article 9 ECHR (which was the primary legal basis on which the case was decided). Third, the ECmHR's language of choice is quite notable[28] (this aspect will be developed in Chapter 3). Fourth, the reference to 'certain religious fundamentalist currents' also implies that wearing a headscarf may amount to pressure on others.[29]

As regards Article 14, the applicant claimed that foreign nationals studying at Turkish universities enjoyed total freedom in respect of clothing, whereas Turkish women students suffered from the above-mentioned restrictions, affecting their freedom of religion (*Karaduman*: 101).[30] This interesting claim was not elaborated any further in the admissibility decision as the ECmHR declared it inadmissible due to non-exhaustion of domestic remedies, according to Article 26 (now Article 35(1)) ECHR.

Eight years later, in 2001, the European Court of Human Rights delivered its decision as to the admissibility of the case of *Lucia Dahlab* v.

25 'La Commission a déjà décidé que l'article 9 ... de la Convention ne garantit pas toujours le droit de se comporter dans le domaine public d'une manière dictée par cette conviction. Notamment, le terme "pratiques", au sens de l'article 9 par. 1..., ne désigne pas n'importe quel acte motivé ou inspiré par une religion ou une conviction.'

26 'La Commission considère que le statut d'étudiant dans une université laïque implique, par nature, la soumission à certaines règles de conduite établies afin d'assurer le respect des droits et libertés d'autrui.'

27 'certains courants fondamentalistes religieux'.

28 And was built upon in the *Denbigh High School* case – Bingham LJ (para 23) described *Karaduman* as 'a strong case' (see Part 2 of this chapter for a discussion).

29 Both non-Muslims and non-practising Muslims – see also *Bulut* v. *Turkey*.

30 'Elle prétend que les ressortissantes étrangères bénéficient d'une liberté totale de tenue vestimentaire dans les universités turques alors que les étudiantes turques subissent les restrictions mentionnées ci-dessus et portent atteinte à leur liberté de religion.'

Switzerland, which involved a public school teacher who had converted to Islam when she married a Muslim man. She had been wearing an Islamic headscarf to work for five years before she was asked to remove it. She relied on Article 9 and Article 14 ECHR, alleging discrimination on the grounds of sex. Like Karaduman's, Dahlab's case was declared 'manifestly ill-founded', but the ECtHR's reasoning in this decision is much more detailed and is generally regarded as a critical point in the development of the ECHR jurisprudence on Islamic headscarves.

The ECtHR agreed with the Swiss Federal Court that the measure was justified by the principles of denominational neutrality and gender equality, protected by the Swiss Constitution. As to the principle of denominational neutrality, the Swiss Federal Court had 'no doubt that the appellant wears the headscarf and loose-fitting clothes not for aesthetic reasons but in order to obey a religious precept which she derives from ... the Koran' (ibid.: 452). Interestingly, this is despite:

> the appellant's main argument ... that her clothing ... should be treated not as a religious symbol but in the same way as any other perfectly inoffensive garments that a teacher may decide to wear for his or her own reasons.
>
> (ibid.)

Despite this ambivalence of the applicant, the ECtHR appears fully to endorse the Swiss authorities' vision of her clothes as prescribed by the Koran (which is in line with the ECmHR's position in *Karaduman*).

Furthermore, the ECtHR did not directly address the applicant's argument that the fact that she had worn the headscarf for more than five years without attracting any complaints was sufficient proof that the beliefs of others were respected. Instead, it appeared to be in tacit agreement with the Swiss Federal Court's speculation that 'some may well have decided not to take any direct action so as not to aggravate the situation, in the hope that the education authorities will react of their own motion' (ibid.: 450). The ECtHR also considered that:

> it is very difficult to assess the impact that *a powerful external symbol* such as wearing a headscarf may have on the freedom of conscience and religion of very young children. The applicant's pupils were aged between four and eight, an age at which children wonder about many things and are also more easily influenced than older pupils. In those circumstances, it cannot be denied outright that the wearing of a headscarf might have *some kind of proselytizing effect*, seeing that it appears to be imposed on women by a precept which is laid down in the Koran...
>
> (ibid.: 463; emphasis added)

Thus, the ECtHR reinforced the perception of the 'Islamic headscarf' not only as a religious symbol per se, but as a threat to others.

As regards the second justification, the principle of gender equality, the ECtHR noted that the headscarf 'appears to be imposed on women by a precept which is laid down in the Koran and which ... is hard to square with the principle of gender equality' (ibid.). This was not further clarified. Interestingly, this pronouncement is at odds with Dahlab's own sex discrimination complaint. The latter was dismissed as the ECtHR considered that the measure 'was not directed against her as a member of the female sex' and that the law 'could also be applied to a man who, in similar circumstances, wore clothing that clearly identified him as a member of a different faith' (ibid.: 460). This is a distinctly 'formal equality', comparator-based type of reasoning, attributable to the generally underdeveloped nature of Article 14 jurisprudence. Despite Dahlab's suggestion of a Muslim man as the appropriate comparator, the ECtHR went for an abstract, 'clearly identifiable' male 'member of a different faith'.[31]

In *Leyla Şahin* v. *Turkey* (2007), the ECtHR finally conceded that prohibitions on wearing Islamic headscarves in educational establishments could raise an issue under Article 9 ECHR. It is thus the first (and so far the most significant) Islamic dress case decided by the ECtHR on the merits.[32] Although Şahin pleaded violations of a number of ECHR articles (such as Article 8, the right to respect for private life, Article 10, freedom of expression, Article 14, prohibition of discrimination in the enjoyment of Convention rights,[33] and Article 2 of Protocol 1, the right to access to education), it is conventional for the ECtHR to concentrate its reasoning on the article which is deemed to be most relevant (Article 9 in Islamic dress cases). The Chamber judgment was delivered in June 2004, after which the case was referred to the Grand Chamber (which functions as a

31 As to the ECtHR's approach to Article 14, see *Abdulaziz, Cabales and Balkandali* v. *UK* (1985), in which the applicants, whose husbands were precluded from joining them in the United Kingdom, alleged discrimination both on the grounds of race and sex. The ECtHR approached the complaint as implying two distinct types of discrimination, despite the interaction of the two as the immigration rule in question relied on gendered stereotypes of immigrants of Asian descent. Only sex (and not race) discrimination was found to have taken place (see further Chapter 4).

32 See also *Tekin* v. *Turkey* (2002), in which a similar Article 9 complaint was declared admissible. The case was however withdrawn by the applicant, without giving reasons (see judgment of 29 June 2004).

33 Şahin claimed that she had been discriminated against on the basis of her religion. This claim was rejected as 'the regulations on the Islamic headscarf were not directed against the applicant's religious affiliation' (para 165 of the Grand Chamber judgment), which suggests a rather underdeveloped, formal-equality type of discrimination analysis, in line with the problematic general (lack of) use of this article. Unlike Dahlab, Şahin did not attempt to plead sex discrimination, which is one of the other prohibited grounds in Article 14.

quasi-appellate authority as regards the lower Chamber's judgments). The Grand Chamber's final judgment was handed down on 10 November 2005, which followed the Chamber's approach quite closely (the only departure being that the circumstances of the case were considered to merit some separate consideration under Article 2 of Protocol 1).

The applicant in this case was a medical student who had worn the Islamic headscarf for four years while studying at Bursa University. Then she transferred to Istanbul University, continuing to wear the headscarf. After that time, the Vice Chancellor of Istanbul University issued a circular, according to which students 'with a beard or wearing the Islamic headscarf' had to be refused access to lectures, seminars and examinations. Accordingly, Şahin was prevented from attending some lectures and examinations because of her attire. She then received a warning from the Dean of Medicine. She also participated in an 'unauthorised assembly' outside the deanery, protesting against the rules. As a consequence, she was suspended for a semester, but was released from that penalty as a result of a general university amnesty. Nevertheless, she left Istanbul University to complete her studies at the University of Vienna.

The ECtHR considered that the applicant's practice of wearing the Islamic headscarf did fall within the meaning of the manifestation of a religion under Article 9 (noting that this did not mean that any wearing of a headscarf would always constitute such a manifestation). However, the restrictions imposed by the university were deemed justified in view of Article 9(2), which provides that the right to manifest one's religion is subject to 'limitations as are prescribed by law and are necessary in a democratic society' in the interests of 'public safety, for the protection of public order, health or morals, or for the protection of the rights and freedoms of others'. Applying the 'legitimate aims' of public order and the rights and freedoms of others to Şahin's case, no violation of Article 9 was found (unanimously by the Chamber and by sixteen votes to one by the Grand Chamber).

The ban was put 'in its legal and social context', that is, Turkey's longstanding commitment to the democratic principles of secularism and gender equality, on the one hand, and the backdrop of burgeoning extremist currents, on the other. Against this backdrop, the message of the headscarf was interpreted as clearly antagonistic to the constitutionally embedded principles of secularism and gender equality, which were seen as foundational to the democratic Turkish state (paras 112–113 of the Grand Chamber judgment; paras 103–110 of the Chamber judgment).

The applicant's practice of wearing the headscarf was believed to threaten the principle of secularism, although the dissenting opinion of Judge Tulkens points out that there appeared to be 'no evidence to show that the applicant, through her attitude, conduct or acts, contravened that principle' (para 7 of the dissenting opinion of Judge Tulkens). Keen to uphold the secularism of the Turkish democracy, the European Court of Human Rights did 'not lose sight of the fact that there are extremist political movements in Turkey which seek to impose on society as a whole their religious symbols and conception of a society founded on religious precepts…' (para 115 of the Grand Chamber judgment, citing para 109 of the Chamber judgment). The dissenting judge, however, pointed out that the applicant did not belong to any such movements or seek to impose her religious views on others (para 14 of the Grand Chamber judgment; see also para 10 of the dissenting opinion of Judge Tulkens). Furthermore, the dissenting opinion of Judge Tulkens makes the point that the ECtHR appears 'paternalistically' to deny the applicant's 'right to personal autonomy [developed] on the basis of Article 8' when it projects an image of Islamic fundamentalism upon her (para 12, citing *Keenan* v. *United Kingdom* 2001, para 92; *Pretty* v. *United Kingdom* 2002, paras 65–67; and *Goodwin* v. *United Kingdom* 2002, para 90).

As suggested earlier, gender equality was another important principle which was considered to justify the interference with the applicant's right to freedom of religion. As regards this principle, the ECtHR reproduced its earlier opinion in *Dahlab* v. *Switzerland* that the headscarf 'appeared to be imposed on women by a religious precept that was hard to reconcile with the principle of gender equality' (para 111 of the Grand Chamber judgment), providing no further clarifications. (This aspect will be explored in Chapter 4.)

The judgment in *Şahin* has been heavily criticised on a number of counts. These include: inadequate application of the margin of appreciation doctrine; narrow interpretation of the freedom of religion; imposition of 'fundamentalist secularism'; adverse implications on Muslim women's right to education and gender equality; and promotion of the image of Islam as a threat to democracy (see, for example, Decker and Lloydd (2004); Gunn (2005); Knights (2005); Lewis (2007); Lindholm (2005); Marshall (2006b); Scolnicov (2005); and Sugden, 1 July 2004). Some of these criticisms are also reflected in the dissenting opinion of Judge Tulkens.

An interesting argument was advanced in the case of *Sedat Şen and Others* v. *Turkey* (2003: 9), in which the applicants had been discharged from the Turkish Army for their alleged fundamentalist leanings (see also *Kalaç* v. *Turkey* 1997; *Çevik* v. *Turkey* 2002; *Dal and Özen* v. *Turkey* 2002; and *Baspinar* v. *Turkey* 2002). Among other claims, they invoked Article 8 ECHR (which protects the right to respect for private and family rights), referring to their wives' headscarves as 'their families' and their wives' way of life and behaviour' (*Şen*: 9). The ECtHR did not respond to this argument, appearing to accept the Turkish Government's contention that 'their wives' and relatives' Islamic scarves had not been taken as the sole basis for their discharge from the army' (ibid.), thus declaring the complaint inadmissible.

In the case of *Nazlı Ilıcak* v. *Turkey*, the wearing of a headscarf by a member of the Turkish National Assembly (who belonged to an 'extremist' political party, *Fazilet Partisi*) to Parliament was argued to raise a freedom of expression issue. Although this complaint was declared admissible (admissibility decision of 6 April 2004), the ECtHR considered that it was not necessary to examine it in the judgment on the merits, in view of its finding of a violation, based on the wider facts of the case, of Article 3 of Protocol 1, which guarantees voting rights.

More recently, the ECtHR has considered a few applications originating from France. *Fatima El Morsli* v. *France* (2008) is an interesting case as it was concerned with Article 8 inasmuch as it was with Article 9 ECHR. It concerned a Moroccan national resident in Marrakesh, who was married to a French national who lived in France. She was a Muslim and wore what is referred to as 'the veil' (*voile*), presumably a form of the full-face veil, as this is distinguished from a headscarf (*foulard*). In 2002, she came to the French Consulate General in Marrakesh to apply for an entry visa, in order to join her husband in France. She was not permitted to enter the consulate compound because she refused to lift her veil so that her identity could be verified. She then sent her application by registered mail, but was refused a visa. Her husband's appeal on her behalf to the appropriate appeal commission was rejected. He then appealed to the Conseil d'État, which rejected the appeal, stating that the wearing of the veil could be made subject to restrictions, and that his wife's visa application had not been made in accordance with relevant regulations. It further stated that, as the applicant refused to comply with such a restriction, she ought to be regarded as having voluntarily abandoned her attempt to apply for a visa in compliance with relevant regulations.

Before the European Court of Human Rights, the applicant claimed a violation of Article 9, stating that she was willing to lift her veil before a woman. She further claimed that her right to lead an effective family life, under Article 8, had been infringed and that she had been discriminated against on the grounds of religion, contrary to Article 14 ECHR. Furthermore, she alleged a breach of Article 2 ECHR (which protects the right to life), as the French authorities had failed to assist her as 'a person in danger', and a breach of Article 2 of Protocol 1, as her children could not come with her to France to be educated there.

The ECtHR decided that Article 9 was engaged, but that the requirement for lifting the veil was designed to achieve at least one of the legitimate objectives, provided in Article 9(2), namely public order or safety. It was considered that identity checks at consular establishments are 'without any doubt necessary for public security', being comparable to security checks at airports (p. 4, citing *Phull* v. *France* 2005). As to the applicant's willingness to lift her veil before a woman, if the consular authorities had been made aware of this (it is not clear whether they actually were), they would have been within the margin of appreciation not to assign this task to a female official. The ECtHR thus concluded that the interference with the applicant's right was not disproportionate, and thus her Article 9 complaint was manifestly ill-founded. The ECtHR rejected the Article 8 complaint for non-exhaustion of domestic remedies, observing that, because the applicant had not complied with the conditions for submitting a visa application, she had thus not brought her Article 8 grievances to the attention of the French authorities (ibid.: 5). This seems rather self-referential and echoes the logic of the Conseil d'État. The remainder of her claims were likewise rejected for non-exhaustion of domestic remedies.

Belgin Dogru v. *France* and *Esma-Nur Kervanci* v. *France* were both decided on 4 December 2008. Both cases involved Muslim schoolgirls who had been expelled from school for refusing to remove their headscarves for physical education classes. They alleged violations of Article 9 and Article 2 of Protocol 1 ECHR (access to education). The European Court of Human Rights declared the case admissible, but found no violation of either of these provisions.

Dogru argued that:

> Despite her proposal to wear a hat or balaclava instead of her headscarf, she had continually been refused permission to participate in sports classes. The teacher had refused to allow her to take part in the class on grounds of her safety. However, when the teacher had been asked, at the session of the pupil discipline committee, how wearing the headscarf or a hat during his classes would endanger the child's safety, he had refused to answer the question. The Government had not provided any further explanations on this point.
>
> (para 44)

These contentions were not addressed. Instead, the ECtHR gave a very wide margin of appreciation to the state, allowing it to both introduce and assess its own evidence (ibid.: paras 72–77), noting that 'an attitude which fails to respect [the] principle [of secularism] will not necessarily be accepted as being covered by the freedom to manifest one's religion and will not enjoy the protection of Article 9 of the Convention' (ibid.: para 72). Although 'the wearing of religious signs was not inherently incompatible with the principle of secularism in schools' (ibid.: para 70), it 'became so according to the conditions in which they were worn and the consequences that the wearing of a sign might have' (ibid.).

The ECtHR then noted that the French secular model properly addresses the concern that the manifestation by pupils of their religious beliefs on school premises does not 'take on the nature of an ostentatious act that would constitute a source of pressure and exclusion' (ibid.: para 71). Although this resulted in the applicants' own expulsion from the school (and the secular model more generally), the ECtHR accepted that this was 'merely the consequence' of their refusal to comply with school rules 'and not of their religious convictions, as they alleged' (ibid.: para 73). As in previous cases, there was very little scrutiny of the link between the applicants' own behaviour and the 'legitimate aim' behind the restriction, with the ECtHR simply concluding that expulsion was not a disproportionate penalty as the applicants had been able to continue their education by correspondence classes.

7 United Nations

There have also been some developments concerning Islamic dress within the United Nations quasi-judicial, treaty-based human rights system. Although it is not possible to suggest that the UN system as a whole has taken a definitive stance on prohibitions of Islamic dress around the world, an overview of the cases presents some interesting indications.

The leading case is *Rayhon Hudoyberganova* v. *Uzbekistan*, which was decided by the Human Rights Committee, the ICCPR monitoring body, at the beginning of 2005. Like in Turkey, the majority of Uzbekistan's population (over 80 per cent) are Muslim. However, Uzbekistan's policies in respect of Islam, although clearly restrictive, are quite different from those in France and Turkey. Rather than being driven by the principle of secularism as understood by the western democratic tradition, the Government in this post-Soviet Central Asian state is trying to reassert an official version of Uzbek identity, which implies a certain rather 'moderate' understanding of Islam.

In the early 1990s, the Muslim Board of Central Asia and Kazakhstan, which was established after the Second World War by the Soviet authorities in order to control Islamic forces in that region, was decentralised, so that the Muslim Board of Uzbekistan was created. This pro-Government body thus became the official authority on Islam in Uzbekistan. At the same time, various 'independent' Islamic practices (including opening mosques and selecting imams) have been proliferating, which is perceived as a political threat by the Government. In this way, Islamic headscarves that are of a solid colour and clasped at the front are perceived as 'foreign' (in contrast with patterned scarves that loosely cover the head, which are considered to be traditional Uzbek headgear). Thus, 'foreign' forms of Islamic apparel are prohibited in public educational institutions. According to a Human Rights Watch report, between 1997 and 1999 at least twenty-eight students were expelled or suspended from schools and universities for wearing headscarves or beards. The majority of these students were female. Others had removed their headscarves following threats of expulsion or arrest (Human Rights Watch 1999).

Hudoyberganova involved one such case. The author of this communication was a student at the Farsi Department of the Faculty of Languages at the Tashkent State Institute for Eastern Languages. In her second year at university, she began to wear what is referred to as 'hijab' in the HRC's views. She alleged that, since September 1997, the administration of the Institute began to seriously limit students' right to freedom of religion, including the introduction of new regulations that prohibited Islamic dress. Students who wore hijab were 'invited' to leave the Institute and to join the Tashkent Islamic Institute instead. Hudoyberganova refused to leave and protested against the new measures. She was eventually excluded from the Institute. The decision to exclude her was based on her allegedly negative attitude towards staff and a violation of the Institute's regulations. She was informed that she could be readmitted if she changed her attitude to hijab-wearing. In May 1998, a Law On the Freedom of Consciousness and Religious Organisations entered into force. Article 14 of this law prohibited Uzbek nationals from wearing religious dress in public places. Students of the Tashkent State Institute for Eastern Languages were informed that all those wearing the hijab would be expelled.

In her petition to the Human Rights Committee, Hudoyberganova complained of breaches of Article 18 ICCPR, which protects freedom of religion, and Article 19 ICCPR, which protects freedom of expression. The HRC found the Article 19 complaint to be unsubstantiated, but it did find a violation of Article 18. The structure of Article 18 ICCPR is slightly different from that of Article 9 ECHR, as it contains a separate provision (in paragraph 2) that prohibits coercion 'which would impair [one's] freedom to have or to adopt a religion or belief of [one's] choice'. It is this part of Article 18 that Uzbekistan was found in breach of.

The HRC considered that 'the freedom to manifest one's religion encompasses the right to wear clothes or attire in public which is in conformity with the individual's faith or religion' and that, in accordance with paragraph 5 of its General Comment 22, restrictions on religious dress 'that have the same intention or effect as direct coercion, such as those restricting access to education', are inconsistent with Article 18(2) (*Hudoyberganova*: para 6.2, citing HRC, General Comment 22). The Committee went on to say that the freedom to manifest one's religion is not absolute and may be subject to limitations listed in paragraph 3 of Article 18. These are, similarly to Article 9(2) ECHR, limitations 'as are prescribed by law and are necessary to protect public safety, order, health, or morals or the fundamental rights and freedoms of others'. However, in the present case, the state party failed to advance any specific grounds in Article 18(3) on which the restriction could be justified, as its argument simply was that the author's expulsion was as a result of her non-compliance with domestic rules. Therefore, the HRC was 'led to conclude, in the absence of any specific justification provided by the State party, that there has been a violation of article 18, paragraph 2' (ibid.).

This has been described as a 'default decision' (McGoldrick 2006: 230), meaning that a violation was found essentially due to the state party's poor arguments. It is also relevant to note that the Human Rights Committee, unlike the European Court of Human Rights, does not operate a concept of the margin of appreciation, which would allow for wide variation in state parties' approaches to ICCPR rights.[34] This, together with the virtually unenforceable nature of the HRC's views,[35] is often considered to underlie the HRC's often more robust approach. However, the HRC emphasised in *Hudoyberganova* that it did not wish to prejudge 'the right of a State party to limit expressions of religion and belief' or 'the right of academic institutions to adopt specific regulations relating to their own functioning' (*Hudoyberganova*: para 6.2).

It was also noted that it was unclear from the evidence before the HRC what kind of Islamic dress exactly Hudoyberganova wore, as both parties referred to her apparel as simply 'hijab'. In particular, Ms. Ruth Wedgwood in her individual opinion considered that the 'facts of this case remain too obscure to permit a finding of a violation of the Covenant' and took the view that:

> a state may be allowed to restrict forms of dress that directly interfere with effective pedagogy, and the covering of a student's face would present a different set of facts. The uncertain state of the record in this case does not provide the basis for adequate consideration of the issue, or even for a sui generis finding of violation.
>
> (ibid., Individual Opinion by Committee Member Ms. Ruth Wedgwood)[36]

She also cited the European Court of Human Rights in *Şahin*, which 'did not lose sight of the fact that ... extremist political movements in Turkey' sought 'to impose on society as a whole their religious symbols and conception of a society founded on religious precepts', as an example of circumstances in which 'a particular garb might cause other persons of the same faith to feel pressure to conform' (ibid.).

Another UN case that merits some attention is that of *Rahime Kayhan* v. *Turkey* (2006), which was brought within the recently launched individual petition system under the Optional Protocol to the UN Convention on the

34 Regarding the absence of the margin of appreciation in the HRC's approach to ICCPR rights, see in particular *Toonen* v. *Australia*, UN Doc CCPR/C/50/D/488/1992, views of 4 April 1994. The HRC's current approach could, however, be contrasted with its earlier case of *Hertzberg and Others* v. *Finland*, UN Doc CCPR/C/OP/1, views of 2 April 1982, which contains an indication of a 'margin of discretion' approach.

35 In contrast with the ECHR system, which is unique among international human rights adjudicating systems as it has a reasonably efficient enforcement mechanism in place, state parties' record of compliance with the ECtHR's judgments is considered to be high.

36 This approach is reminiscent of those in the British *Azmi* case and the Dutch Equal Treatment Commission, Opinion 2003–40 (see Parts 2 and 4 of this chapter).

Elimination of All Forms of Discrimination Against Women (CEDAW). This Convention is not a typical human rights treaty as it was designed specifically to tackle the widespread and deeply structural discrimination and stereotyping that women encounter in all spheres of life. It thus does not have a clear public/private separation characteristic of most human rights instruments. Another remarkable feature is that it contains civil and political as well as economic, social and cultural rights. After the entry into force of the Optional Protocol, individuals can bring complaints against state parties that have ratified it. They can either allege violations of specific articles or of the Convention as a whole. The CEDAW Committee has also adopted an unusual approach as, in its recommendations to the state party, it does not limit itself to particular circumstances of the case, but also urges the state to take general action in order to tackle the structural causes of the situation.[37] These factors make the CEDAW procedure quite innovative.

For cases involving prohibitions of Islamic dress, this presents a possibility of more creative arguments (as opposed to the token freedom of religion one). Indeed, *Kayhan* v. *Turkey* was such a possibility. The author of the communication was a public school teacher, teaching religion and ethics, who had worn an Islamic headscarf from the age of sixteen. She was first appointed as a teacher in 1991, and had worn the headscarf since. In 1999, she received warnings and deductions were taken from her salary. In 2000, she was informed that an investigation against her had started on the allegation that 'she did not obey regulations on appearance, that she entered the classroom with her hair covered and that she spoiled the peace, quiet, work and harmony of the institution with her ideological and political objectives' (*Kayhan*: para 2.4). In the same year, she was dismissed from her job and had permanently lost her status as a civil servant. She had also lost a number of employment-related social benefits and alleged that she became virtually unemployable as this was 'the gravest of disciplinary penalties' (ibid.: para 2.8).

Kayhan alleged a violation of Article 11 CEDAW, which prohibits discrimination against women in employment. She alleged that Turkey had violated 'her right to work, her right to the same employment opportunities as others, as well as her right to promotion, job security, pension rights and equal treatment', as her dismissal was on account of her wearing a headscarf, a 'piece of clothing that is unique to women' (ibid.: para 3.1). She argued that 'her right to a personal identity includes her right to choose Islamic attire without discrimination' (ibid.: para 3.2). Furthermore:

37 This has happened, for example, in a series of cases concerning domestic violence: see *AT* v. *Hungary* 2005; *Goekce* v. *Austria* 2007; and *Yildirim* v. *Austria* 2007.

> [h]ad she not considered the headscarf so important and vital, she would not have jeopardized her family's income and future. The author considers that the act of forcing her to make a choice between working and uncovering her head violates her fundamental rights that are protected in international conventions.
>
> (ibid.)

This is clearly an unusual legal argument, facilitated by the innovative character of the CEDAW. Unfortunately, the CEDAW Committee did not express a view as to the merits of this argument as it considered the communication inadmissible due to non-exhaustion of domestic remedies. Although Kayhan had properly exhausted all judicial remedies available to her in respect of her dismissal, she did not plead sex discrimination before domestic courts as her arguments were (rather understandably) focused on the direct grounds of her dismissal.

8 Concluding remarks

To sum up this overview, Islamic veiling has enjoyed a remarkable degree of domestic as well as international attention in the current political climate. The developments recounted in this chapter demonstrate a range of legal approaches, as well as political constitutional backgrounds, to the handling of the issue by courts, legislatures, human rights activists, the media and within the public debate more generally. At the same time, several common themes can be said to emerge, which will be explored in more detail in the rest of the book.

Inevitably, some of the developments overviewed in this chapter will merit more attention than others. In particular, the French, British and ECHR developments will serve as the primary material for the exploration that the book pursues. The other developments, however, form part of the contemporary context and a useful comparison point, and as such will reappear at various junctures of the ensuing analysis.

Chapter 3

Autonomy and choice

So far, the book has been concerned with laying out conceptual and factual background for its analysis of the three frames of the Islamic veiling debate in legal discourse, which is carried out in the remaining three chapters. This chapter considers the first frame – that is, the rhetoric of autonomy and choice. The central argument is that conventional western liberal notions of autonomy and choice have come firmly to frame the views and arguments of both the proponents and opponents of various restrictions on Islamic veiling, as overviewed in Chapter 2. The aim is to expose the limitations of this autonomy/choice model, in which the rational, self-contained, autonomous individual is treated as an ideological given, existing prior to her choices. It is argued that the normative parameters of this framework need to be exposed and interrogated.

To this end, Part 1 of the chapter provides an account of the rhetoric of autonomy and choice as it shines through the judgments and views of those who support various restrictions on Islamic veiling. Part 2 turns to the views of the opponents of these restrictions, highlighting how these as well are articulated within the same conceptual framework. Part 3 then takes a step back, in order to consider the limitations of this preoccupation with autonomy and choice. Part 4 highlights what the rhetoric of autonomy and choice might eclipse – the possibility of conceptualising religious agency in different terms.

1 Islamic veiling as a lack of autonomy and choice

Let us briefly recall the Beit Shemesh affair recounted at the start of the book. The 'Jewish burka', adopted by a group of Israeli women, was met with general distaste as at first they were assumed to have been forced into such behaviour by the males of their ultra-orthodox community. But the news that they were in fact choosing such attire in spite of their more moderate husbands and community leaders was hardly perceived as a mitigating factor. Rather, secular feminists called on the Edah Haredit rabbinical court – hardly a liberal institution in any sense of the word – to repress the practice. These feminists, of course, had a point that such 'extreme' covering had its roots in the more mainstream religious ideas on the necessity of women's modesty and thus a logical consequence of a patriarchal order (e.g. Sztokman, 7 April 2010). Yet, the strange irony is that the rabbis sided with the husbands who complained, prohibiting the women from doing something they chose for themselves.

As to the question of choice in Islamic veiling, the British *Denbigh High School* case (2006) provides a good start. To refresh the more detailed account provided in Chapter 2, the case concerned a schoolgirl, Shabina Begum, who at the age of thirteen decided to wear a jilbab (a dress/cloak covering most of the body) to school. The House of Lords ruled that the school's refusal to accommodate this desire did not amount to a violation of Shabina's right to freedom of religion under Article 9 ECHR. Reading the judgment, one cannot help wondering whether teenage Shabina Begum might have been manipulated in her apparently sudden radicalisation[1] by her 'quite unnecessarily confrontational' (Lord Scott: para 80), Islamic activist older brother. The Law Lords' depiction of the September 2002 incident, when Shabina, dressed in a jilbab for the first time, was 'escorted' to school by her brother and 'another young man', exudes empathy for the assistant headteacher, Mr Moore, who, 'one would imagine, was having a busy morning' (Lord Hoffmann: para 46). Apparently, Mr Moore 'felt that their approach was unreasonable and ... felt threatened' as the men 'talked of human rights and legal proceedings' (Lord Bingham: para 10). Lord Scott was of the opinion that 'the confrontational nature of the peremptory manner in which the *jilbab* issue was raised with the school' was 'very unlikely to have been chosen by Shabina, not yet 14 years of age' (para 80). He also considered it 'extraordinary' that Shabina did not regard the shalwar kameeze as sufficient for the purposes of her religion (para 83).

This is not to say that questions of Shabina Begum's choice and agency were irrelevant. Indeed, the media widely reported that she had been influenced in her beliefs by her brother, a known Islamic activist, who also acted as her litigation friend. Rather, the Law Lords' allusions to a young schoolgirl being duped into dangerous Islamic radicalism sit uncomfortably with their endorsement of the consequences she should be prepared to suffer as part and parcel of her 'freely chosen' religious beliefs. Indeed, Lord Bingham asserts that 'it was ... open to the respondent, as she grew older, to modify her beliefs, but she did so against a background of *free and informed consent* by her and her family (para 25, emphasis added).

In *Denbigh High School*, the House of Lords reinforced the message that (some) 'people sometimes have to suffer some inconvenience for their

1 'For two years before September 2002, the respondent wore the shalwar kameeze happily and without complaint' (Lord Bingham, ibid. at para 9).

beliefs' because of the choices they make (Lord Hoffmann: para 50), a position derived from the 'expectation of accommodation, compromise and sacrifice' in relevant ECHR jurisprudence (ibid.: para 54). Indeed, this appears to be the general approach to Article 9 that the Strasbourg authorities have long taken regarding issues involving accommodation of various religious requirements, such as alteration of working hours (*Ahmad* v. *UK* 1982; *Kalaç* v. *Turkey* 1997; *Konttinen* v. *Finland* 1996; *Stedman* v. *UK* 1997) or special dietary needs (*Cha'are Shalom ve Tsedek* v. *France* 2000). Lord Bingham referred to *Karaduman* v. *Turkey* (1993), which he described as 'a strong case' (para 23). In this case, the European Commission on Human Rights referred to the applicant's 'choice' to study at a secular university, which by its very nature implied submission to certain rules (i.e. not to wear Islamic clothes) (p. 100). The ECmHR's abstract language of 'choice' suggests a firmly entrenched presumption that individuals function as rational agents virtually free from structural constraints; there was no discussion of whether the applicant had a realistic option of obtaining the same kind of education elsewhere. This simple choice paradigm reinforces the legitimacy of existing social arrangements, thus averting any questioning of whether they are appropriate or fair.

Karaduman seems particularly extreme, which could be blamed on the generally underdeveloped nature of ECmHR jurisprudence. However, a brief look at recent ECHR cases concerning Islamic dress reveals that the European Court of Human Rights has not departed from that very limited understanding of autonomy and choice. In *El Morsli* v. *France* (2008), it agreed with the Conseil d'État's assessment that the applicant's attempt to apply for a French visa should be regarded as 'voluntarily abandoned' as, by refusing to remove her veil, she had not complied with relevant regulations. In this logic, the nature of the choice between complying with one's religious convictions and administrative regulations of a state is completely unproblematic. Similarly in *Dogru* v. *France* (2008) and *Kervanci* v. *France* (2008), it was accepted that the applicants' expulsion from school was 'merely the consequence' of their refusal to comply with school rules (i.e. to remove their headscarves) 'and not of their religious convictions, as they alleged' (para 73). The ECtHR did not address the rather obvious fact that the applicants' refusal to comply with the rules was a direct consequence of their religious convictions.

The *Denbigh High School* case is not quite as unsatisfactory as the ECHR jurisprudence as it was elaborated that there were other schools in the area in which the wearing of a jilbab was permitted or would not be a religious requirement (i.e. female-only schools). In *X* v. *Y School* (2007), availability of an alternative school was also a significant factor. However, the House of Lords in *Denbigh High School* found 'no evidence to show that there was any real difficulty in her attending one or other of these schools' (para 25). It is interesting to explore what level of difficulty would have been considered real enough. It has been argued that the assumption of their Lordships that 'enrolling a child at a particular school is underpinned by informed consent and unconstrained choice appears to ignore the difficulties involved in sending a child to a different school', as well as the emotional and social costs of an alternative, such as the risk of ghettoisation (Gies 2006: 385–386).

The rhetoric of choice also underpins the concurring opinion of Baroness Hale, albeit in quite a different vein. Rather than finding justifications for her position in doctrinal ECHR law, Hale's opinion is explicitly, if rather unusually, informed by feminist and multicultural theory. Her speech expresses concerns over the 'free will' of Muslim schoolgirls who adopt such radical attire as Shabina's. She states: 'If a Sikh man wears a turban or a Jewish man a yamoulka, we can readily assume that it was his free choice to adopt the dress dictated by the teaching of his religion' (para 94). Baroness Hale is prepared to 'make the same assumption about an adult Muslim woman who chooses to wear the Islamic headscarf' (para 94), but not about a Muslim schoolgirl like Shabina, because 'genuine individual consent to a discriminatory practice or dissent from it may not be feasible where these girls are not yet adult' (para 98, citing Raday 2003: 709). On the contrary, the role of the school is to teach equality of men and women (para 97). The gender equality aspect will be explored in more detail in the next chapter, but for present purposes it is noteworthy that teaching such equality would enable Muslim girls to make the 'right' kind of choices.

In Baroness Hale's judgment, the two 'conflicting policy priorities' of gender equality and cultural diversity were to be balanced 'in a specific social environment', which was 'exactly what [Denbigh High School] was trying to do when it devised the school uniform policy' (para 98). This means 'the elevation of the unity of the community – the commonality and cohesion produced by the school', which dresses up 'the exigencies of sustaining a particular formation of the political – the cohesive multicultural state ... as a defence of *individual autonomy*, or the *protection of vulnerable girls*' (Motha 2007: 144). Notably, these two aims are in contradiction with each other as protection of vulnerable girls implies certain paternalism, which is hardly conducive to enhancing individual autonomy.

Baroness Hale's argument appears to be informed by a deep-seated assumption that something is inherently wrong with Muslim dress, and hence it can hardly be a 'free' choice. Indeed, writing over a decade ago, Hirschmann noted that western reactions to 'veiling' are 'fairly universal':

> Feminists as well as non-feminists often assume that veiling is in and of itself an inherently oppressive practice. Many view it like domestic

> violence: just as staying with an abuser seems beyond comprehension, so does 'choosing' to veil. Women are seen as brainwashed or coerced, and the veil is seen as a key emblem of this oppression.
>
> (1998: 349)

'Veiling' has long stood for the archetypal anti-liberal practice signifying total restraint of autonomy and choice. It is instructive that the paradigm of women's choice is often used by (liberal) feminists to sheath western cultural chauvinism. Mainstream feminists construct culture and gender as complete antagonisms, with 'culture' being decidedly non-liberal and thoroughly conflated with 'religion' (e.g. Okin 1999). At the same time, this antithesis sustains the belief that western liberal legal orders are uniquely capable of upholding and advancing gender equality. Both culture and patriarchy thus are positioned as 'always elsewhere from liberalism' (Brown 2006: 195), and their perpetuation of women's subordination in the rest of the world (or, for that matter, in minority communities within the West) is deemed so uniquely serious because their law 'openly avows its religious and cultural character' (ibid.: 197); in other words, the individual and the background are not clearly separated. Veiled women are thus deemed to be completely saturated by their oppressive material conditions that generate false consciousness.

Such deeply held perceptions of 'veiling' as total lack of autonomy and choice paint a rather skewed picture of a Muslim woman's agency. When interpolated into judicial reasoning, they ensure that the Muslim woman is treated as a priori incapable of passing the required threshold, as is subtly demonstrated in the speech of Baroness Hale. On the one hand, she is required to demonstrate 'conscious, rational and unimpeded decision-making' (Gies 2006: 384) – an arguably higher standard than applicable to hypothetical Jewish or Sikh men. On the other, the inherently irrational and anti-egalitarian nature of her belief makes her choice already suspect, as Raday's article, quoted by Baroness Hale, suggests persistently. Hence, a Muslim woman's consent is treated as incapable of ever being 'free', 'informed' and 'genuine'.

In the debate surrounding the much-publicised case of Aishah Azmi (2006/2007), the teacher who was sacked for wearing a veil in the classroom, concerns over a Muslim woman's 'free choice' took grotesque proportions. The Employment Appeal Tribunal recorded that she did not wear the veil to her job interview because 'her husband had suggested to her that she should go unveiled' (2007: para 8), which was generally perceived by the media as undermining her claim to be exercising an autonomous choice. Although Azmi herself had maintained that her decision to 'veil' was a personal choice, the press reported that she was in fact obeying a fatwa from her local cleric, Mufti Yusuf Sacha, who apparently 'follows the teachings of the Tablighi Jamaat, a hardline Muslim group, elements of which are suspected by western intelligence agencies of having links with terrorism' (Taher, 29 October 2006). This raises the question of whether the two accounts should necessarily be mutually exclusive: surely one's personal choices are never formed in isolation from one's environment, and hence can hardly ever be considered completely 'free' or 'autonomous', as much of the classic liberal tradition would have it? Rather, it appears that it is the inherent unintelligibility to western liberal sensibilities of the decision to veil that ensures that it is refused to be comprehended as a valid 'choice'.

The 'coerced/freely chosen' binary is also vivid in the debate around the 2004 French law banning 'ostentatious' religious symbols from public schools and the 2010 law banning 'concealing the face' in public. The choice/coercion, or *individual autonomy versus cultural compulsion* (Scott 2007: 127), framework has been prominent in parliamentary as well as popular discussions of why Muslim girls and women in France may veil. A major justification of the law, advanced by the Stasi Commission, was that girls were coerced into wearing headscarves by their families. Not dissimilarly to Baroness Hale's opinion, Asma Jahangir, UN Special Rapporteur on Freedom of Religion, commended the French ban on Islamic veiling in schools as 'it takes into account the autonomy of a female child who may be subjected to gender discrimination at a stage when she is unable to realize the consequences of being lured or forced into wearing a headscarf' (UN Press Release, 30 September 2005).

This is not to deny that some, or indeed many, girls and women may in fact have been coerced into wearing some form of Islamic dress by their families or wider communities. Yet there tends to be a sweeping assumption that all Islamic veiling practices signify total restraint of freedom and choice, while any attempt to justify the practice is seen as false consciousness, as exemplified in the following account by the Chair of the Netherlands-based International Network of Women from Turkey:

> Restrictions such as wearing headscarves are made up by men who are using women as marionettes. Next, women declare that they like to wear a scarf and that they do so out of their free will. Thus, they are denying their submission in order to embellish their situation. In their denial they resign themselves to their fate. They maintain that their scarves are a purely voluntary affair, for they do not want to be repudiated by their family and community.
>
> (Arda, 22 March 2001, as cited in Maris 2007: 14)

Such a stance has prevailed in the evidence of the Stasi Commission. Although it was admitted that some (*certains*) girls may regard the *foulard* as voluntary and even emancipatory, many felt that it was oppressive (Debré 2003, vol 1: 103–104). According to the Commission:

> There are pressures constraining young girls to wear religious signs. Their family and social environment impose on them a choice that is not their own. The Republic cannot remain deaf to these girls' cry of distress. The space of the school must remain for them a place of liberty and emancipation; it must not become a place of suffering and humiliation.
>
> (Stasi 2004: 128)

The Stasi Commission interviewed only a few girls who wore headscarves, 'in private session, away from audiences that might have been swayed by what they said' (Scott 2007: 124). Expert opinions were overwhelmingly in favour of banning headscarves, with accounts as extreme as 'a veil is a rape' ('un voile est un viol') or the veil being a form of 'psychological, sexual and social mutilation', denying girls any possibility of 'becoming a human being' (ibid.: 133, 158). Thus, no statistics were considered necessary to support Bernard Stasi's conclusion that '[o]bjectively, the veil stands for the alienation of women'. It would be a step too far to assert that such a conclusion was prompted by a deliberate desire to misrepresent the facts. Rather, it is indicative of the deep-seated inability to comprehend veiling as a free, rational choice. Arguably, it is the entrenched nature of this inability that is more troubling. The Stasi Commission's stance could be compared with the majority judgment of the German Federal Constitutional Court in *Ludin* (2003), according to which the relevant test is one of the 'objective', or 'neutral', observer, but the subjective intentions of the wearer are to be taken into account. The latter is a rather atypical clarification, which is to be welcomed.

As to individual cases, that of *Mme M*, decided by the French Conseil d'État in June 2008, has some of the strongest anti-veiling rhetoric so far, couched as a concern with women's autonomy. According to the Conclusions of the Government Commissioner, Mme Prada Bordenave, Mme M:

> lives in total submission to the men of her family, which manifests itself in the wearing of her clothes as well as in the organisation of her daily life; and … she finds this normal and … it never even crossed her mind to challenge this submission.
>
> (p. 4)[2]

For the record, Mme M herself was reported to consider the Conseil d'État's assessment wrong and 'humiliating for her':

2 'Elle vit dans la soumission totale aux hommes de sa famille, qui se manifeste tant le port de son vêtement que dans l'organisation de sa vie quotidienne et les propos qu'elle a tenus aux services montrent qu'elle trouve cela normal et que l'idée même de contester cette soumission ne l'effleure même pas.'

> Everything is wrong! I am not submissive to the men of my family, I don't lead a secluded life and I go out when I want to. I take my niqab off when driving my car. It is solely myself who decided to wear it, after reading some books. I respect the law and my husband respects my decisions.
>
> (Naudé 2008)[3]

In this way, a woman is told that she is incapable even of understanding the total submission she lives in and so her own views on the matter are simply irrelevant.

The refusal to validate the wearing of Islamic dress as a legitimate choice also manifests itself in the milder version of the coercion argument – that of peer pressure, which is routinely raised in the debate. According to Patrick Weil, a member of the Stasi Commission, the law would protect those girls who did not wish to wear headscarves from *social and family* pressure (Weil, 25 March 2004). In the *Denbigh High School* case, Lord Hoffmann reiterated that the school was 'in the best position to weigh and consider' its 'wish to avoid clothes which were perceived by some Muslims (*rightly or wrongly*) as signifying adherence to an extremist vision of the Muslim religion and to protect girls against external pressures' (para 65, emphasis added). According to Lord Bingham, 'a number of Muslim girls at the school have said that they do not wish to wear the jilbab and fear they will be pressured into wearing it' (para 18).

In the High Court case of *X* v. *Y School*, 'avoiding applying pressure on girls to wear a niqab' (para 65) was cited as a factor potentially justifying the interference with the claimant's Article 9 rights. She argued that when her three sisters, who went to the same school, wore the niqab between 1995 and 2004, there was no evidence that any other pupils were pressured to follow their example. Silber J rejected this argument, considering that there was:

> a difference between, on the one hand, the situation in a school when the niqab is worn by only one or two sisters and when there is no mention of whether niqabs can be worn and, on the other hand, a situation when it is *expressly* stated that niqabs can be worn which is what will occur if the claimant is successful. In the latter case, many Muslim girls might become subject to pressure to wear the niqab.
>
> (para 92)

3 'Tout est faux! Je ne suis pas soumise aux hommes de ma famille, ne mène pas une vie de recluse et sors quand il me plaît. Quand je conduis ma voiture, j'enlève mon niqab. C'est moi seule qui ai décidé de le porter, après la lecture de certains livres. Je respecte la loi et mon mari respecte mes décisions.'

Mme M's husband 'confirmed laughingly': 'Vous avez déjà vu une Marocaine soumise?'

It was further stated that the headteacher would know best, reiterating Lord Bingham's opinion that 'it would be ... irresponsible of any court lacking the experience, background and detailed knowledge of the head teacher ... to overrule their judgment on a matter as sensitive as this' (para 34, cited in *X* v. *Y School*: para 93). Similar, 'protection of the rights of others', arguments were advanced in *Şahin* v. *Turkey* (2007) – although, as pointed out by the dissenting judge, there was no concrete evidence to justify such a perception.

In neither of these cases was it explained why banning certain clothes would be the best way of protecting girls from 'external pressures', let alone why pressure to practise some sort of Islamic veiling might be worse than the pressure not to. Whether or not such a hierarchical distinction between different types of pressure is justifiable, it is routinely taken for granted. In effect, this means unscrutinised prioritisation of one kind of individuality, autonomy and choice – indeed of one kind of social pressure – over another. Scott's observation that it is only the individuality of 'those who had made the right choice' that receives legal recognition and protection (2007: 131) is certainly applicable beyond France.

2 Islamic veiling as a positive choice

Although the proponents of Islamic dress restrictions, as described above, refuse to admit that wearing some form of Islamic veiling may signify a positive, autonomous and perfectly legitimate choice, there is no shortage of evidence to support such an idea. To return to the *Denbigh High School* case, one cannot help admiring the defiant stance that the schoolgirl in question, Shabina Begum has, over years, taken in respect of her point of wearing the jilbab. Although she was assisted by her older brother, who acted as her litigation friend (and apparently authored the speech she read out after her victory in the Court of Appeal; BBC Online News, 2 March 2005), she gave numerous interviews which suggest a rather strong character and remarkable determination regarding the issue. In the aftermath of the House of Lords judgment, which had overruled the Court of Appeal, Shabina was reported to say that she would consult her lawyers about the possibility of taking the case to the European Court of Human Rights, but in any case she was happy to have made 'a stand':

> I had to make a stand about this. Many women will not speak up about what they actually want. I still don't see why I was told to go home from school when I was just practising my religion. I'm just a teenager – not many teenagers go out there and challenge the system.
>
> (BBC Online News, 22 March 2006)

Arguably, this is indicative of conscious, strategic deployment of the human rights avenue in a society where dominant ideology requires that conflicts are channelled that way. Ironically, the House of Lords was rather disapproving of Shabina Begum's brother's '[talk] of human rights and legal proceedings' (*Denbigh High School*: para 10). Likewise, the headteacher in *X* v. *Y School* thought it was 'regrettable' that the claimant's family had consulted solicitors (*X* v. *Y School*: para 10).

However, Baroness Hale, who ultimately doubts whether a choice such as Shabina's can be free, acknowledges that, in some circumstances, it might. She admits that Muslim women and girls may choose to adopt certain forms of Islamic veiling for reasons of political defiance (meaning most obviously resistance to westernisation and anti-Muslim prejudice) (*Denbigh High School*: para 94, citing Alibhai-Brown 2000: 246). Among others, she cites British multicultural theorist, Parekh's (1997) response to Okin's notorious *Is Multiculturalism Bad for Women?*, according to which 'several Muslim girls freely wore the hijab' to resist the imposition of a westernised identity, or to indicate 'to white boys how they wished to be treated' (para 94). As the hijab is now more popular among the younger generation, it could also be, ironically, an exercise of individual choice in the face of parental disapproval. The Lévy sisters, who were at the centre of controversy in France in 2003, are a prominent example of such a scenario.

Furthermore, there is much support, particularly within what has come to be known as Islamic feminism, for the view that Islamic veiling should be seen as symbolic of resistance to patriarchy, rather than of the repression by it (as much mainstream opinion would have it), and hence as a perfectly acceptable, even commendable, choice. According to a note summarising the proceedings of a conference on headscarves held several years ago at the European University Institute:

> The 'new veil' is the most conspicuous sign of Islamic feminism. Women choose to wear it, and will not remove it in any circumstance, including in women-only gatherings or in foreign countries. This is a way of freeing themselves from a male-imposed feminine model that allows them to remove the veil in private settings, since its main function is to conceal women from men who are not their relatives. By retaining the veil, they show that it is not imposed by men but *chosen* by them.
>
> (Lyon and Spini 2004: 344; original emphasis deleted, emphasis added)

The debate around the introduction of the French law prohibiting religious symbols in public schools is replete with affirmations of veiling as a positive choice, although these often tend to be muffled or silenced so that the views discussed in Part 1 of this chapter remain predominant.

Writing about the French situation, Benhabib (2002) describes the 'complex symbolic negotiations' 'behind the simple act of veiling' (p. 97). Interestingly, these 'complex symbolic negotiations' are configured by the same normative parameters which frame the views of the proponents of the law. Benhabib appears to share the vision of the veil of the French sociologists Gaspard and Khosrokhavar (1995) as '*the vehicle of passage to modernity* within a promiscuity which confounds traditional distinctions, of an access to the public sphere which was forbidden to traditional women as a space of action and the *constitution of individual autonomy*' (pp. 44–45, translated by Benhabib 2002: 97, emphasis added. See also Werbner 2007). According to another account, the veil is the expression of 'the *autonomy* of newly urbanized youth of rural origin, or of young people from modest urban backgrounds ... who *demand social recognition*' (Chafiq and Khosrokhavar 1995: 163, cited in Scott 2007: 138). Here, modernity, autonomy and recognition are key terms that ensure that the argument in defence of veiling is comprehensible within a western liberal paradigm.

It is noteworthy that other, more explicitly liberal, commentators openly insist that, for Islamic veiling codes to become fully acceptable, Islam needs to reinvent itself in a way compatible with the 'fundamental principles of Europe', of which autonomy and individualism are one (e.g. Gallala 2006: 593). In this way, the acceptability of the practice of 'veiling' depends on its ability to be presented as a symbol of Muslim women's liberal transformation, their transition to modernity – and accordingly their ability to make good autonomous choices for themselves.

Interestingly, the position of those who opposed the French ban could still be informed by a belief that Islamic veiling is not a good choice – insofar as it is constructed as *a* choice. In 2003, prominent French sociologists and philosophers called on feminists, parents, students and teachers to mobilise against the ban, presenting their case in *Libération*: 'In all cases, it is in welcoming them [girls in headscarves] to the secular school that we can help emancipate them, by giving them the means of achieving autonomy' (20 March 2003, as cited by Scott 2007: 140). The authors 'gestured to a *choice* to wear a headscarf', and thus constructed the girls as ripe for the emancipation of the republican education system, because 'some kind of autonomy was already at work' (Scott 2007: 140). Likewise, Baroness Hale in *Denbigh High School* states:

> If a woman freely chooses to adopt a way of life for herself, it is not for others, including other women who have chosen differently, to criticise or prevent her. Judge Tulkens, in *Şahin* v. *Turkey* ... draws the analogy with freedom of speech. The European Court of Human Rights has never accepted that interference with the right of freedom of expression is justified by the fact that the ideas expressed may offend someone. Likewise, the sight of a woman in full purdah may offend some people, and especially those western feminists who

> believe that it is a symbol of her oppression, but that could not be a good reason for prohibiting her from wearing it.
>
> (para 96)

Even if the choice is still considered 'wrong', what makes it comprehensible is that it is made for plausible reasons (Scott 2007: 136) – such as political protest, resistance, quest for recognition, autonomy – in other words, known liberal goods. Right or wrong, the choice to veil in this strand of argument remains a matter of individual autonomy, and hence ought to be protected.

Indeed, autonomy is such an important value in the western liberal legal tradition that it is now considered to undergird a number of human rights. In particular, the dissenting opinion of Judge Tulkens in *Şahin* v. *Turkey* makes the point that the majority of the ECtHR 'paternalistically' deny the applicant's 'right to personal autonomy [developed] on the basis of Article 8 [which protects the right to respect for private and family life]' when they project an image of Islamic fundamentalism upon her (Dissenting Opinion of Judge Tulkens: para 12; citing *Keenan* v. *UK*: para 92, *Pretty* v. *UK*: para 65–67; *Goodwin* v. *UK*: para 90; citations deleted).

An important indicator of the overwhelming purchase of the normative values of autonomy and choice is the enthusiasm with which many postcolonial (as opposed to liberal) feminists have hailed practices of veiling as positive, affirmative choices for women in the Islamic world. In her piece 'Post-colonial Feminism and the Veil: Considering the Differences', published in the early 1990s, Abu-Odeh confronts her unease in respect of Arab women who choose to veil themselves. She notes how the veil has been a very concrete gain for women in many Arab societies as it provides, among other things, protection from harassment on the streets. Abu-Odeh concludes that the practice of veiling is far more diverse, ambiguous and empowering than the liberal feminist might intuitively be inclined to admit. According to her, '[v]eiled sexuality ... reveals a multiplicity that is beyond the feminist's wildest expectations' (1992: 1535), whereby the veil creates a space for women to cultivate their individuality free from public scrutiny.

There is indeed much to be gained from such insights about women's resilience in the face of patriarchal oppression, and about the possibilities that the veil allows precisely because it creates 'portable seclusion' (Papanek, cited in Shaikh, 20 March 2002). Informative historic accounts have shown how in many Islamic societies veiled women traditionally enjoyed a degree of freedom in their day-to-day activities which had become unthinkable after the colonial unveiling campaign – precisely because unveiled women were thought to be much more dangerous and hence in need of stricter social control mechanisms (see Chapter 4 for a more detailed exploration of this aspect).

Accounts such as Najmabadi's (1993), Kandiyoti's (1998) or Abu-Lughod's (1998) work to problematise the traditional equation of veiling with the total lack of autonomy and thus can hardly be accused of oversimplifying reality. There has, however, been much scholarship that does just that by underplaying, if not completely erasing (intentionally or not), the rigid structural limitations in which women in Islamic societies function. Moghissi forcefully criticises what she sees as radical anti-Orientalism[4] converging with 'postmodern relativism', which unwittingly colludes with 'fundamentalist conservatism' and is characterised by 'an uncritical pursuit of the culturally exotic and the untouched' (1999: 47).[5] According to her, 'there is a profound failure to draw a clear distinction between the position of fundamentalists and that of a large number of anti-representational post-colonial feminists' (ibid.). She highlights how strict Islamic dress codes have hardly protected women from (often extreme) physical and sexual violence across many of the contemporary Islamic states (ibid.: 42–47). Indeed, no amount of wishful thinking can recast reactionary impositions of rigid dress codes in places like Afghanistan and Algeria as enhancing women's autonomy.[6]

Although Moghissi's conclusions may be debatable (she advocates a return to some variant of a classic liberal feminist agenda as applicable to Islamic societies as it is in the West), her warning against taking Orientalism to its logical extreme is apposite. In other words, an over-enthusiastic celebration of the choice to veil, be it in western liberal democracies or in Islamic societies, may be just a reversal of the coercion argument, and thus does little to investigate the workings of power in this free choice/total compulsion binary. As Abu-Lughod suggests, 'we need to ask some hard questions about what we actually mean when we use words like "agency" and "choice" when talking about human beings, always social beings always living in particular societies with … variable meanings of personhood' (Shaikh 2002).

4 The term 'Orientalism' was coined in Said (1978). Originally, it was meant as ironic criticism of the then accepted field of 'Orientalism' that was concerned with studying 'Oriental' people and culture. It denotes an 'imaginative geography' involving a strongly essentialised division between western superiority and eastern inferiority, in which western representations of the East and Islam are formed with no or little engagement with what is being represented. Similar theories to Said's were formulated in Asad (1968) and Hentsch (1992). Said has been criticised for 'Orientalism-in-reverse': see Al-Azm (1981) and Ahmad (1992).

5 Moghissi cites the following: Ahmed, A. (1992); Afshar (1994); Hoodfar (1993); Ramazani (1993); and Tohidi (1994), although her assessment is not necessarily endorsed here.

6 Compare, however, Hirschkind and Mahmood (2002), who point out that, although 'Taliban policies had made conditions much worse for urban women, they did not substantially affect the lives of the vast majority of rural women either because many of the Taliban edicts already mirrored facts of rural life, or because those edicts were never enforced' (p. 346).

3 What is wrong with autonomy and choice?

As is implicit in the arguments cited earlier in the chapter, autonomy is a foundational normative value of western liberal democracies, and thus also of international human rights regimes. Its origins go back a long time; the etymology is from the ancient Greek αυτο = self and νόμος = law. Autonomy thus means self-legislation, the rational capacity to derive the source of one's constitution from oneself. For present purposes, the version of autonomy prevalent today can be traced to early modern ideologues of liberalism, such as Thomas Hobbes and John Locke. In this classic version, autonomy denotes an atomistic, 'relentlessly self-interested' (Brown 1995: 25), pre-social individual, largely independent of and easily separable from the conditions he lives in. Many feminist critiques in particular have highlighted the exclusionary nature of the concept of autonomy in western liberal thought, as it becomes a blatant fiction whenever applied to anyone other than the archetypal male citizen figure. At the same time, much of feminism has sought to 'retain the value' of autonomy, 'while rejecting its liberal incarnation' (Nedelsky 1989: 7). Most feminists today recognise the role that social conditions play in shaping people's circumstances, but would still regard choice and autonomy as important tools of women's empowerment. Yet, as the preceding discussion shows, the arguments prevalent in the Islamic veiling debate tend to discount these developments in feminist theory, holding on to a most skewed version of autonomy when applied to Muslim women.

But there is a more significant line of enquiry pursued here: the limitations of the autonomy framework itself. For this purpose, it is worthwhile to highlight Brown's (2006) take on liberal autonomy, in which she interprets Freud's (1952; 1961; 1975) seminal account of group psychology. Freud's theory implicitly underlies the late modern configuration of the group as the antithesis of individual autonomy. In liberalism, the opposition between the group/community/culture and individual moral autonomy ('individuation') requires that culture must be subdued by autonomy. This is made possible by the strong Kantianism underlying liberalism's ideology, in which liberalism figures as uniquely capable of being 'culturally neutral and culturally tolerant' (Brown 2006: 151). Within liberalism, the possibility of an 'optional relationship' with 'culture' is secured by the conceit that 'the individual *chooses* what he or she thinks' (ibid.: 152), which figures 'culture' as extrinsic to the subject. In this scheme, it is only liberal individuals for whom culture and religion become mere 'background', a house one can enter and exit; while for 'organicist' creatures, such as non-western peoples, culture is 'saturating and authoritative' (ibid.: 153). As highlighted in the first part of this chapter, this is well manifested in the Islamic veiling debate where individual autonomy is routinely cast against cultural compulsion. The axiom that autonomy and choice are themselves (western) cultural beliefs completely escapes the proponents of Islamic veiling bans.

Freud's work provides an interesting vantage point for liberalism's distinction between the 'liberal self and its ... organicist Other' (ibid.: 154), in other words between individual autonomy and cultural compulsion. According to Freud, the modern individuated subject emerges out of its earlier organicist (i.e. collectivised) state. On the other hand, the self is always prior to the group (the lone savage). Thus, in a group (in other words, *culture*), the unindividuated man is regressed to his *own* more instinctual psychic state, to a lowered superego. If this is right, any individual, no matter how educated or 'civilised', can regress to such an organicist state, a kind of emotional childhood in which rational capacity and impulse control are radically diminished. Indeed, this ever-present possibility is vividly demonstrated by the recent history of European totalitarianism. This valuable aspect of Freud's theory, however, tends to be underplayed in liberal thinking. Indeed, there is 'huge resistance, both moral and political, to exploring the historical causes of the Nazi genocide' (Mamdani 2004: 4). Abu-Ghraib and the killing of Baha Musa in Iraq are more recent examples of atrocities perpetrated by western people, which tend to be explained away as absolutely exceptional pathology. Similarly, Razack (2004) argues in the context of the Canadian 1990s peacekeeping operation in Somalia that the typical, recurrent nature of imperial violence and its obsessive photographing and video-recording make it difficult to believe that such events are exceptional.

Rather, liberalism hinges on Freud's pathologisation of the group and 'cultural' behaviour as inherently dangerous. And, thus, liberal ideology seems to perpetuate the myth that it is non-liberal people, saturated with their 'culture', who intrinsically suffer from diminished rational capacity and destructive behaviour. Accordingly, 'organicist' societies are problematic because this primordial affect saturates their public sphere and formal laws – unlike in liberalism that purports, rather unsuccessfully, to confine affect (i.e. culture) to its proper place – the private and familial domains. Thus, non-liberal orders (such as Islamic societies) are dangerous simply because they signify an uncivilised condition, in contrast with civilised individuated individuals who are rational and self-regulating. By extension, the same applies to minority communities in western liberal democracies (such as Muslims), in which individuals purport to refuse to be self-regulating.

Although it may seem obvious that autonomy can never be absolute, noteworthy is the denial of the inherent limitations of the western liberal secular autonomy framework, as espoused by many liberal theorists, including liberal feminists. This denial may itself be libidinally charged as western women need a standard against which to gauge advances in their own emancipation (see e.g. Spivak 1985, Mohanty 1988, Ahmed 2000 and Kapur 2005). For example, Kapur (2005) argues that many western liberal feminists have long deployed what she terms 'the tragedy of victimisation rhetoric' in respect of Third World women, who are seen as the ultimate victim subject – what Spivak (1985) called 'saving brown women from brown men'. (This point will be returned to in Chapter 4.) These postcolonial scholars have problematised the West's conceit that western women are 'secular, liberated, and [have] control over their own lives' (Mohanty 1988: 74) as a fantasy sustained by the figure of its putative opposite, the Third World (or for that matter, ethnic minority) woman oppressed by her culture and ultimately lacking in agency. However, the effect of this deeply entrenched conceit is such that even someone as sympathetic to the cause of Muslim women and girls as Baroness Hale betrays certain paternalism when it comes to the 'choice' to veil.

The idiom of women's choice often acts to channel the West's cultural chauvinism towards what is seen as inherently non-liberal, 'cultural' practices, such as Islamic veiling codes enacted by religious law. Western women's 'choices' are somehow seen as 'freer', if not absolutely free, despite the fact that they are, in their own way, constrained by western ideas of what is feminine, fashionable and appropriate. In the West, there are different forms of nearly compulsory feminine dress, not to mention invasive cosmetic surgery that is increasingly becoming the norm. Another prominent example of unfreedom is the largely private character of childcare in most western societies, in which women are still presumed to be primary child-carers. That, in effect, means that most women are faced with a choice of either not working (and thus sacrificing possible professional fulfilment and career prospects) or leaving their children in paid care (expensive and potentially engendering feelings of guilt and maternal failure). It is hard to see how being faced with this kind of choice is necessarily better than choosing whether or not to veil.

Perhaps acknowledging forms in which western women are oppressed would undermine the western sense of superiority. One is inclined to agree that 'we *need* fundamentalism, indeed, we project and produce it elsewhere, to represent ourselves as free' (Brown 2006: 189). Surely, there are serious differences between western and Islamic dress codes, and it is not the intention here to collapse them. But the problem is that one kind of dress code is automatically presumed to be better and freer than the other.

It could be something to do with the fact that the *formal existence of choice* within liberalism is valued regardless of its actualisability, reinforced by its 'strict quantification of sexism' ('more there, less here') and 'inattention to the *varieties* of male superordination' (ibid.: 195–196). Indeed, even the more sensitive and culturally attuned liberal feminists speak in terms of *degrees* of choice: according to Nussbaum (1999), for example, 'religious systems of family law ... may severely limit women's degree of choice in and consent to marriage' (p. 98). There is a pervasive tendency to equate freedom with choice, which 'sets loose, in a depoliticized underworld, a sea of social powers nearly as coercive as law, and certainly as effective in producing subjectivated subjects' (Brown 2006: 197). Choice becomes fetishised, which 'both cloaks and potentially eroticizes the powers it engages' (ibid.). It seems that the West considers itself to be free(r) as it still believes, rather naïvely, that power is mostly associated with law and sovereignty, rather than is complex, diffused and decentralised. As veiling is presumed to be 'imposed' by a religious law, it is believed to be coercive and oppressive. Western feminine dress, in contrast, is dictated by secular and market considerations of compliance with social and professional conventions. That, however, is disguised as freedom and a pathway to success, and hence not seen as problematic.

While this sort of critique is most obviously directed at those feminists who refuse to comprehend Islamic veiling as a valid 'choice', it also applies to the other side of the binary – that is, celebratory representations of Islamic veiling as a positive, autonomous choice. This is not to say that individuals ought not to be entitled to argue their case in these terms. Rather, the point is that legal, popular and academic accounts of Islamic veiling as a choice, which underplay structures, conditions and circumstances in which choices are made, entrench the normative parameters of the debate in which formal availability of choice is the definition of freedom.

The problem has been signalled in a different context:

> consider a contradiction that we have not adequately confronted in our politics, the contradiction between our belief in the need to assert and protect the autonomy of the individual citizen and our simultaneous belief in the operation of the hegemony of dominant power-laden values that makes the 'freedom to choose' so problematic.... When, for instance, a woman chooses to abort a fetus because of its female sex, or to acquiesce to a marriage in which her natal family will be made bankrupt by dowry requirements or to participate in a beauty contest, what operates is not free will in the feminist/modernist sense, but at the same time, the situation is so complicated that it cannot simply be characterised by a *lack* of free will either.
>
> (Menon 2005: 219)

Even more striking is the Beit Shemesh scenario of women voluntarily choosing to cover their bodies and faces in many layers of fabric, despite the clear message from rabbinic authorities that that was not necessary. On the one hand, the women sought to assert themselves and their decision to take on additional stringencies in stark defiance of male authority. On the other, their decision, although extreme, stemmed from the entrenched culture of the necessity of female modesty, perpetuated by the male religious authorities they sought to oppose. It is an attractive solution to label these women deluded and suffering from a severe form of false consciousness. But that does not get us very far: 'false consciousness' is not just patronising; it assumes to know for sure what kind of consciousness is good or bad for women, regardless of any particular woman's own self-perception and ways of relating to the world. It is not just that the conditions these women live in need changing. It could be that they genuinely find self-fulfilment and self-assertion within and despite them, however incomprehensible that may be to the western secular feminist.

To sum up, we would do well not to rush to construct the veiled woman as an autonomous subject whose behaviour could be explained away as either oppressed by or resisting the norm. Both sides of the binary present an inadequate account of agency, failing to acknowledge that something more complex is at work, as agentic choices are 'conditioned ... but not overdetermined' (Motha 2007: 150) by one's circumstances.

4 Towards a different view of religious agency

One alternative way of conceptualising religious agency, as it is implicated in the practice of Islamic veiling, has been developed in Mahmood's scholarship on the politics of Islamic Reformation (2006) and the Islamic Revival movement (2001; 2005). It provides a particularly constructive counterpoint to the prevailing parameters of the veiling debate as it helps understand how the paradigm of autonomy and choice may not be an adequate tool to comprehend *religiousness.* This is especially valuable as religion remains notably undertheorised in feminist theory (which, by and large, tends to bundle it together with culture).

Constructions of Islamic veiling as a sign of women's autonomy or transition to modernity, discussed earlier, are indicative of a particular 'singular relationship' between the subject and a religious text whereby the text is a collection of signs to be interpreted by the subject. In effect, this is simply a reversal of the vision of Islamic veiling as signifying religious fundamentalism and/or oppression of women ('ostentatious religious signs', according to the French law). Such 'secular hermeneutics' are essential to 'remaking certain kinds of religious subjectivities ... so as to render them compliant with liberal political rule' (Mahmood 2006: 328). Mahmood argues this in the context of the US policy of promoting a more 'liberal', 'rational' and 'modern' version of Islam in the Middle East, which is seen as essential for world peace and stability. Yet, there are remarkable similarities in the Islamic veiling controversies as they have arisen around Europe, which presents fertile ground for critique.

To come back to Baroness Hale's speech in *Denbigh High School,* she says: 'If a Sikh man wears a turban or a Jewish man a yamoulka, we can readily assume that it was his free choice to adopt the dress dictated by the teaching of his religion' (para 94). (She is prepared to 'make the same assumption about an adult Muslim woman who chooses to wear the Islamic headscarf' (ibid.)). There is a kind of contradiction there: how does one 'freely choose' what one believes is 'dictated' by a higher authority? Perhaps religiousness is more accurately described by what political philosopher Michael Sandel calls 'encumbered' personhood, where individuals are 'claimed by duties they cannot renounce, even in the face of civil obligations that may conflict' (1998: 87). The religious self is constituted by religious norms, rather than by its own authority, as the autonomy framework would have it – hence the liberal need to 'remake' religious subjectivities as compatible with secularism (this will be explored in more detail in Chapter 5). Baroness Hale's 'ready assumption' promotes a particular 'religious subject who understands religion – its scriptures and its ritual forms – as a congeries of symbols to be flexibly interpreted in a manner consonant with the imperatives of secular political rule' (Mahmood 2006: 344).

This does not mean that the understanding of religiosity where the self is constituted by religious norms, rather than by one's own, colludes with the total lack of choice approach. Questioning the liberal view of autonomy does not necessarily imply dissolving individual responsibility. It is useful to recall that the idea of free will is key to Abrahamic religious traditions, which understand agency as predicated on voluntary choices – hence the concept of reward and punishment. Yet these traditions also acknowledge that the choices one makes in the exercise of free will are always already grounded in individual circumstances; hence everyone's challenges are different. In other words, it is misleading to assume that religious subjectivity is saturated by religious law in a way that precludes any meaningful choice or decision-making.

Writing to define the Islamic *umma*, Asad (2003) notes that it is a 'theologically defined space', a crucial point about which is 'not that it is imagined but that what is imagined predicates distinctive modes of being and acting'. As such, it:

> presupposes individuals who are *self-governing but not autonomous*. The *sharī'a*, a system of practical reason morally binding on each faithful individual, exists independently of him or her. At the same time every Muslim has the psychological ability to discover its rules and to conform to them.
>
> (p. 197, emphasis added)

Although Asad's choice of the term 'self-governing' may not be entirely fortunate as the meaning is rather close to the Greek *αυτονομία*, it could perhaps be understood as 'conditioned, but not overdetermined' by one's sources of constitution. In this way, religion provides a series of practices for one's realisation, a kind of 'habituated learning', in which 'the outward behavior of the body constitutes both the potentiality, and the means, through which an interiority is realized'. The veil thus may be 'a means both of being and becoming a certain kind of person' (Mahmood 2001: 215, 214).

To return to Mahmood's observations, they are grounded in her field work in the women's mosque movement in Egypt. They are of wider validity, though, as they touch upon the important general questions of religiosity and agency. Her study shows how qualities such as modesty, docility and patience, which are willingly and consciously cultivated in the course of such 'habituated learning', are not at all those usually approved by the traditional liberal autonomy framework. For the traditional feminist in particular, modesty, docility and patience signify submission to patriarchy, false consciousness and a near-total lack of freedom and choice. This may be a rather short-sighted preconception: for religious women, docility and patience are not natural or social givens, but acquired qualities which require much will-power and determination to cultivate. In this way, 'habituated learning' is an ultimately agentic, although not necessarily 'autonomous', practice.

Unlike many 'religion-friendly' feminists, Mahmood's approach is not quite concerned with the question of what 'conceptual and practical resources [religious traditions] offer to women, and [what] possibilities of redirecting and recoding these resources in accord with women's own "interests and agendas"' (2005: 6). The agentic practice of habituated learning does not necessarily presume women's 'own interests and agendas' distinct from those of their religion or religious communities. Rather than striving for a better system of gender arrangements, it could be described as being about self-fulfilment and spiritual betterment.

Interestingly, such a conception of agency does not necessarily fit with poststructural feminism, such as Judith Butler's. Butler's work is famous for rejecting what she calls 'an emancipatory model of agency', which presumes that all humans are 'endowed with a will, a freedom and an intentionality' whose workings are 'thwarted by relations of power that are considered external to the subject' (Benhabib *et al.* 1995: 136) – precisely the liberal autonomy/choice framework criticised here. But Butler locates her concept of agency within Foucauldian notions of power and subjectivation and Lacanian notions of foreclosure and abjection. She thus emphasises the utterly constructed nature (*performativity*) of gender and the destabilising potential of various gender performances, wherein every repetition carries the possibility of failure, and thus of resignifying the dominant meaning. It is through such resignification that the dominant gender system can be subverted. For Butler, 'the iterability of performativity is a theory of agency' (Butler 1990/1999: xxiv). Although of tremendous radical potential, Butler's theory features norms as *either* consolidated *or* subverted. In contrast, Mahmood is more interested in the 'work norms perform beyond this register of suppression and subversion within the constitution of the subject' (2005: 22), and that interest is shared here.

Veiling is indeed a prime example of such work as:

> the veil [may be] a necessary component of the virtue of modesty because the veil both expresses 'true modesty' and is the means through which modesty is acquired. They draw, therefore, an ineluctable relationship between the norm (modesty) and the bodily form it takes (the veil) such that the veiled body becomes the necessary means through which the virtue of modesty is both created *and* expressed. In contrast with this understanding is a position (associated with prominent secularist writers) that argues that the virtue of modesty is no different than any other human attribute ... it is a facet of character but does not commit one to any particular expressive repertoire such as donning the veil.
>
> (ibid.: 23)

Similarly:

> ritual transforms the subject by giving him or her a world to inhabit that is shifted away from the empirical, social, and pragmatic world – hence also shifted vis-à-vis the world of conscious or unconscious rationality. Not that it eliminates the latter; rather, it relates to them in concealments or displacements, thus coloring life and action.
>
> (Hammoudi 2006: 275)

Thus, a richer concept of agency needs to be attuned to the work Islamic veiling may be doing for those who practise it. It is illuminating that allusions towards such an understanding have tentatively been made in the Islamic veiling debate in Europe. A book published in France in 2004, *Ordinary Girls* (*Des filles comme les autres*) is a series of interviews with sisters Alma and Lila Lévy, who had been expelled from their suburban school for wearing headscarves. The girls were born to secular, non-Muslim parents and had converted to Islam against the wishes of their family. Their account indicates that the:

> authority to accept religious prescription ... lies in the willing self. ... What they are after seems more often an abandonment of ego than an assertion of it; at the same time, the self is very much at the center of how they conceive of what they do.
>
> (Scott 2007: 142)

Perhaps Alma Lévy's own words describe her experience better:

> I began by praying.... In order to pray, you have to cover your head. Quickly, I found it impossible to put on the veil when I prayed and to take it off when I went outside. Undressing in order to go out seemed incongruous to me: the headscarf was a part of myself.
>
> (Lévy and Lévy 2004: 63, translated by Scott 2007: 143)

Another book published in France at approximately the same time, *One Veiled, the Other Not* (*L'une voilée, l'autre pas*) (2003), is an exchange between two Muslim women on the topic of Islamic veiling. According to the veiled author, Saïda Kada, the founder of French Muslim Women in Action (*Femmes françaises et musulmanes engagées*):

> One is a Muslim first; one adheres to a certain philosophy of life and, in this context, one wants to wear a headscarf. The discovery of Islam is marked by a series of steps that successively fashion your identity by leading you to find an equilibrium in yourself, in God, and with others.... You can't understand the headscarf without talking about the whole spiritual progression that goes with it. For a young girl the logic is not 'with or without the headscarf.' She begins to feel herself 'with' it in a progressive journey of faith, where she discovers things strongly linked to spirituality.
>
> (Bouzar and Kada 2003: 25, translated by Scott 2007: 143)

These accounts are perfectly in line with what Mahmood describes as a 'concordance of inward motives, outward actions, inclinations, and emotional states through the repeated practice of virtuous deeds' (Mahmood 2001: 215). There is also some corroboration of such an understanding of religious agency in the case-law. The most notable is the approach taken by the Norwegian Ombud in cases involving restrictions on the wearing of headscarves, as she takes the view that the hijab is part of the wearer's personal integrity (as described in Chapter 2).

In *Dahlab* v. *Switzerland* (2001), the ECHR case that involved a public school teacher (herself a convert to Islam) who was told to remove her headscarf while at work, the applicant argued 'that her clothing ... should be treated not as a religious symbol but in the same way as any other perfectly inoffensive garments that a teacher may decide to wear for his or her own reasons' (p. 452). It is at least arguable that such ambivalence about 'reasons' is indicative of a more complex view of agency, which involves reluctance to think of religion as a 'symbol' to be put on and off. As discussed earlier, this argument was rejected by the Swiss Federal Court (and then by the ECtHR), which had 'no doubt that the appellant wears the headscarf and loose-fitting clothes not for aesthetic reasons but in order to obey a religious precept which she derives from ... the Koran' (ibid.). This is very much the way of secular understanding Mahmood critiques: there is a singular text to be interpreted by the rational subject, and the ECtHR asserts the 'correct' interpretation.

Finally, the case of *Kayhan* v. *Turkey* (2006), which was brought to the Committee on the Elimination of Discrimination Against Women by a teacher who had permanently lost her status as a civil servant because of wearing a headscarf, turns the classic choice argument, conventionally deployed in human rights litigation, on its head as the author considered that 'the act of *forcing her to make a choice* between working and uncovering her head violates her fundamental rights that are protected in international conventions' (para 3.2, emphasis added). It is unfortunate that the communication was inadmissible due to non-exhaustion of domestic remedies, so that the Women's Committee did not have an opportunity to address this argument and perhaps envisage a more complex picture of religious subjectivity.

5 Concluding remarks

This chapter has been concerned with the first 'frame' of the Islamic veiling controversy, namely the rhetoric of autonomy and choice. This is currently a predominant modality in which arguments both for and against various restrictions on Islamic veiling are formulated. There is certainly no shortage of arguments that veiling signifies a near-total lack of autonomy and choice and therefore needs to be discouraged and prohibited. At the same time, the position taken in mainstream human rights jurisprudence is that rational, autonomous individuals are to be expected to prioritise their choices – *either* wear the hijab *or* go to a certain school or university. In contrast, those who oppose the restrictions commonly argue that the decision to veil is a positive, autonomous choice, which is to be understood and celebrated.

This chapter has been sceptical of both sides of the debate. The position that veiling always signifies a total lack of choice is clearly unsustainable. The opposite argument, although perhaps more convincing, still stays within the same classic western autonomy/choice paradigm, as do the arguments of those who believe that veiling can never be a free, autonomous choice. This chapter has called for interrogation of the framework as such. Although a total break may not be possible or even desirable, a reflective enquiry into what the Islamic veiling issue has come to stand for would be served well by exploring possibilities for alternative ways of conceiving of human agency, which the preoccupation with the classic autonomy/choice framework eclipses. Such an exploration has been carried out towards the end of the chapter. This does not mean that the terms 'autonomy' and 'choice' could not be meaningfully used in the Islamic veiling debate or elsewhere. Rather, the chapter's argument has been that it is appropriate to question the wisdom of fetishising these concepts as the default hermeneutic tool for making sense of human experience. Not to do so would be to risk mistaking choice for freedom.

The next chapter draws and builds on this analysis, but concentrates on a rather different aspect. If this chapter has been primarily concerned with the individual, agentic dimension of Islamic veiling, Chapter 4 looks at the broader picture as it considers the gender equality argument as such, which is the second 'frame' containing the debate. The structure of Chapter 4's analysis is quite similar to that of the present chapter: the uses of the gender equality argument on both sides of the debate are outlaid, followed by a more in-depth interrogation of such uses, as well as of the principle of gender equality itself. Inevitably, there is a certain overlap between these two chapters, with the same material sometimes being engaged in both. Whenever this happens, however, there is a different purpose, and different emphasis and different points are made.

Chapter 4

Gender equality

This chapter explores the second framework that contains the Islamic veiling debate – that of gender equality. Islamic veiling is an obvious candidate for a gender analysis as it is women and their bodies that are at the centre of veiling controversies. Much has been written on how religious movements use women's bodies symbolically to advance certain political and social agendas (e.g. Werbner 2007; Ahmed, L. 1992; Kandiyoti 1991; Mernissi 1991; Ong 1990; Pourzand 1999; Yuval-Davis 1992). The chapter is not going to elaborate on this, fairly uncontroversial, point much further. Instead, it pursues a different line of enquiry, which is believed to be underexplored. It aims to show how gender equality has become an indispensable argument *both for and against* Islamic veiling restrictions in Europe. It aims to trace the deployment and subtle workings of the gender equality argument on both sides of the Islamic veiling debate as it is currently conducted in western liberal secular, human rights environments. It argues that the contemporary unprecedented status of gender equality is a sign of the times, indeed an important achievement of feminism. However, the somewhat dogmatic character of much of the feminist project will be shown to be problematic.

On the one hand – and most prominently – gender equality is commonly treated as a major foundational value in liberal democracies and international human rights regimes, whereas various forms of Islamic veiling are considered incompatible with this value. A key element in this type of argument is the pitching of gender *against* culture and religion, which are in turn conflated. An account of this type of argument, as it is deployed in the relevant cases and the surrounding debate, is given in Part 1 of the chapter. On the other hand, others – a growing minority – insist that the 'veil' symbolises women's equality and emancipation, rather than submission to patriarchy, and as such should be celebrated. This type of position provides the focus of Part 2 of the chapter. Part 3 then contains a more in-depth critique of these two positions, highlighting problems with both. The use of the gender equality argument in support of Islamic veiling restrictions is problematic as it has strong racist and colonialist undertones. The use of gender equality rhetoric by the other side – that is, Islamic feminists who defend veiling – also has its problems as it tends to mythologise Islam as a hotbed of feminist ideas. Part 4 argues that both types of views, together with some other examples, point to the firm normative entrenchment of 'gender equality' in contemporary social, legal and political theory as well as popular discourse. Possible reasons for this entrenchment are explored, as well as its implications. Ultimately, the chapter interrogates the normative purchase of gender equality, which tends to penalise and discipline the very women it is supposed to benefit.

1 Islamic veiling as subordination of women

There is no shortage of representations of Islamic veiling as symbolising total oppression of women. Commenting on the *Aishah Azmi* case (2006), which concerned a teaching assistant who wore a full-face veil, the journalist Minette Marrin wrote in the *Sunday Times*:

> What Mrs Azmi stands for, so to speak, is what many people fear about Muslims, no matter how tolerant they would like to feel. A woman shrouded in veils represents deliberate cultural separation, voluntary apartheid, a pre-Enlightenment religion and *a view of relations between the sexes that the mainstream culture in this country can no longer accept and rejects in law.*
>
> (Marrin, 22 October 2006, emphasis added)

This rhetoric is noteworthy not just for its rather strong anti-Muslim sentiments, but, more relevantly for this chapter, for the specific way in which Islam is linked with backwardness and thus a blatant lack of gender equality. Indeed, Islamic veiling has come to be viewed as a perfect embodiment of the near-total conflict between 'culture, religion and gender', in which the West is presumed to be the neutral standard and thus to have no real 'culture'. According to Frances Raday, an ex-member of the UN Committee on the Elimination of Discrimination against Women, whose article on culture, religion and gender was cited by Baroness Hale in the *Denbigh High School* case (2006):

> The conflict between culture, religion, and gender has arisen as a constitutional issue, not in the theocratic Islamic states, which mandate women's dress codes with extremely severe penalties for any breach, but, rather, in secular countries in which religious Muslim communities demand that their women and girl children observe the dress code.
>
> (Raday 2003: 690)

This is quite in line with the general stance of the Council of Europe on gender and religion (which in turn informs the approach of the European Court of Human Rights in Islamic veiling cases, as the European Convention on Human Rights is a Council of Europe treaty). For example, the Council of Europe Parliamentary Assembly's recent Resolution on Women and Religion in Europe proclaims that the 'influence [of religion on the lives on women] is seldom benign', and that 'it is the duty of the member states of the Council of Europe to protect women against violations of their rights in the name of religion and *to promote and fully implement gender equality*' (PA Resolution 1464, 2005: paras 2, 6, emphasis added).

In turn, the ECtHR has proclaimed that gender equality is a fundamental value underlying the ECHR. This is so despite the notable lack of such intent at the time of the drafting of the Convention (see e.g. Baer 2004). It was thc case of *Abdulaziz, Cabales and Balkandali* v. *United Kingdom*, decided in 1985, which provided the first major occasion for the ECtHR to affirm the normative value of the goal of the 'advancement of the equality of the sexes', for both individual member states of the Council of Europe and the ECHR legal system itself (para 78). The application of this goal in the *Abdulaziz* case itself was not uncontroversial: the case concerned immigration rules that allowed Asian wives, but not husbands, to join their spouses in the United Kingdom. Both gender and race discrimination were pleaded, but only the former succeeded as the ECtHR noted the particular importance of eliminating gender discrimination in the member states of the Council of Europe.

The goal of the 'advancement of the equality of the sexes' has since been keenly upheld in ECtHR case-law. Indeed, gender equality has firmly secured the top position in the hierarchy of equalities in Europe and beyond. An overview of respective ECHR jurisprudence reveals that 'religious equality' – or indeed any other type of 'equality' – has not enjoyed a comparable level of protection. Quite in contrast, cases involving discriminatory aspects of Article 9 ECHR, which protects freedom of religion, demonstrate that there is a certain expectation of unequal treatment in respect of 'minority' religions (this will be explored in more detail in Chapter 5). This inevitably means that gender equality is understood through the prism of the dominant western cultural norm.

Most ECHR cases dealing with Islamic veiling issues cite the principle of gender equality as an important consideration justifying restrictions on women's freedom of clothing. The decision of the European Commission on Human Rights in the earlier case of *Karaduman* v. *Turkey* (1993), which concerned a university graduate who could not obtain a provisional graduation certificate because she would not submit a photograph with an uncovered head, contains a rather underdeveloped reasoning. Raday, however, believes that '[a]lthough no direct reference was made to the issue of women's equality [in *Karaduman*], this issue has been seen as intrinsic to questions of women's dress and modesty' (Raday 2003: 693).

The reasoning of the ECtHR in the case of *Dahlab* v. *Switzerland* (2001), which involved a public school teacher who was asked to remove her headscarf, is more elaborate and is often regarded as a turning point in the development of the ECtHR's approach to Islamic veiling. Two justifications for the restrictive measure were cited by the ECtHR (following the Swiss Federal Court): denominational neutrality and gender equality. The justification of gender equality is of particular interest here: the ECtHR noted that the headscarf:

> appears to be imposed on women by a precept which is laid down in the Koran and which … is *hard to square with the principle of gender equality*. It therefore appears difficult to reconcile the wearing of an Islamic headscarf with the message of tolerance, respect for others and, above all, equality and non-discrimination that all teachers in a democratic society must convey to their pupils.
>
> (ibid.: 463. See also *Şahin* 2007: paras 112–123)

In this way, the headscarf is cast as irreconcilable with the uncontested democratic virtue of gender equality and therefore cannot be tolerated. Gender equality is treated in a rather abstract way and is, interestingly, at odds with Dahlab's own contention, under Article 14 ECHR, that the requirement that she stop wearing the headscarf discriminated against her as a woman. This was dismissed as the ECtHR considered that the measure 'was not directed against her as a member of the female sex' and that the law 'could also be applied to a man who, in similar circumstances, wore clothing that clearly identified him as a member of a different faith' (which was chosen despite Dahlab's suggestion of a *Muslim man* as the appropriate comparator) (*Dahlab* 2001: 464). Thus, a distinctly 'formal equality' comparator-based type of reasoning was applied, which is characteristic of the generally underdeveloped nature of Article 14 jurisprudence.

The strong normativity of the ECtHR's rhetoric of gender equality is quite in contrast with the notoriously inefficient nature of the ECHR equality/non-discrimination provision, Article 14. The application of Article 14 ECHR depends on the applicability of another, 'substantive', article of the ECHR, as it can only be utilised in conjunction with such other substantive right. In most cases where a violation of a substantive provision of the ECHR has been found, the ECtHR considers addressing Article 14 unnecessary. Cases in which application of Article 14 led to a finding of a violation of this non-discrimination provision (in conjunction with another substantive right) are rather rare. Generally, the ECtHR has adopted a 'formal equality' type approach to this article, interpreting discrimination as a 'difference in treatment', capable of being justified by an 'objective and reasonable justification' pursuing a legitimate aim, provided there is a 'reasonable relationship of proportionality between the means employed and the aim sought to be achieved' (*Belgian Linguistic Case* 1968: para 10. On Article 14, see e.g. Arnardóttir 2009).

Similarly to the *Dahlab* decision, in *Şahin* v. *Turkey*, which involved a medical student who was prevented from attending lectures and examinations because of wearing a headscarf, the message of the headscarf was interpreted as clearly inimical to the constitutionally embedded principles of secularism and gender equality (paras 112–123). The headscarf was thus understood as a religious item detrimental to gender equality, which suggests that gender and religion operate as abstract and unrelated to each other.[1] In respect of gender equality, the ECtHR reproduced its earlier opinion in *Dahlab* that the headscarf 'appeared to be imposed on women by a religious precept that was hard to reconcile with the principle of gender equality' (*Şahin* 2007: para 111), providing no further clarification. Despite the considerable length of the *Şahin* judgment, the ECtHR did not attempt to give the principle of gender equality any specific content, which might have included some elaboration on whom exactly this principle is intended to benefit. As noted in the previous chapter, this can be contrasted with the majority judgment of the German Federal Constitutional Court in *Ludin* v. *Land Baden-Württemberg* (2003), according to which the subjective intentions of the wearer, although not decisive, should be taken into account, with the relevant test being that of the 'neutral observer'.

This suggests that the 'gender' in 'gender equality' operates as a highly abstract concept, bearing little or no reflection on the specific applicants or any other women. Obviously, this approach of the ECtHR is unsatisfactory. The applicants in both the *Dahlab* and *Şahin* cases did not appear stereotypically oppressed as they went all the way to Strasbourg to make their point. Both asserted that they wore the headscarf voluntarily and not because of subordination to men. The ECtHR seems to disregard this completely, choosing to see the headscarf as evidence of the women's acceptance of gender inequality or, worse, of seeking to impose this inequality on the rest of society (Evans 2006). Indeed, Judge Tulkens in her dissenting opinion in *Şahin* v. *Turkey* points out that there was nothing in the case to suggest that the applicant justified the majority's projection of the headscarf as symbolising gender inequality. According to her:

1 Note, however, the dissenting opinion of Judge Tulkens in *Şahin* at para 5: 'In a democratic society, I believe that it is necessary to seek to harmonise the principles of secularism, equality and liberty, not to weigh one against the other.' On this point, see further Vakulenko (2007).

> Equality and non-discrimination are subjective rights which must remain under the control of those who are entitled to benefit from them. Paternalism of this sort runs counter to the case-law of the Court…
>
> (Dissenting opinion of Judge Tulkens: para 12)

Not dissimilarly to the rhetoric of the ECtHR, the debates around the French laws prohibiting 'ostentatious' religious symbols in public schools and niqabs anywhere in public, are replete with representations of the headscarf as institutionalised oppression of women. As was mentioned in the previous chapter, the Stasi Commission concluded, without much evidence, that '[o]bjectively, the veil stands for the alienation of women' (Stasi 2004: 128). Thus, a certain 'objective' truth on gender equality is prescribed.

According to Elisabeth Badinter, a French feminist philosopher who was vocal in the debate:

> Soon feminists in the rest of Europe will realise the headscarf is a terrible symbol of submission. You cannot denounce what has been going on in Afghanistan while tolerating the veil in Europe – *even if women claim they are wearing it voluntarily.*
>
> (Smith, 1 February 2004, emphasis added)

In fact, this attitude has been common among feminists in France since the 1980s. Gisèle Halimi, a leading feminist lawyer of Tunisian origin, resigned from the anti-racist organisation *SOS-Racisme* when it defended the girls excluded from school during the 1989 *foulard* affair, arguing that '[t]here cannot be integration without respect for the laws of the receiving country. There cannot be a change in mentalities without women's dignity equalling that of men' (*Quotidien de Paris,* 2 November 1989, cited in Freedman 2007: 38). A former Minister of Women's Rights claimed that accepting Islamic headscarves would be 'equivalent to saying yes to the inequality of women in French Muslim society' (*Quotidien de Paris,* 6 November 1989, cited in Freedman 2007). Many of the French teachers 'who fired the conflict by excluding young women wearing headscarves from their classes or by taking industrial action and striking in protest at the wearing of headscarves, did so out of supposedly feminist sensibilities' (Freedman 2007: 39). One teacher, who had asked a pupil to take off her headscarf, summarised her reaction as '[m]ore feminist than secular to tell the truth: a thirteen-year-old girl wearing a headscarf seemed evidently unacceptable to me' (Altschull 1995: 11). Fadela Amara, the then leader of the feminist group *Ni Putes Ni Soumises* ('Neither Whores Nor Submissives'), which had strongly supported the ban, believed that the mandatory headscarf-wearing that many girls in France face implies, among other things, constant surveillance by brothers, forced marriages and virginity monitoring (*Dimanche Ouest France*, 28 December 2003, cited in Wing and Smith 2006: 767–768). A petition widely circulated by *Ni Putes Ni Soumises* asserts that 'the Islamic veil subjects *all of us*, Muslim and non-Muslim alike, to an intolerable discrimination against women' (Guénif-Souliamas and Macé 2004: 9, emphasis added). This very strong rhetoric is not unlike the Dutch films *Submission* and *Fitna*, in which Islam is crudely portrayed as inherently violent and misogynist (see Chapter 2). As will be elaborated in Part 3 of this chapter, feminism hereby becomes an authoritarian discourse on truth and what is good for women and society.

Another notable feature of the debate is that the visibility of the female body (which is what Islamic veiling covers) becomes coterminous with gender equality. In the French debate, this attitude was exemplified by the psychoanalyst Elisabeth Roudinesco, who was 'absolutely convinced that the real problem posed by the veil is that it covers over a sexual dimension. It denies the equality between men and women upon which our society rests' (Debré 2003, vol 2: 52). According to her, the veil interferes with the 'natural psychological process' of feminisation, in which feminine identity is conferred by male desire.

More generally, it is quite noteworthy that, like in the Council of Europe legal order, in the French debate, gender equality is assumed to be a foundational value of the French republic, on a par with *laïcité*, despite such a strong emphasis on sexual equality being a rather recent phenomenon (see Fassin 2006). The then Minister of the Interior and now President of the French Republic, Nicolas Sarkozy, summarised this in 2005:

> We are proud of the values of the Republic, of equality between men and women, of laïcité, and of the French ideal of integration. So let us dare to speak of these to those we welcome here. And let us bring pressure to bear so that the rights of French women apply also to immigrant women.
>
> (9 June 2005)[2]

The Conseil d'État case of *Mme M* (2008) contains some of the most extraordinary uses of the gender equality principle so far. The unsuccessful applicant, a Moroccan woman who wore the niqab, was refused French citizenship due to 'insufficient integration, other than linguistic competence'. This was because she 'adopted a radical practice of her religion, incompatible with the essential values of French society, notably with the

2 'Nous sommes fiers des valeurs de la République, de l'égalité entre les hommes et les femmes, de la laïcité, de l'idéal français d'intégration. Alors, osons en parler à ceux que nous accueillons. Et agissons pour que les droits de la femme française s'appliquent aussi aux femmes de l'immigration' (Sarkozy, 9 June 2005, translated by Scott 2007: 162)

principle of the equality of the sexes' (ibid.).[3] The ruling relies on the Conclusions of the Government Commissioner, Mme Prada Bordenave,[4] who examined Mme M's 'dossier' (consisting of three transcripts of interviews with social services and police).

The dossier reveals a great deal of detail about Mme M's lifestyle and daily routine, which betrays a certain discomfort with the niqab, despite the Commissioner's assurance, at the outset of her analysis, that the wearing of the veil as such does not amount to insufficient assimilation (*Mme E.Y.*, 3 February 1999, cited in Conclusions: 3). Apparently, Mme M would wear a niqab each time she turned up for an interview at the Prefecture's department. The interviewing officers (in all cases female) testified that:

> Mme M only accepted to lift this piece of cloth in the office after their express request, when they told her that they had to be able to identify her and that, as soon as the interview was over, before even crossing the doorstep, she would put it back on, walking down the corridors of that establishment in this way.
>
> (Conclusions: 3)[5]

The Commissioner then noted that Mme M's own statements indicate that she 'adopted this costume' only upon her arrival in France and at the request of her husband (a French citizen). She had said that she wore it 'out of custom rather than conviction. She puts it on as soon as she leaves her home and, even in her apartment, she puts it on when she has male visitors who are not related to her or her husband' (ibid.: 3–4).[6]

3 'Elle a cependant adopté une pratique radicale de sa religion, incompatible avec les valeurs essentielles de la communauté française, et notamment avec le principe d'égalité des sexes.'

4 Conclusions of a Government Commissioner, who is considered to be a neutral adviser to the Conseil d'État, rather than a representative of the Government as a party to the dispute, are part of the proceedings before this quasi-judicial institution. The Conclusions normally contain much more detailed information and reasoning than Conseil d'État rulings, which are usually very brief.

5 'Mme M. s'est rendue à plusieurs reprises à un entretien en préfecture, à chaque fois elle s'est présentée recouverte du vêtement des femmes de la péninsule arabique : longue robe unie sombre ou kaki tombant jusqu'aux pieds, voile masquant les cheveux, le front et le menton et, combinée avec le voile, une autre pièce de tissus masquant le visage et ne laissant voir les yeux que par une fente qui dans cette région s'appelle le Niqab. Les agents qui faisaient l'entretien étaient dans tous les cas des femmes, elles notent que Mme M. n'a accepté de relever cette pièce de tissu dans le bureau qu'à leur demande expresse, lorsqu'elles lui ont fait remarquer qu'il fallait qu'elles puissent l'identifier et que dès que l'entretien a été fini, avant même de franchir la porte, elle l'a remis, circulant ainsi dans les couloirs de cette administration.'

6 'Elle dit le porter plus par habitude que par conviction. Elle le met dès qu'elle sort de chez elle et, même dans son appartement, elle le met lorsque viennent des hommes qui ne sont pas de sa famille ou de celle de son mari.'

The 'positive' points that Mme M scored were her good French, the education of her two young children in a municipal school and (most puzzlingly) her examinations by a male gynaecologist during her pregnancies (ibid.: 4). These, however, were not enough to outscore her apparently nearly total seclusion:

> it remains the case that, according to her own statements, she leads an almost imprisoned life, isolated from French society: she does not receive visitors at her home; in the morning she does her chores, goes for a walk with her baby or her children; in the afternoon she visits her father or her father-in-law. As far as shopping is concerned, she indicates that she can do shopping on her own, but admits that more often than not she goes to the supermarket in the company of her husband.
>
> (ibid.)[7]

This leaves one wondering what kind of life a housewife and mother of three young children, let alone a woman of an economically disadvantaged minority background, is supposed to lead in a society where childcare is, despite all the advances of feminism, still a largely private matter. The Commissioner referred to no evidence of any measures taken by the state to help 'assimilate' Mme M into the French way of life, thus presenting 'assimilation', or lack of it, as a one-way process.

The Commissioner concluded that Mme M:

> has not made the values of the Republic, and in particular equality of the sexes, her own. She lives in total submission to the men of her family, which manifests itself in the wearing of her clothes as well as in the organisation of her daily life; and ... she finds this normal and ... it never even crossed her mind to challenge this submission.
>
> (ibid.)[8]

The previous chapter noted the Conseil d'État's blatant disregard for the applicant's own views on the matter, but its more general gender equality rhetoric is more central here. What is even more noteworthy is that Mme

7 'Il reste que, d'après ses propres déclarations, elle mène une vie presque recluse et retranchée de la société française : elle ne reçoit personne chez elle, le matin elle s'occupe de son ménage, se promène avec son bébé ou ses enfants, l'après midi elle va chez son père ou son beau père. Pour les courses, elle indique qu'elle peut faire des achats seule mais admet qu'elle va le plus souvent au supermarché en compagnie de son mari.'

8 'Mme M. n'a pas fait siennes les valeurs de la République et en particulier celle de l'égalité des sexes. Elle vit dans la soumission totale aux hommes de sa famille, qui se manifeste tant le port de son vêtement que dans l'organisation de sa vie quotidienne et les propos qu'elle a tenus aux services montrent qu'elle trouve cela normal et que l'idée même de contester cette soumission ne l'effleure même pas.'

M's *internalisation* of the French value of gender equality – rather than just her outward compliance with it – was under investigation. Furthermore, it is a characteristically French feminist version of gender equality that she was expected to adhere to.

As to the debate around Islamic veiling in Britain, Baroness Hale in the *Denbigh High School* case speaks of the balancing of the 'conflicting priorities' of gender equality and cultural diversity. She quotes Raday's article, according to which a 'mandatory policy that rejects veiling in state educational institutions may provide a crucial opportunity for girls to choose the *feminist freedom* of state education over the patriarchal dominance of their families' (para 92, citing Raday 2003: 709, emphasis added).

At the same time, both Raday and Hale appear to agree that such a prohibition risks offending against 'cultural and religious diversity'. The conflation of religion and culture in this account, although uncontroversial insofar as religious practices may also be cultural or culturally specific, is quite symptomatic of the wider tendency in much of feminism to counterpose gender against culture *and* religion, in which the last two are treated as largely coterminous and even interchangeable. It is useful to recall Brown's (2006) explanation of how this conflation reflects liberalism's amalgamation of 'beliefs' with 'practices', thus performing liberalism's classic move of essentialising difference: 'The practice or attribute is seen as issuing from the identity and as constitutive of certain kinds of experiences, and the combination of the identity and the experiences is treated as the fount of certain views or beliefs' (p. 42). The same type of conflation was salient, for example, in the political response to the French riots in October–November 2005: although the rioters were 'decidedly multicultural and multiethnic', the appropriate response from the state was meeting with 'mosque leaders, rather than consulting a broader constituency' (Al-Azmeh 2007: 212).

Indeed, framing the question as one of cultural(/religious) difference versus gender equality, as exemplified in Baroness Hale's speech, appears to assume that Shabina Begum's desire to wear a jilbab to Denbigh High School was an expression of her 'culture' – which is rather at odds with the other Law Lords' accounts of Shabina's apparently sudden radicalisation, as discussed in the previous chapter. The public debate around the *Denbigh High School* case was saturated with a kind of benign culturalism, neglecting the obvious fact that the jilbab, adopted by Shabina Begum at the age of thirteen, is a type of dress traditional in Arab countries, not Bangladesh from where Shabina's family came to Britain. Thus, 'by no stretch of the imagination could it be considered part of "her" inherited tradition' (Mufti 2007: 21). Finally, Baroness Hale believes that the two 'conflicting policy priorities' of gender equality and cultural diversity are to be balanced 'in a specific social environment', which is 'exactly what [Denbigh High School] was trying to do when it devised the school uniform policy' (para 98).

To sum up, Baroness Hale's otherwise sympathetic account espouses, first, a strong normative vision of the 'feminist freedom' to be free of the false consciousness associated with Islamic veiling (as will be explored later in this chapter, the mandatory nature of this 'freedom' is not unproblematic). Second, there is a rather strong underlying, although unarticulated, assumption that culture and gender are separate formations functioning in isolation from each other. Third, there is also a conviction that they are invariably in competition and therefore in need of balancing. All these features are also salient, often in much stronger terms, in the Islamic veiling debate as it is conducted elsewhere, most notably in the ECHR jurisprudence and in France.

2 Islamic veiling as emancipation of women

The view that Islamic veiling symbolises gender inequality and the subjugation of women, as outlined in Part 1 of this chapter, is by far the most widespread and influential. Yet, there is also some not inconsiderable support for the opposite view, namely that the hijab should be seen as symbolic of resistance to patriarchy, rather than of the repression by it. This is the possibility expressly recognised in *Ludin* v. *Land Baden-Württemberg* (2003) by the German Constitutional Court, which is unique among the selection of cases discussed in Chapter 2 in admitting that wearing Islamic dress is as likely to symbolise women's emancipation as the lack of it (para 52). Lucia Dahlab, the applicant in the ECtHR case of *Dahlab* v. *Switzerland* (2001), even argued that the requirement that she stop wearing a headscarf at work amounted to gender discrimination (p. 464).

In her well-known piece, 'Postcolonial Feminism and the Veil: Considering the Differences', a personal narration published in the early 1990s, Abu-Odeh confronted her unease about Arab women who had recently chosen to veil. Her research concludes, rather surprisingly to her, that '[u]nless I engaged in intellectual elitism and accused those women of false consciousness and of not knowing their own good, there was no way that I could point to instances of the disempowerment of the veil' (1992: 1532). She made an observation that veiled women may:

> differentiate themselves from others in their environment by wearing the veil, using it as *a statement on female subordination* in the non-fundamentalist (pseudo-secular, pseudo-religious) Arab households in which they find themselves. Wearing the veil allows them to have a singular and individual voice: 'You are not wearing the veil, but I am. I am powerful enough to do it, and this is how I carve myself a space you cannot reach. I disapprove of what you are, who you are, and what you think.'
>
> (ibid.: 1536)

A more recent article summarising the proceedings of a conference on headscarves, held at the European University Institute in Florence, asserts:

> The 'new veil' is the most conspicuous sign of Islamic feminism. Women choose to wear it, and will not remove it in any circumstance, including in women-only gatherings or in foreign countries. This is a way of freeing themselves from a male-imposed feminine model that *allows* them to remove the veil in private settings, since its main function is to conceal women from men who are not their relatives. By retaining the veil, they show that it is not imposed by men but chosen by them.
>
> (Lyon and Spini 2004: 344)

This extract was already cited in the previous chapter for what it says about choice, but is worth reproducing here as it indicates that the veil, worn as a 'conspicuous sign' of Islamic feminism, signifies women's emancipation, rather than perpetuation of patriarchy. This type of account contains an interesting, even obstinate, reversal of the gender equality argument to the point of the exact opposite: the veil would not be removed 'in any circumstance' *because* 'a male-imposed feminine model' makes allowances for such a possibility.[9] In this way, the normative value of gender equality itself is preserved intact, while the putative symbolic meaning of veiling is reversed from anti- to pro-equality.

While full historic and socio-political reasons for the relatively recent emergence of Islamic feminism are outside the scope of this book, it is fair to say that the movement as a whole, although surely not internally uniform, can be characterised by an adherence to an Islamic religious framework, as well as a commitment to the improvement of the social, political and legal situation of Muslim women. According to El Guindi (1999):

> It is feminist because it seeks to liberate womanhood; it is Islamic because its premises are embedded in Islamic principles and values. Yet in some senses, the liberal Western-influenced feminism of the aristocracy and the Islamic one are not far apart. Both are about the emancipation of women.
>
> (p. 184)

Thus, there is a fundamental similarity with classic western feminism insofar as there is a quest for women's emancipation. This is so even if the

9 The rule that women may appear unveiled before certain male relatives is contained in Sura 24:31 and is also associated with the incest prohibition in Sura 4:27.

precise definition of emancipation may be different and Islamic veiling may be taken to signify opposite things.

To be sure, there is also an undeniable tension with western, or secular, feminism. Afshar and Maynard (2000) summarise the position of 'Muslim women who have been made invisible by a veil of misunderstanding and Islamophobia' as follows:

> The development of an Islamic feminist discourse has been located not only in contestation with the West, but also with Westernized feminists in Islamic countries. The tensions between the two groups have in the first instance resulted in a return to generalities and to grand narratives, with the 'modernists' looking West and the 'traditionalists' looking East, each constructing an essentially new vision of feminism and its relation to new constructions of faith, culture, femininity and the analysis of religious meanings.
>
> (p. 811. See also Afshar 1998; Barlow and Akrazadeh 2008)

However, despite a clear conflict with the values and preferences of western feminism, the Islamic feminism Afshar and Maynard describe is still committed to a (certain) vision of women's equality as such feminists use:

> the theological basis of Islam to carve their own path towards freedom.... They have argued that Islam, as a religion, has always had to accommodate women's specific needs. Since the first convert to Islam was the Prophet's redoubtable and wealthy wife Khadija, no religion which she accepted could discriminate against women.
>
> (Afshar and Maynard 2000: 811)

The phenomenon of subjecting Islamic sacred texts to reinterpretation is the key method of Islamic feminism. Feminist scholars and activists across the Islamic world have recently asserted the imperative of engaging with the Islamic framework as the only viable option to advance women's cause. Indeed, in view of the resurging importance of religion in these countries and communities (as well as worldwide), turning away from Islam is something women simply cannot afford to do (see e.g. Sadiqi 2006; Mir-Hosseini 1999). Women's help has been enlisted strategically to advance Islamic causes. The 1979 Islamic Revolution in Iran was a prominent example, when the 'opposition of traditional women to the shah's un-Islamic monarchy was represented through the figures of Fatima and Zeinab (the daughter and granddaughter of the prophet), Shia icons of female resistance to oppression' (Shaditalab 2006: 16).

Apart from such prominent female figures from early Islamic history, the Islamic tradition of women's economic independence, which is not relinquished even in marriage, the notion of marriage as a contract between consenting partners, remuneration for motherhood and domestic work and an emphasis on the sexual pleasure of both sexes are often cited (Afshar 1998; Ahmed, L. 1992; Shaditalab 2006). These factors lend support to the argument that Islam provides a better framework for a feminist agenda than the western, or westernised, secular liberal framework. The argument goes that the Islamic framework, 'unlike capitalism and much of Western feminist discourse', is more suited to the recognition of 'the importance of women's life cycles' as 'it offers them different roles and responsibilities at different times of their lives and at every stage they are to be valued, respected and financially rewarded for what they do' (Afshar and Maynard 2000: 812). Furthermore, Mernissi's (1991) analysis suggests that a revisionist interpretation of Islamic texts can even lead to political equality between the sexes in Islamic states. The phenomenon of Islamic veiling thus comes to symbolise this alternative vision of feminism and gender equality, achieved through a process not unlike the western preference for a 'modernised' Islam characterised by (re)interpretative practices, as described in the previous chapter.

There are also practical instances of women's empowerment procured by the veil. Abu-Odeh discusses what she understands as Arab women's longstanding ambivalence about their bodies, which the new veiling in the 1980s was ultimately related to, rather than being 'a radical transition from "revealment" to "concealment"' (1992: 1529). In this context, 'public sexual harassment' reinforces the non-veiled woman's insecurities, 'making her powerless in the face of unwelcome intrusions'. Conversely:

> The problem does not seem to exist for veiled women, since adopting the veil was meant to shield them from such sexual approaches; when such approaches are actually made, they are looked upon as being simply outrageous, both by the veiled women themselves and the public.
>
> (ibid.: 1530–1531)

In this way, protection from sexual harassment can be seen as a very concrete gain for women, a practical solution which 'has come to remedy the uncomfortable daily lives of single, young women, who are leaving the house seeking work and education' (ibid.: 1534).

Another argument to bolster the veil's empowering, 'pro-feminist' potential is that '[v]eiled sexuality … reveals a multiplicity that is beyond the feminist's wildest expectations':

> Once secure in the company of women, they reveal bodies that are more colorful, lively, and sexual. One is surprised at the shift their bodies make when they remove the veil. The bland face becomes

> colorful with creative make-up. The loose dress of the veil, once taken off, reveals fashionable clothing underneath, making more of an individual and personal statement than the collective, public one of the veil. Their sexuality appears to be more forthcoming, assertive, and joyful. Once together, their interaction with each other is not devoid of seductiveness and flirtation. Their private bodies are almost unrelated to their public ones.
>
> (ibid.: 1535)

This account alludes to the values of individuality central to classic western feminism and connects to the constructions of Islamic veiling as a positive choice, as discussed in the previous chapter. This depiction of female sexuality 'behind the veil' also distinctly resonates with historical accounts of Muslim women in the period preceding the colonial and/or modernising unveiling campaign. In her seminal study of women and gender in Islam, Leila Ahmed (1992) reveals how much of the orthodox western assumption that veiling denotes the total oppression of women does not survive closer scrutiny. Ahmed's general account, as well as more specific ones, such as by Najmabadi (1998) and Sullivan (1998) in respect of Iran, Shakry (1998) and Abu-Lughod (1998) in respect of Egypt and Kandiyoti (1998) in respect of Turkey, show that women in fact enjoyed a greater degree of freedom in their day-to-day activities and notably in connection with their sexual expression. As was mentioned in the previous chapter, and in contrast with the received view, unveiled women became subjected to much stricter social control mechanisms as their sexuality was thought to be more dangerous.

For example, Najmabadi's (1993) informative account shows how the 'Woman Question' and its attendant modernisation in the late nineteenth and early twentieth century in Iran had led to the openly sexual, earlier women's language becoming sanitised. References to sexual organs became 'conspicuously absent' in the 'modern discourse', with many traditional Persian words being replaced with more 'decent' French words, 'disconnecting the associative chains between a word and all its vast, multilayered culturally scripted erotic meanings' (ibid.: 489). Exclusively female gatherings, with traditional female plays, dances and songs, which were 'highly sexual in their language, gestures, and expressed emotions' had 'no modern equivalent' (ibid.). All these changes appear to be the side effect (or perhaps the other side) of the unveiling process, which was supposedly designed to do away with the 'chains of female enslavement' (ibid.: 487) and to open the public sphere to women. In this way, 'when the female voice found a public audience, it became a veiled voice, a disciplined voice' (ibid.: 489). These insights reinforce the point that the veil has offered Muslim women much emancipating potential, both in the preunveiling period and in the present.

3 What is wrong with the gender equality argument?

So far, the chapter has provided an account of the uses of the gender equality argument as it is made on both sides of the Islamic veiling debate. This part of the chapter adds a further dimension to the analysis, by highlighting factors that discredit such uses on both sides. It begins with highlighting the hidden underpinnings of the gender equality argument as it is made by those who are against Islamic veiling, followed by refocusing on the other side's deployment of the same.

Postcolonial theory has highlighted how Islamic veiling practices have been a prime site of western incomprehension and criticism. It is noteworthy that such derision of 'the Orient' was routinely framed as concern with women's rights and welfare. A little historical analysis reveals some disturbing racist and imperialist connotations of this (pseudo-)feminist rhetoric, which to a large extent discredits its modern-day deployment to oppose Islamic veiling. Detailed and comprehensive analyses of this history have been carried out by historians, literary scholars and postcolonial theorists (see e.g. Bullock 2007 for a particularly extensive account). The following is only a brief selection.

Although the Orient had fascinated the European imagination for much longer, the Enlightenment provides particularly ripe ground for discovering historical parallels with the current rhetoric. The arts, literature and even the philosophical and political writings of the European Enlightenment contain many references to Oriental gender practices as a metaphoric reference point for Europe's ontological superiority. In his *Persian Letters*, for example, Montesquieu (1973) recounts the story of a lascivious eastern despot and his seraglio to warn of the dangers of authoritarian political rule. In this story, the Oriental harem serves as a model of gender despotism, which in turn stands as a metaphor for the despotism of absolute monarchy, which only civilised European nations are capable of moving beyond (see further Mosher 1994). In such constructions, the confined chastity and enforced purity of Oriental wives stand for sexual slavery and degradation of women. It is remarkable that back in Europe these same qualities were vigorously promoted by great post-Enlightenment philosophers such as Rousseau and Schopenhauer, whose work betrays a strong belief in the innate inferiority of women (Osborne 1979: 113, 231–234).

In her famous 1792 manifesto, *Vindication of the Rights of Women*, the early feminist thinker Mary Wollstonecraft refers to the 'true style of Mahometanism' as a powerful rhetorical device to depict the appallingly unequal treatment that women are subjected to in such civilised nations as Britain and France. It is noteworthy that Islam is central to such projections of Europe's Oriental other. As Said (1978) highlights, in such instantiations of Orientalism assumptions are made on the basis of 'a logic deliberately outside Islam'.

Orientalism reached its zenith with the ascendance of European colonial rule. The figure of the veiled woman especially has featured as the archetypal expression of 'the harem fantasy' of European imperialism (Kabbani 1986), 'the most visible marker of the differentness and inferiority of Islamic societies' (Ahmed, L. 1992: 152). British colonial presence in late nineteenth century Egypt is often highlighted as a particularly illuminating manifestation of the western fascination with this 'eastern' practice. Lord Cromer, the colonial governor of Egypt (1883–1907), considered that veiling and the seclusion of women it represented were 'the fatal obstacle' to the 'attainment of that elevation of thought and character which should accompany the introduction of Western civilisation' (ibid.: 153). It is rather telling that, back in Britain, Lord Cromer was a 'founding member and sometime president of the Men's League for Opposing Women's Suffrage' (ibid. See further Shaikh 2002; Valenta 2006). It is conceivable that Lord Cromer was sincere in both his pursuits, yet it highlights some remarkable selectivity about which feminist causes are taken up and which opposed or ignored – the kind of selectivity which we still see in the Islamic veiling debate today.

Anglo-Christian missionaries, and in particular women missionaries, played an important part in the colonial unveiling campaign, of which attacking and denigrating Islam was an important part. Ahmed cites the proceedings of a missionary conference held in London in 1888, at which it was observed that:

> Muhammad had been exemplary as a young man but took many wives in later life and set out to preach a religion whose object was 'to extinguish women altogether'; and he introduced the veil, which 'has had the most terrible and injurious effect upon the mental, moral and spiritual history of all Mohammedan races.'
>
> (Ahmed, L. 1992: 153–154, citing Johnston 1889: 18–19)

For British Empire officials, Christian missionaries and feminists alike, women and their veiling practices were central to civilising 'backward' Muslim races. Targeting women was advocated as a subtle and indirect, but sure, way of undermining Islam as women mould future generations. It is noteworthy that both Christian and early feminist critics of Islamic gender arrangements pointed out that Islam 'gave license to "lewdness"', and marriage in Islam 'was "not founded on love but on sensuality", and a Muslim wife, "buried alive behind the veil," was regarded as "prisoner and slave rather than ... companion and helpmeet"' (Ahmed, L. 1992: 154). Egyptian girls and women were pro-actively persuaded, by western missionaries and feminists alike, to rebel against their families and not wear the veil, which was seen 'as the essential first step in the struggle for female liberation' (ibid.). In 1899, the Egyptian reformer Qasim Amin published *Tahrir al-Mar'a (The Liberation of Women)*, a treatise profoundly influenced by such ideas of modernity and colonial feminism. It is quite ironic that the contemporary Islamist movement that advocates veiling is deeply, if rather unrecognisably, indebted to earlier modern western feminist ideas of this sort, in particular on matters such as marriage and family. Abu-Lughod's (1998) study of Islamic political currents in twentieth century secular Egypt highlights the dynamics of what she calls 'selective repudiation': as colonial western feminist ideas on exclusive companionate marriage and informed child rearing have fundamentally reshaped Egyptian society, much of today's Islamist family ideology bears a hidden mark of modern liberal values (see also Hatem 1994). This problematises the liberal demonisation of Islamic fundamentalism as inherently misogynist and anti-liberal.

French colonialism has followed a similar pattern of obsession with women's veiling. Lazreg describes 'the most spectacular example of the colonial appropriation of women's voices' during a French generals' demonstration in Algiers on 16 May 1958 when 'a few [Algerian] women ... were solemnly unveiled by French women' in a 'well-choreographed ceremony' (Lazreg 1994: 135. See also El Guindi 1999; Scott 2007), a gesture which is being symbolically repeated in much of the current debate in France.

This early feminist rhetoric is strikingly patronising, self-righteous and permeated by a deeply embedded sense of the superiority of the western, Christian (now turned secular – see Chapter 5) and modern way of life. There is a remarkable emphasis on 'rescuing' Oriental Muslim women by their western 'sisters' from 'ignorance and degradation'. The spectacular title of the proceedings of a missionary women's conference held in Cairo in 1906, *Our Moslem Sisters: A Cry of Need from the Lands of Darkness Interpreted by Those Who Heard It*, encapsulates this attitude perfectly. Compare this to the Stasi Report: 'The Republic cannot remain deaf to these girls' cries of distress. The space of school must remain for them a place of liberty and emancipation; it must not become a place of suffering and humiliation' (2004: 103–104). It seems that not so much has changed after all: now, as then, feminism is used to consolidate, rather than disrupt or transform, western cultural ways of being in its preoccupation with reforming gender relations 'elsewhere'.

Spivak (1985) famously referred to this process as 'saving brown women from brown men'. As highlighted in the previous chapter, postcolonial insights such as Spivak's, Mohanty's (1988), Ahmed's (2000) and Kapur's (2005) show how colonial feminism is far from extinct today. Kapur argues that many western liberal feminists continue to deploy 'the tragedy of victimisation rhetoric' in respect of the ultimate victim subject, Third World women. The figure of the poor Third World (or ethnic minority, as the case may be) woman, oppressed by her religion/culture, has long been the ultimate embodiment of gender inequality, sustaining the western feminist fantasy that western women are equal with men, emancipated and suitably empowered about their own lives. Thus, the effect of the feminist demonisation of the veil and the paternalistic victimisation of those who wear it (as it is reflected in the case-law and the surrounding debate) is a profound denial of the persisting gender inequality in the West.

The mainstream feminist approach assumes a 'strict quantification of sexism' ('more there, less here') and a certain 'inattention to varieties of male superordination' (Brown 2006: 195–196). To be sure, there are very important differences between the various forms that gender inequality takes in different societies, and indeed the achievements of western feminism have been significant. However, what is objectionable is a certain feminist orthodoxy that casts the situation of western women as in all respects better, more emancipated and more equal to men than that of their non-western counterparts. That obviously eclipses the many areas in which western women are constrained (the discussion in the previous chapter mentions western feminine dress, cosmetic surgery and childcare). Arguably, more attention to the *varieties* of gender oppression could lead to strategies that would address the inequality of Muslim women in non-racist ways, as well as promote a more balanced reflection on the situation of western women.

Furthermore, the equation of the visibility of the female body with emancipation and gender equality, so salient in the debate, is only sustainable if one accepts a view of gender relations in which the body has to signify accessibility to the other sex (Scott 2007: 155) – otherwise, a covered body is as capable of being emancipated. Such an emphasis on sexual accessibility is what enables us to make sense of the Government Commissioner's approving mention of Mme M's examinations by a male gynaecologist. Another example is the case of 'Monsieur X', highlighted in Chapter 2, in which a Moroccan man was denied French citizenship for, among other things, 'display[ing] in an everyday manner a discriminatory attitude towards women, *going as far as* refusing to shake their hands' (Davies, 2 February 2010, emphasis added). Here, routine physical contact with the opposite sex is presumed to be such a fundamental sign of equality that not having such contact is seen as outrageously discriminatory. It is not clear why no physical contact with unrelated people of the opposite sex (a basic rule in Islam as well as other 'traditional' religions) could not be seen as signifying respect for each other and hence pro-equality.

Commenting on the contemporary French debate, Badiou asserts ironically:

> Everywhere you hear it said that the 'veil' is the intolerable symbol of control of feminine sexuality. Is it that you imagine feminine sexuality

is not controlled in our day and age, in our societies? Such naivety would have really made Foucault laugh. Never has feminine sexuality been scrutinized with such meticulousness, had so much expert advice thrust on it, been subject to such fine discriminating between its good and bad uses. Enjoyment has become a sinister obligation. The universal exhibition of supposedly exciting bits is a duty more rigid than Kant's moral imperative. Besides, Lacan some time ago established the fact that, between the 'Enjoy yourselves, women!' of our gossip rags and the imperative 'Do not enjoy!' of our great-grandmothers, there is a strict isomorphism. Market control is more constant, surer, more massive than patriarchal control ever was.

(Badiou 2006: 104)

In this respect, it can be argued that the feminist gloss of Islamic veiling bans has patent capitalist undercurrents as they prescribe that 'femininity be *exhibited*', that the putatively emancipatory 'circulation of the feminine body necessarily comply with the market paradigm' (Badiou 2006: 103). Indeed, the body, and in particular the female body, is now a crucial advertising and marketing tool in the West, which sells almost anything from food staples to package holidays and real estate. Refusal to publicise the body's erotic and market appeal is perceived as backward and oppressed. And thus the Islamic 'covered' gender system, exemplified by veiling practices, may be so intolerable also because it confines women to a 'restricted economy', thus resisting the hegemonic 'generalized model' of 'prostitutional circulation' (ibid.: 102, 104).

Scott points out that 'there was not much discussion in France of the limits of Western dress',[10] with the question of equality becoming not one of the equality of women and men, but 'that of Muslim *women* and French *women*' (2007: 161, 162). In this equation, it is the western sartorial practices that are the standard of equality. Thus, differences *among* both Muslim and western women become erased or muted, with only two contrasting categories standing out: sexually liberated western women and veiled, sexually oppressed Muslim women (ibid.).

The two contrasting categories of the liberated western woman and the oppressed Muslim woman are not unlike 'the mother and the whore' binary, which Badiou says 'must be rejected', but:

Not however by the 'neither ... nor...,' which only ever perpetuates on neutral ground ... what it professes to contest. Saying 'neither mother, nor whore' is simply pathetic. As is 'neither whore, nor

10 For an example of such discussion in the Netherlands, see L. Duits and L. van Zoonen (2006) 'Headscarves and Porno-Chic: Disciplining Girls' Bodies in the European Multicultural Society', *European Journal of Women's Studies*, 13: 103.

> submissive' [an allusion to *Ni Putes Ni Soumises*], which is quite absurd: is not a 'whore' generally submissive...?
>
> (2006: 104)

An important feature of the gender equality argument as it is used by the proponents of Islamic veiling restrictions today, as was described earlier in the chapter, is a conviction that gender and culture/religion are antagonistic categories. This orthodox view is traceable to early feminist days and is still rarely challenged in mainstream feminism as well as human rights jurisprudence. Clearly, it ignores the fact that the principle of gender equality, as we know it, is also embedded in culture. More often than not, western liberal legal orders (and, for that matter, international human rights law) are stripped of their historical cultural origins. Despite being shaped so obviously by the values of the European Enlightenment, such formations are commonly believed to be acultural. Proponents of liberal toleration and multiculturalism routinely assume that western liberal societies have departed from their patriarchal past (because they prescribe gender equality in the law) while non-western 'cultures' are stuck in theirs simply by virtue of not adopting a set of liberal legal values. As Brown (2006) suggests, when the existence of gender inequality in the West is acknowledged, it is attributed to 'some cultural remainder that the law has not yet managed to reform or extinguish' (p. 193). This unfailing belief that liberal orders are gender- and culture-neutral ignores the tradition of feminist critique that exposes liberalism as itself deeply inscribed with hidden but pervasive signs of male dominance (e.g. Brown 1995; Scott 2005. See also Munro 2007; Charlesworth and Chinkin 2000).

A related effect of the use of the gender equality argument to support Islamic veiling restrictions is the total eclipsing of the other, in many instances much more pertinent, factors that perpetuate the unequal position of Muslim women both in western democracies and in the Islamic world. A prime example of such eclipsing is the contemporary neo-imperial linkage of veiling with Islamic fundamentalism and terrorism. The veil, in its different forms, typically stands for the twin objectives of oppression of women and destruction of the western civilisation, which are allegedly espoused by Islamic terrorists. This is what enabled Laura Bush, the wife of the former President of the US, George W. Bush, to say in her radio address in November 2001 that '[t]he fight against terrorism is also a fight for the rights and dignity of women'. Her straightforward account, shared by much of the western 'war on terror' rhetoric, reinvigorated in connection with the 9/11 trauma, presents the Taliban and Al-Qaeda as not only the most relevant, but *the* single cause of the oppression of Afghan women. Furthermore, it claims that the US military intervention in Afghanistan had removed this oppression,[11] completely discounting western imperialism, neoliberalism and globalisation as possible contributing factors to gender inequality around the world.

Finally, prohibitions of Islamic veiling suffer from certain myopia insofar as some immediate sartorial symbolism is accorded too much weight. Even if one accepts that Islamic veiling is an embodiment of a deep-seated belief in the inferiority of women and it merits discouragement, it is not clear why prohibiting it is the best way to confront the belief. To the contrary, prohibitions of Islamic veiling often mean further marginalisation of Muslim women as some form of Islamic veiling may often enable women to enter the education system and occupations they would not otherwise consider accessible, not to mention the degradation associated with requirements to remove what one considers an essential element of one's appearance or identity. In Mme M's case, it remains hard to see how the ideal of gender equality is advanced when a woman is denied citizenship. It appears then that the idea of gender equality has assumed an existence of its own, largely separate from and even incompatible with the needs and interests of real women.

If gender equality is taken as a serious normative ideal, then surely it needs some more consistent and thoughtful implementation, which would take into account women's realities, rather than penalise them for non-compliance with dominant ideology. Arguably, out of all the legal developments reviewed in Chapter 2, only the Norwegian Ombud takes these factors into account: she has considered Islamic veiling restrictions to be *incompatible with*, rather than justified by, the principle of gender equality as their practical effect is to exclude women from work life which 'would then be twice as oppressing' (UNHCR, 3 February 2004).

So much for the gender equality argument as it is used by those who disapprove of Islamic veiling. But the use of the gender equality card by the other side in the debate has its problems also. To return to the contemporary Islamic feminism, as discussed in Part 2 of this chapter, there is indeed much merit in an approach that highlights positive, potentially empowering aspects of Islamic veiling. Islamic feminism has made an important point dislodging classic western feminist assumptions and cornerstones – 'views that placed the family as *the* site of oppression, regarded employment as the path to liberation, and envisaged patriarchy as an uncomplicated singular force' (Afshar and Maynard 2000: 810). This

11 'Because of our recent military gains in much of Afghanistan, women are no longer imprisoned in their homes. They can listen to music and teach their daughters without fear of punishment' (Bush 2001). See also G.W. Bush, 'State of the Union Address', 29 January 2002 (no longer available online). For poignant critiques of the conflation of veiling with terrorism in such representations, see, e.g. Shaikh (2002); Ayotte and Hussain (2005); Hirschkind and Mahmood (2002); Ho (2007); Kapur (2002).

enriches feminism in general. However, there are aspects in the feminist defence of veiling that are to be taken with a pinch of salt.

While one can be as sexual as one likes underneath the veil, its purpose remains the exclusive preservation of female sexuality for the familial, private domain, which has for centuries sustained a patriarchal system of male domination. As far as protection from harassment is concerned, Abu-Odeh, whose 'pro-veiling' piece was extensively cited in the previous part of the chapter, herself acknowledges that the feminist undertones of 'the veiled position' are self-deconstructing insofar as it 'assumes that women should be ideally inconspicuous' (1992: 1534), and it is women's responsibility to shield their bodies from the gazes of men. While the hijab may work as far as mundane harassment on a public bus goes, it is a rather questionable shield from serious sexual violence against women, which is as real in Muslim countries as it is elsewhere. Although on a practical level the veil may mean access to certain occupations, the ideology associated with it presumes a rather significant degree of gender segregation in the public sphere and in the workplace, with positions of power often being out of reach for women (ibid.).

An overemphasis on colonialism and colonial feminism as the main cause of the position that Muslim women around the world currently find themselves in is problematic. Although the historic effects of colonialism are undeniable, postcolonial studies are not immune to analytical reductivism as much of it tends to justify Islamic societies' resistance to women's equality as a reaction against colonialism and imposed western values. Although this may be true to an extent, an exclusive emphasis on colonialism often implies a rather idealised view of the pre-colonial Islamic world, which is as skewed as the West's unthinking demonisation of Islam and its gender practices. Mirza (2000) highlights 'the contemporary accent on the trope of authenticity', characteristic of both political Islamists and Islamic feminists, who share a certain 'doctrinal absorption with the inception of Islam as an ideal past, as a "luminous purity" that has arisen from the defining moment of Islam's origin' (p. 187). Indeed, excessive valorisation of veiling as a 'reconstructed tradition' tends to mythologise the Islamic religious framework as a hotbed of gender equality and feminist ideas. It is wishful thinking insofar as such ideal feminist moments are a fantasised view of history.

There were different patterns of European colonisation throughout the Islamic world, and indeed major political powers such as Turkey or Iran were never colonised. Despite these significant differences, it is not too much of a leap to assert that 'Islamic societies, with some exceptions, disclose greater similarities than differences in their rigidity in the treatment of women' (Moghissi 1999: 19). There is an important point in this generalisation. Although much of Islamic feminism, as shown in the previous part of the chapter, insists that an Islamic religious framework celebrates female sexuality, the constructions of a Muslim woman's body as 'a temple of her family's honor' (Minai 1981: 100) have for centuries justified strict surveillance and mobility restrictions. Although the practice of policing female sexuality can be found, in one form or another, across the different religious and cultural traditions, the specifically Islamic outlook on human sexuality may have interesting implications for women.

It is fair to generalise that the Christian tradition on the whole disapproves of sex and sexual pleasure. Sex is acceptable in church-sanctioned, heterosexual marriage and for procreation purposes, and is otherwise inherently sinful. Although there may be important differences between Catholicism and Orthodox Christianity in respect of procreation being the primary purpose of marriage, neither regards sex as vital. To Christians, the idea of a sexless marriage is not an oxymoron, but a spiritual union between two individuals, not contaminated by lust. Celibacy is the standard for Christian monastic orders and for Catholic priests. Strands of other major world religions, including Buddhism and Hinduism, also encourage celibacy. This is not at all so in Islam, which is, as far as generalisations go, 'a sex-affirming cultural and religious tradition' (Moghissi 1999: 21).

In Islam, sex and sexual pleasure are a legitimate right of the believer, with sex itself – as opposed to reproductive sex only – being regarded as 'a sacred function'. Celibacy is strongly disapproved, with marriage being commendable even for a man 'who has strong will to control his sexual desire, who has no wish to have children, or who feels that marriage will keep him away from his devotion to Allah' (Doi Abdul Rahman 1989: 33–34). The Islamic concept of paradise is a place where good believers are rewarded by eternal sexual pleasure, consisting of unrestricted access to the fair, wide-eyed, eternally young *huri*. These paradisal creatures represent ideal female material, 'created to be consumed as a sexual partner, [their] value comes from [their] physical beauty' (Sabbah 1988: 96–97).

The *huri* of the Islamic paradise reflects a distinct sexual hierarchy between men and women. Indeed, while approving of sex and sexual pleasure, Islam is also very strict in allocating sexual roles between men and women, in paradise as well as this world. Notably, both men and women in Islam have a right to sexual fulfilment. Female sexuality, however, is clearly subservient to that of men. Although the husband is required not to abandon intercourse with his wife for longer than four months (Sura 2:226), the wife's sexual duties are more burdensome. The wife is to provide sexual gratification to her husband at any time when he so desires (Sura 2:223), except during menstruation (Sura 2:222). There is also normative recognition that a man has sexual drives that cannot be satisfied by one woman at a time, hence the Islamic tradition of polygamy, which allows a man to have up to four wives (Sura 4:3). More generally, the Koran is clear that '[m]en are superior to women on account of the qualities with which God hath gifted the one above the other' (Sura 4:38), and thus men have the power, and the duty, to chastise disobedient wives (ibid.).

The point here is not to use a sacred text as proof that Islam is inherently misogynist, but rather highlight the *specificity* of this tradition's attitude to female sexuality. The situation is not the same, for example, in Judaism, with which Islam shares common Abrahamic ancestry. Although Judaism is also a 'sex-affirming' tradition, traditionally there is much more emphasis on the importance of pleasing the wife and unacceptability of sexual coercion. To be sure, an orthodox Jewish approach to sexuality relies on patriarchal gender roles just as Islam – or indeed any other religious tradition – does. However, there is something different about the way that Muslim women are imbued with 'the primary responsibility for maintaining the sanctity of relations between the sexes ... because the juristic Islamic tradition assumes that women are the objects of sexual desire and men the desiring subjects' (Mahmood 2005: 110).

That being so, nearly unconditional, self-effacing submissiveness to their husbands becomes the only route through which Muslim women's sexuality can be channelled legitimately. It has even been suggested that this contradiction between, on the one hand, an acknowledgment of the sexual potential of women, and, on the other, rigid restrictions on its realisation accounts for Islam's special attitude to women as liable to inevitable sexual transgression (Moghissi 1999: 24). The inevitability of female deviation then justifies the constant policing of women and to some extent absolving men of the responsibility to control their own sexual drives. This attitude to (female) sexuality has clearly been there long before the forces of colonialism and modernisation might have provoked a reactionary response.

It is true that Islam, as any other religion, is mediated through cultural constructions and is continuously subjected to (re)interpretation. It has been pointed out, for example, that, according to the practice of *fegh-e pouya* (dynamic jurisprudence), 'Islamic texts should be understood and interpreted within the context of their time and location' (Shaditalab 2006: 16). A popular Islamic feminist method is distinguishing between contextual and normative Koranic verses, arguing that verses evidently unfavourable to women should be explained by their historic context, while those that speak of the equal rights and duties of men and women should be seen as normative and thus applicable at all times (see Mirza 2000). Yet, 'not all gender roles in Islamic society are subject to the same evolutionary processes', whereas 'innate gender differences are expressed within the family structure and cannot be changed' (Shaditalab 2006: 16). Although women in Islam are indeed entitled to economic independence, this primarily comes from the financial support they are supposed to receive in return for the sexual gratification of their husbands and their mothering duties (Sura 2:233. See further Ahmed, L. 1992; Afshar and Maynard 2000; Shaditalab 2006). Perhaps more importantly, great weight is attached to the value of compliance itself – that is, the kind of agentic practices discussed in the final part of the previous chapter.

Whether or not Islam is misogynist is the wrong question to ask. Neither is it the answer that '"secular humanism" could gradually rid itself of such views, whereas "Islamism" ... did not' (Joppke 2009: 9). First, the ability of 'secular humanism' or liberalism ever to be gender-neutral is questionable. Second, as will be explored in Chapter 5, the valorisation of secular progress is itself problematic. Rather, the point is simply that there are certain fundamentals in the Islamic outlook on gender relations, that may be difficult to superimpose with a feminist framework. This, however, is not necessarily a criticism of Islam. The point is that it need not be objectionable in the first place for women not to be interested in reforming gender relations in society.

At the moment, however, there is a rather symptomatic situation that the strategic alliance between Islam and feminism helps to sustain. The flipside of the false consciousness trope, still espoused by a great many mainstream feminists, is the equally widespread, if more recent, perception that any view a woman consciously holds or defends is feminist by default. One might wonder whether the adjective 'feminist' functions to validate, politically, legally and popularly, views and positions that may otherwise be unusual or even incomprehensible. This question is explored in the next part of the chapter.

4 Why gender equality at all?

So, rather than asking 'why feminists in the Muslim world have gone Islamic' (Mir-Hosseini 1999; Moghissi 1999; Sadiqi 2006), it might be more insightful to ask 'why Islamic positions need to be justified as feminist at all'. This part of the chapter suggests that the reasons for this might not be far off the reasons underlying the deployment of the gender equality argument by those who oppose Islamic veiling. An exploration of these reveals something important about the strong normative status that feminism has achieved around the world today.

As highlighted earlier in the chapter, gender equality is invariably represented as a foundational value of western liberal democracies as well as international human rights law. This is interesting as it is only rather recently that the idea of gender equality began to be treated seriously on the international human rights agenda. Although 'gender mainstreaming' is now believed to underlie all United Nations action, it was in fact the 1995 United Nations Fourth World Conference on Women in Beijing that formally launched the concept.[12] Indeed, the Beijing Conference was an unprecedented feminist

12 According to, for example, the Report of the United Nations Economic and Social Council for 1997, A/52/3.18, September 1997, at 28:

> Mainstreaming a gender perspective is the process of assessing the implications for women and men of any planned action, including legislation, policies or programmes, in all areas and at all levels. It is a strategy for making women's as well as men's concerns and experiences an integral dimension of the design, implementation, monitoring and evaluation of policies and programmes in all political, economic and societal spheres so that women and men benefit equally and inequality is not perpetuated. The ultimate goal is to achieve gender equality.

success, following a concerted effort of a number of academic and activist networks (Otto 1996; Riles 2002). In the Council of Europe, a major first mention of the goal of the equality of the sexes came about in the 1980s, which was not however followed by much concrete action (see Part 1 of this chapter). Despite these developments being so relatively recent, gender equality is now being constructed in the Islamic veiling debate, as well as elsewhere, as having always been a foundational principle and value. As highlighted earlier, this is implausible insofar as the gender neutrality of liberal legal orders (on which international human rights law is also modelled) is itself a fiction.

This new mythology reflects the international success of what Halley (2006) terms 'governance feminism', a term which cuts across a range of liberal, radical, cultural and other types of feminism. Arguably, governance feminism is considerably co-extensive with what Brown (1995) calls 'feminist foundationalism', although the emphasis is on a different aspect. Feminist foundationalism refers to a strong modernist ethos, converting gender 'to a "center" of "selves" understood as foundational' (Brown 1995: 40), prescribing a particular narrative of gender as truth. As Parts 1 and 3 of this chapter have shown, there is often a certain, western liberal, kind of gender equality that is imposed on Muslim women. 'Feminist foundationalism', which cuts across different varieties of feminism, insists on equating subjectivity with truth, normativity and – perhaps most problematically – feminist politics. For example, Benhabib, a leading Habermasian feminist, cannot conceive of feminist politics 'without positing [in some form] norms of autonomy, choice and self-determination' (1992: 16) – the classic liberal values associated with subjectivity. This implies a strangely restrictive view of feminist politics. Arguably, the epistemological crisis of subjectivity ought not to neutralise the political validity of feminist engagement with law (Drakopoulou 2000).

'Governance feminism', on the other hand, is a feminism that 'rules' and '*wants* to rule' (Halley 2006: 22), even if (or perhaps particularly if) this is 'power masquerading as servitude' (Cossman *et al.* 2003: 608). The most important common feature of governance feminism and feminist foundationalism is that both suffer from what Halley calls 'paranoid structuralism'. This is a tendency to see and explain everything in the world through the prism of some variant of a gender subordination theory – as Halley puts it, 'a distinction between something m and something f; a commitment to be a theory about, and a practice about, the subordination of f to m; and a commitment to work against that subordination on behalf of f' (2006: 4–5).

Here is the paradox: on the one hand, feminism is by definition an oppositional politics, as it is directed at disrupting male hegemony. On the other, it has achieved a certain degree of normative acceptance in the legal and political mainstream in the West and, to a certain extent, worldwide. Feminists today have their fair share in the new global and local governance – which is often 'done through informal, opaque, ideologically committed "nongovernmental organizations" that strategize hard – sometimes successfully – to become indispensable when major new fluidities in formal power emerge' (ibid.: 21). Indeed, there are aspects over which feminism colludes with the traditionally 'male' discourses of liberalism, secularism and human rights, so that a certain mythology of a secular liberal order (or international human rights regime), which respects/has always respected gender equality, is created. Moreover, colonial or radical anti-Islamic feminism have on occasions colluded with politically influential, deeply conservative forces within the West on issues such as foreign and immigration policy. As the preceding discussion in this chapter has shown, Islamic veiling is an issue where this collusion is demonstrated particularly well. Chapter 2 contains an account of how the anti-Islamic activism of Ayaan Hirsi Ali, Dutch feminist, politician and scriptwriter of the controversial film *Submission*, was co-opted by right-wing political forces in the Netherlands and United States.

An important qualification is in order: it is not the intention to blame feminism exclusively for this collusion. There is certainly something about the way in which strange discourses, such as feminism, are processed by the mainstream, so that only the most familiar and intelligible elements are recognised and picked up. In other words, it is the most traditional, western, secular, liberal or universalist feminism that tends to make its way into judicial pronouncements such as the ECtHR's judgments in *Şahin* and *Dahlab* or Conseil d'État's in *Mme M.* (Baroness Hale in *Denbigh High School* and Judge Tulkens in *Şahin* are more nuanced.) The result is processed feminism in its most skewed and crude form, which serves to solidify, rather than challenge, the reigning order, by penalising real women for their non-compliance with highly abstract 'feminist' ideas. Yet, the 'paranoid structuralism' of much of contemporary feminist activism and scholarship is itself a force worth exploring.

Of course, not all feminist varieties are resolvable into Halley's formula of governance feminism or paranoid structuralism, preoccupied with the subordination of women to men. She appears to gloss over some important critiques of feminists' entrenchment of female ontological subordination, which have emerged from within feminism (with postcolonial feminist varieties being especially instrumental). Furthermore, her outlook is distinctly North American. However, the type of feminism she deplores has, without doubt, become the most influential globally. This is not at all to say that feminism has completely achieved its objectives or that a vision of the world as based on gender hierarchy is dated or irrelevant. Rather, it is the pervasiveness and exclusivity of such a vision and its strong, almost dogmatic normativity, which are the object of critique here. The normativity of feminist theory is not itself a problem – indeed, most political movements are defined by a cause. Rather, what is taken issue with here is the *dogmatism* of 'feminist foundationalism' and 'governance feminism' in respect of both its normative hold and its inability to imagine women's experience in terms other than the oppression/emancipation paradigm.

To be more precise, the argument is that the international success of the feminism of the criticised type might explain the normative purchase of the gender equality argument as it is used on both sides of the Islamic veiling debate, as shown earlier in the chapter. This might be problematic insofar as feminism might not (and ought not to) have unique epistemic purchase on women's condition. Rather, as Halley suggests, 'no one theory, no one political engagement, is nearly as valuable as the invitation to critique that is issued by the simultaneous incommensurate presence of many theories' (2006: 9). This might imply putting feminist 'truths', however valuable, to one side, in order to make room for other possibilities, insights and perspectives. It is also arguable, after Halley, that 'taking a break from feminism' would ultimately be of benefit to feminism itself. As Denise Riley (2003) famously put it, '[t]o lead a life soaked in the passionate consciousness of one's gender at every single moment, to will to be a sex with a vengeance – these are impossibilities, and far from the aims of feminism'.

As discussed in Chapter 3, the liberal secular human rights discourse has notable difficulties when it comes to 'choices' which do not square with its values. Likewise, feminism faces a genuine dilemma when it is confronted with agentic female behaviour which consolidates, rather than subverts, patriarchy and male hegemony. To recall the case of *Mme M*, discussed in some length in Part 1 of this chapter, those feminists who supported Mme M tended to do so on grounds that French citizenship would empower her to challenge her submission to her husband. What to make then of Mme M's own apparent affirmation of it: '"I don't want to draw men's looks," she said. "I want to belong to my husband and my husband only."' (Bennhold, 19 July 2008)? And what of the Beit Shemesh women, whose story was a gateway into the book's themes in Chapter 1, who insisted on hiding their faces from men completely, thus ostensibly refusing to be feminist? The stock feminist response was a call to ban this kind of female self-expression.

Feminist politics is by definition oppositional, so that subverting hegemonic, dominant norms often becomes an aim in itself. As Brown has argued throughout much of her work, feminism's oppositional status gives it its high moral ground. This sort of moralism is traceable to Nietzschean slave morality, in which the subject (of feminism in the present case) feels morally right and politically righteous *because* she is oppressed by the dominant, hegemonic norm. It can be said, after Brown after Nietzsche, that the *ressentiment*-inflicted subject prefers 'a negative form of action' (Brown 1995: 70), which implies denouncing the hegemonic norm as morally wrong and valorising opposition to that norm. In this way, even the most poststructural or non-modernist feminist strategies can be co-opted by feminist foundationalism insofar as their ostensible purpose is to subvert or resignify the dominant norm. As Mahmood shows in her study of the women's mosque movement in Egypt, pious women present a challenge to feminist theorising, however 'poststructural' or 'Islamic', as their 'performance' of gender, unlike Butler's (1993) drag queens, 'does not put the structure that governs its normativity at risk but rather consolidates it' (Mahmood 2005: 164).

Thus, piety, embodied in the practice of Islamic veiling, cannot quite be constructed as enhancing gender equality, yet thinking of it as the ultimate oppression of women is not adequate either. Configuring Islamic veiling as on one or the other side of this binary would be 'to reinscribe a familiar way of being human that a particular narrative of personhood and politics has made available to us, forcing the aporetic multiplicity of commitments and projects to fit into this exhausted narrative mold' (Mahmood 2005: 154–155). Rather than seeking 'to embrace such movements as forms of feminism, thus enfolding them into a liberal imaginary' (ibid.: 155), it may be worthwhile suspending feminist judgment for a while. This is not to suggest that feminism is completely redundant in an issue such as Islamic veiling, but to acknowledge non-feminist possibilities for making sense of female experience. Loosening the analytical noose around the axis of gender oppression would also serve feminism well as an 'approach to knowledge and its evaluation which is tentative, revisionist, and relentlessly self-critical' (Conaghan 2000: 381). In other words, it may be useful to think of Muslim women who practise Islamic veiling in less definitive terms, not as 'either/or', but as simultaneously both or neither. Thus, Mahmood insists on her 'refusal to recuperate the members of the mosque movement either as "subaltern feminists" or as the "fundamentalist Others" of feminism's progressive agenda' (2005: 154).

There is a notable parallel with gender equality dogmatism as it appears in the current Islamic veiling debate – the 1980–1990s' influential anti-pornography campaign of radical feminism, as espoused by Catharine MacKinnon and Andrea Dworkin (Dworkin and MacKinnon 1994; MacKinnon 1987, 1993). In both cases, there is a strong presumption that the practice (be it Islamic veiling or pornography) is inherently harmful in itself and to all womanhood, so that individual consent to it can never be endorsed as valid. It is this strong normative vision of such special gender harm, constituting the female subject, which enables the European Court of Human Rights or the Conseil d'État to justify discrediting the practice of veiling by an abstract principle of gender equality, even if the woman concerned does not seem to subscribe to this particular understanding of gender equality or even to the principle itself. The individual wearer does not enter the equation as 'the Islamic veil subjects *all of us*, Muslim and non-Muslim alike, to an intolerable discrimination against women' (Guénif-Souliamas and Macé 2004: 9, emphasis added); or '*[o]bjectively*, the veil stands for the alienation of women' (Stasi 2004: 128, emphasis added). This is much the same as the US Antipornography Civil Rights Ordinance, drafted by Dworkin and MacKinnon, which casts (a rather broad definition of) pornography as a violation of *all* women's civil rights.

As far as the pornography issue is concerned, there is, of course, much feminist opposition to the MacKinnon/Dworkin very strong feminist foundational stance (see e.g. Cornell 2000). However, it is notable that such opposition tends to concentrate on transforming pornography into a more 'women-friendly' practice, rather than engaging with the more difficult question of what psychic (as opposed to some immediate economic) value the mainstream, male-centred pornography can possibly have for women. Arguably, this type of argument is largely absent because of the difficulty a feminist consciousness would have conceiving of female agency consciously consolidating, rather than disrupting or subverting, male sexual dominance (but see Vance (1984) for some earlier, generally more adventurous views). Furthermore, Halley points to an even more general lack of feminist engagement with heterosexual pleasure. She believes that '[a]ny leftist with a serious heterosexual fetish for the erotic connection between masculine men and feminine women' (Halley 2006: 206) would not quite fit in with any 'progressive', leftist sexual politics, which is preoccupied with the subversion or reconfiguration of dominant norms.[13] In much the same way, a defence of Islamic veiling can only be palatable if it is framed as some sort of pro-feminist reconfiguration.

Another example elucidating the success of 'governance feminism' is a Dutch case, *Clara Wichmann Foundation* v. *The Dutch State*, in which state subsidies to a religiously conservative political party, *Staatkundig Gereformeerde Partij* (SGP), which would not give women full membership rights, were found in breach of the UN Convention on the Elimination of All Forms of Discrimination against Women. The feminist organisation that initiated the proceedings, Clara Wichmann Foundation, was unable to persuade any women members of the party to join the legal action, but it however claimed 'to be representing the interests of SGP women who disagreed with the party rules but are *under special pressure* not to challenge them' (Davies 2006a: 154, emphasis added). Davies argues that the only group the decision was supposed to benefit was exactly the women within the party who chose to pursue the gender debate internally, rather than bringing a legal action. Thus, in this case as well as in the Islamic veiling debate, gender equality becomes an important normative emblem and a

13 For an exploration of the problematic of female submissiveness, see Benjamin (1988). On feminism and psychoanalysis more generally, see Mitchell (1974).

tool of social engineering, with women being 'the manipulable objects of the law, not people with protected rights of their own' (ibid.: 165).

These analogies point to the strong normative purchase that *dogmatic* feminism has achieved today, as well as expose its unwillingness to have an analytical approach not structured along the oppression/emancipation axis. Arguably, feminism itself would benefit from acknowledging its limits and making room for alternative discourses, which would not revolve around 'the passionate consciousness of one's gender at every single moment'.

5 Concluding remarks

This chapter has been concerned with exploring the gender equality argument as it is used on both sides of the Islamic veiling debate. The most common use is the deployment of the principle of gender equality, both in judicial and popular discourses, to justify various restrictions on Islamic veiling. This line of argument tends to construct Islamic veiling as profoundly antithetical with the ideal of gender equality and thus deserving disapproval, regardless of the ideas or normative attachments of those who wear it. A notable feature of this argument is its near-total counterpositioning of gender with religion and culture, which in turn tend to be conflated. The other, although less prevalent, use of the gender equality argument asserts the opposite – namely, that Islamic veiling symbolises women's quest for equality and liberation, rather than their submission to male dominance.

The chapter has argued that there are problems with both these uses. Most prominently, the gender equality argument employed by proponents of Islamic veiling restrictions has some longstanding colonial and racist connotations, which makes its present-day utilisations suspect. By concentrating on the 'exotic' practice of Islamic veiling, it works to eclipse all other, more important and persistent, varieties of gender inequality. The use of the gender equality card by the Islamic feminists who defend Islamic veiling practices, although not without merit, is not unproblematic either as it tends to create a certain mythology of Islam as a pro-feminist religious framework. It has been suggested that this strategic coupling of Islam and feminism can be explained, to a certain extent, by the strong normative hold that feminism has acquired over popular imagination. The chapter's ultimate objective has then been to interrogate the normative purchase of gender equality itself. In doing so, it has asked whether it might be better to suspend feminism's normative vision of the world as permeated with gender oppression, in order to make some room for acknowledging the ultimate richness of human experience.

Chapter 5

Religion and secularism

This final chapter addresses the third 'frame' of the Islamic veiling debate – secularism and its flipside, religion. It shows how Islamic veiling is being either demonised or 'reinterpreted' in order to repudiate the charge of fundamentalism and be made compatible with secular liberal rule. The chapter argues that the currently dominant modality of secularism that enables this process is problematic in various ways. Far from being universal, it represents a rather particular historical formation and political rationality, which implies a peculiarly modern counterpositioning of religion and secularism, rooted in certain versions of Christianity. This being so, Islam has become the perfect 'other' of the secular West. Yet – arguably more significantly – the sort of difficulty secularism is currently having with religion is not resolvable into its conflict with Islam alone. Although the latter certainly enjoys a special status in the current, post-Cold War, post-9/11 era, it is the contemporary secular understanding of religion as such which provides for a more illuminating enquiry.

The chapter proceeds in much the same way as the previous two, first by outlining positions on both sides of the debate and then exposing the underlying currents. Part 1 outlines the argument, as it informs the law and surrounding public debates, that Islamic veiling is the ultimate expression of Islamic radicalism threatening secularism and associated foundational values of the West. Part 2 presents the opposite position – the argument that veiling is simply a legitimate exercise of one's freedom of religion, a valued right in democratic societies and international human rights regimes. Part 3 then explains the structure of freedom of religion itself, which makes such constructions possible. Part 4 then explores what makes the two seemingly opposing positions possible. In brief, it is a certain 'compartmentalisation' of religion as something essentially private, largely irrelevant to the material world and not to be interpreted literally, which informs dominant modes of secularism across the western world. To support the point, the chapter explores secularism's evolution, showing how the currently dominant version is not only Christian in origin, but represents certain currents within Christianity itself, in contradistinction to other forms of religiosity.

1 Islamic veiling as dangerous Islamic radicalism

Already in the early 1990s, the European Commission on Human Rights was concerned with the danger of 'certain religious fundamentalist currents' (*Karaduman* v. *Turkey* 1993: 101). As recounted in Chapter 2, the Commission declared the *Karaduman* case inadmissible. It concerned a university graduate who could not obtain a provisional degree certificate because the photograph she provided for this purpose featured her in a headscarf. The ECmHR did not think that wearing the headscarf was even within the definition of freedom of religion as 'the term "practice", in the sense of paragraph 1 of Article 9 ... does not denote any act motivated or inspired by a religion or a conviction' (ibid.: 100). Thus, Article 9 'does not always guarantee the right to behave in public in a way dictated by this conviction' (ibid.). The ECmHR also referred to the importance of upholding rules at a secular university, in order 'to ensure respect for the rights and freedoms of others' (ibid.: 101) – a recurrent theme in subsequent cases. Although the existence of 'certain religious fundamentalist currents' in Turkey seemed to justify the outcome, the ECmHR did not explain the link between them and Karaduman's photograph.

In 2001, the European Court of Human Rights declared inadmissible *Dahlab* v. *Switzerland*, a case that involved a public school teacher who was prevented from wearing a headscarf at work. Two justifications for the restrictive measure were accepted: denominational neutrality and gender equality. While gender equality has already been considered in the previous chapter, denominational neutrality is the Swiss version of secularism and thus is a primary concern for the present discussion. Dahlab tried to argue that she wore the headscarf for aesthetic, as opposed to religious, reasons. The Swiss Federal Court, the final instance in domestic proceedings before the case reached Strasbourg, was unwilling to accept this. It described the headscarf as a 'manifest religious attribute' (pp. 452–453) that derives from passages of the Koran (ibid.: 448–449), which 'may even be said to constitute a powerful religious symbol' (ibid.), incompatible with denominational neutrality. The ECtHR appeared to be in agreement with these findings.

The applicant argued that the fact that she had worn the headscarf for more than five years without attracting any complaints was sufficient proof that the rights of others were not interfered with. The ECtHR was not prepared to accept this, instead tacitly agreeing with the Swiss Federal Court's speculation that 'some may well have decided not to take any direct action so as not to aggravate the situation, in the hope that the education authorities will react of their own motion' (ibid.: 450). As an improvement on the *Karaduman* decision, there was some attempt here to supply a link between the headscarf and the rights of others. It was, however, purely speculative – others failing to react in order not to aggravate matters. A further point is whether it is acceptable simply to pander to prejudice, rather than scrutinise the content of the alleged objection to headscarves.

The Swiss Federal Court went on to say of the applicant, '[a]dmittedly, she is not accused of proselytising or even of talking to her pupils about her beliefs'. It continued:

> However, the appellant can scarcely avoid the questions which her pupils have not missed the opportunity to ask. It would seem somewhat awkward for her to reply by citing aesthetic considerations or sensitivity to the cold – the approach she claims to have adopted to date, according to the file – because the children will realise that she is evading the issue.
>
> (ibid., Swiss Federal Court: 452–453)

Thus, the very fact of Islam's visibility is considered sufficiently antithetical to the interests of the pupils in the school. The ECtHR reinforced the perception of the Islamic headscarf as a threat to others, especially to Dahlab's pupils aged between four and eight (ibid.: 463). It considered that 'it cannot be denied outright that the wearing of a headscarf might have *some kind of proselytizing effect*, seeing that it appears to be imposed on women by a precept which is laid down in the Koran' (ibid.). It also noted: 'It ... appears difficult to reconcile the wearing of an Islamic headscarf with the message of tolerance, respect for others and, above all, equality and non-discrimination that all teachers in a democratic society must convey to their pupils' (ibid.). Thus, the headscarf itself is understood to be incompatible with these western democratic values.

Şahin v. *Turkey* (2007) is a landmark ECHR case on the issue of Islamic headscarves. As described in Chapter 2 in more detail, the case concerned a medical student at Istanbul University who was prevented from attending classes and examinations due to wearing a headscarf. She complained, in particular, of a violation of her rights under Article 9, which protects freedom of religion. The case was declared admissible under Article 9, which meant that wearing an Islamic headscarf could, in principle, be within the meaning of the manifestation of a religion under Article 9 (although it was emphasised that this would not always be so). However, Şahin lost on the merits as the university's restrictions were believed to be justified by Article 9(2). The latter specifies that the right to manifest one's religion is subject to 'limitations as are prescribed by law and are necessary in a democratic society' in the interests of 'public safety, for the protection of public order, health or morals, or for the protection of the rights and freedoms of others'. The relevant 'legitimate aims' were those of public order and the rights and freedoms of others.

Of special significance to the ECtHR was the longstanding commitment of the democratic Turkish state to the principle of secularism. The applicant's headscarf was considered to be incompatible with this principle, particularly in view of the 'burgeoning extremist currents' in Turkey (Grand Chamber: paras 112–113; Chamber: 103–110) – mirroring the ECmHR's reference in *Karaduman* to 'certain religious fundamentalist currents'. The ECtHR did 'not lose sight of the fact that there are extremist political movements in Turkey which seek to impose on society as a whole their religious symbols and conception of a society founded on religious precepts...' (para 115) as a danger justifying banishing headscarves from the public space. This is despite the fact that the applicant did not belong to any such movements or seek to impose her religious views on others (para 14). Like in previous cases, it is the wearing of the headscarf as such which is regarded as detrimental to democracy, with no further evidence necessary.

Şahin also pleaded a violation of Article 14 ECHR, claiming that she had been discriminated against on the basis of her religion. This was rejected as 'the regulations on the Islamic headscarf were not directed against the applicant's religious affiliation' (para 165). Such a straightforward assertion suggests obliviousness to the complex discriminatory effects that a facially neutral provision might have. Obviously, it was Muslims who were more likely to be affected; indeed the 'burgeoning extremist currents' refer to Islamist political movements.

The cases of *Dogru* v. *France* (2008) and *Kervanci* v. *France* (2008) hardly improved the position. Two Muslim schoolgirls had been expelled from school for refusing to remove their headscarves for physical education classes. (The events in both cases predated the 2004 law, under which it became illegal to wear headscarves to school in general, not just physical education.) The European Court of Human Rights recognised that this could raise an Article 9 issue, but found no violation on the merits. It did not address Dogru's contentions that she had been refused permission to participate in sports classes despite suggesting an alternative (to wear a hat or balaclava instead of a headscarf) and that the teacher did not explain how the student's safety would be endangered; nor further explanations had been provided by the respondent Government (para 44). Instead, a rather wide margin of appreciation was given to the state, as it was in a position to both introduce and assess its own evidence as to what sort of conduct is incompatible with *laïcité* (paras 72–77). The ECtHR was keen to emphasise that 'an attitude which fails to respect [the] principle [of secularism] will not necessarily be accepted as being covered by the freedom to manifest one's religion and will not enjoy the protection of Article 9 of the Convention' (para 72).

As a positive development, the European Court of Human Rights explained that 'the wearing of religious signs was not inherently incompatible with the principle of secularism in schools' (para 70). But the effect of this was undone by the ensuing, largely unscrutinised assertion that it 'became so according to the conditions in which they were worn and the consequences that the wearing of a sign might have' (ibid.). Such conditions and consequences were not explained, nor whether the girls' actual attitude was 'anti-secular'. The ECtHR simply noted that the French secular model as a whole properly addresses the concern that the manifestation by pupils of their religious beliefs on school premises does not 'take on the nature of an ostentatious act that would constitute a source of pressure and exclusion' (para 71). Although this resulted in the applicants' own expulsion from the school (and arguably the secular model more generally), the ECtHR accepted that this was 'merely the consequence' of their refusal to comply with school rules 'and not of their religious convictions, as they alleged' (para 73). As in previous cases, there was very little scrutiny of the link between the applicants' own behaviour and the 'legitimate aim' behind the restriction, with the ECtHR simply concluding that expulsion was not a disproportionate penalty as the applicants had been able to continue their education by correspondence classes. Thus here, as in previous cases, headscarves are simply taken to be incompatible with secularism, regardless of the wearer's attitude or intentions.

The debate around Islamic veiling in France is even more permeated with a vision of Islamic veiling as an aggressive religious threat to secularism. Prior to the introduction of the 2004 law, President Chirac asserted that it was to target the 'Islamist veil', 'an aggressive, ostentatious sign of religious proselytism' (BBC Online News, 17 December 2003). The law itself was worded to ban '*ostentatious*' (*ostensible* in French) 'religious signs and dress' in public primary and secondary schools. Interestingly, not all of the Stasi Commission recommendations were followed; for example, it was decided not to recognise 'the most important Jewish and Islamic holy days as national holidays in the school and workplace calendars' (Stasi 2004). In 2006, the French National Assembly awarded its annual prize for the best book on politics to Caroline Fourest, a high-profile feminist known for her support of the Islamic veiling bans. Her book *The Obscurantist Temptation (La tentation obscurantiste)* (2005) fiercely opposes 'religious fundamentalism', allegedly espoused by Islamic veiling, and defends *laïcité*.

The case of Mme M, considered by the Conseil d'État in June 2008, contains some very strong *laïcité* rhetoric, disapproving of veiling as such – as opposed to in the public sphere only. To expand on the account provided in Chapter 2, a Moroccan woman was refused French nationality for wearing the niqab as this was considered indicative of 'insufficient assimilation'. She had been told by the French Government, which refused her citizenship application, that she had 'preserved very strong ties with [her] culture of origin' and that her dress and daily conduct was indicative of 'a radical religious practice incompatible with the essential values of French society' (Conclusions of Mme Prada Bordenave: 2). In response, and before the Conseil d'État, Mme M argued that preserving ties with one's culture of origin was not incompatible with French nationality; that she had never sought to undermine the fundamental values of the Republic; and that, in contrast, she believed in the values of *liberté, égalité, fraternité* and above all of *laïcité*, which in fact was an opportunity for her to practise her religion. She also asserted that the exercise of religious freedom is guaranteed by the French Constitution as well as the European Convention on Human Rights, which is directly applicable in France. This argumentation was dismissed as 'very summative and very general', as no evidence was produced by Mme M concerning her 'personal situation, which would support her contestation'. It is interesting what kind of evidence would be considered appropriate or convincing to support one's belief in *laïcité*. It seems that some kind of *laïcité*-inspired conduct is required, in the same way as religious belief is seen as inspiring certain conduct.

The Conseil d'État ruling itself is brief. Essentially, it concludes that, despite possessing a good command of French, Mme M 'however adopted a *radical practice of her religion*, incompatible with the essential values of French society' (emphasis added). More clues in respect of her incompatibility with *laïcité* are contained in the Conclusions of the Government Commissioner, Mme Prada Bordenave, on which the Conseil d'État ruling relies. The Commissioner notes previous Conseil d'État jurisprudence, according to which the fact of wearing a veil, even with reference to a strict religious practice, cannot in itself justify a finding of insufficient assimilation. Nonetheless, additional evidence contained in Mme M's 'dossier' (consisting of three transcripts of interviews with social services and police) was found to constitute sufficient proof, with the Commissioner concluding that 'it is the combination of Mme M's conduct in her daily life and her statements that reveal a lack of adhesion to certain fundamental values of French society'.

The dossier reveals that Mme M and her husband 'spontaneously come across as Salafists' and 'claim to belong to a group which, according to the Prefecture's department, won over some of the youth from the area where they live, following the appearance of a particularly vehement Imam' (Conclusions: 4). The interview Mme M gave to the *New York Times* records her and her husband's discontent with the term 'Salafist', which they see as associated with violent, political Islam; instead they prefer to characterise their religiousness simply as 'a literalist interpretation of the Koran' (Bennhold, 19 July 2008). Interestingly, the believability of Mme M's own legal argumentation is discredited in the Commissioner's Conclusions because she had 'spontaneously stated', in earlier interviews with social services and police, that she 'had no idea about *laïcité* or the right to vote', so that her legal submissions are to be regarded with suspicion as they 'without a doubt do not reflect [her] personal convictions' (p. 4).

This kind of assessment of one's plausibility as a potential citizen seems to assume that legal avenues, frameworks and norms are there to be earnestly believed in, rather than available structures and formulas to fit one's case into in order to achieve a desired outcome. Far from being a neutral framework facilitating co-existence of various religions, secularism comes to compete with religion as a world view and system of societal organisation. The current President of the French Republic, Nicolas Sarkozy, commented back in 2003 on the new law prohibiting headscarves in schools: 'If I enter a mosque, I take off my shoes. If a young Muslim enters school, she has to take off her veil' (*Le Figaro*, 12 September 2003, as cited in Joppke 2009: 36). Clearly, secularism here is on a par with religion, with a secular school to be treated like a sacred space. In Mme M's case, *laïcité* goes even further, being an authoritative life- and thought-governing code as one faces adverse consequences for non-compliance with it in one's mind and daily life (as opposed to the public sphere only). Thus, Mme M is not simply rejected for her public actions or sartorial choices, but for the entire way she is. The Conseil d'État thus examined not only Mme M's outward compliance with *laïcité*, but her internalisation of it, her 'making it her own'. Her full body and face covering were deemed to be the key symbol of her rejection of French values, with a state minister referring to her way of dressing as a 'prison' and a 'straightjacket', 'not a religious insignia but the insignia of a totalitarian political project' (*Parisien*, as cited in BBC Online News, 16 July 2008).

In October 2010, a new law penalising 'the concealment of the face in public space' was passed with overwhelming majority by both chambers of the French Parliament. The law was framed as a defence against the growing threat of Islamic radicalism, threatening essential French values of *laïcité*, individualism and gender equality. Again, the veil was seen as a key emblem of this threat, despite the fact that only a few hundred Muslim women in France are believed to cover their faces. So great was this perceived threat that the law was passed despite the Conseil d'État's recommendation to the contrary. It contains a broad definition of 'public space', including streets, markets, open spaces, public transport and 'places affected by a public service' – in sum, almost anywhere outside one's home. Although the law is framed in neutral terms, it clearly targets Islamic veiling. A number of exceptions from liability are provided, such as covering the face for medical or artistic reasons. The most relevant exception concerns clothes worn 'in the context of festivities (disguise for a carnival or as Father Christmas) ... or traditional expression (processions, particularly religious)'. Father Christmas, a permutation of a Christian saint figure (Saint Nicholas), obviously is not seen as threatening *laïcité* – rather, it is a central part of modern secular culture. The exception granted to 'traditional religious processions' is even more candid: it clearly refers to traditional Catholic processions, popular in France. Again, organised Catholic expression does not seem to threaten *laïcité*, while a handful of individual women wearing niqabs do. This special protection for Catholic religious expression is also a telling contrast with the Paris ban on Muslim street prayers enacted in late 2011 (BBC Online News, 16 September 2011). Although the phenomenon of street prayers is believed to be linked to insufficient mosque space, praying outside is considered as acceptable in Islam. The reaction of the French Minister of the Interior was that '[p]raying in the street is not dignified for religious practice and violates the principles of secularism' (Samuel, 15 September 2011), thus betraying an incomprehension of a religion which does not have a familiar separation between the sacred and secular space. And yet, Catholic street processions are not seen as undignified or deserving prohibition.

Other places in Europe also display similar discomfort with Islamic veiling as a radical religious practice. Much anti-Muslim rhetoric has centred around veiling in the Netherlands, which has recently seen the introduction of a national proposal to ban full-face veils. As recounted in Chapter 2, these measures have been pushed by Geert Wilders' Freedom Party, which has a strong populist, anti-immigrant and anti-Muslim agenda. Wilders himself made the notorious film *Fitna* in 2008, which crudely portrays Islam as inherently anti-secular, violent and fundamentalist, likening 'Islamic ideology' to 'Communism' and 'Nazism'. A few years earlier, the film *Submission* was made by (subsequently murdered) Theo van Gogh, which featured fictional female characters wearing a transparent covering over the naked body, recounting their poeticised stories of brutal violence and abuse against women in the name of Islam. In this film scripted by Ayaan Hirsi Ali, a Dutch feminist who had denounced her Islamic faith, a clear link is made between veiling and oppressive fundamentalist mentality – much the same link that was thought to justify a national veil ban.

In Germany, the dynamic is somewhat more nuanced. There is no state ideology of secularism, like in France. Religion is not considered automatically prejudicial to the public sphere; however, there is a framework of 'neutrality, non-discrimination and tolerance in religious matters'. In the landmark case of *Ludin* v. *Land Baden-Württemberg* (2003), which concerned a public school teacher who wore a headscarf, the Federal Constitutional Court openly addressed the symbolism of this garment. The list of possible meanings included adherence to tradition, refusal to westernise, women's sexual purity and religious or cultural identity (para 52). It was ruled that what the headscarf actually symbolises could only be determined with reference to the wearer, but her subjective intentions were not decisive. The relevant test was the 'neutral observer' (*objektiver Empfängerhorizont* in German) and her 'objective understanding' (ibid.). On the facts of the case, it was concluded that the headscarf did not automatically contradict the German Constitution and its wearing could not be limited without an appropriate legal basis (which was then hastily introduced). However, the minority judgment considered the headscarf objectively to symbolise political Islamism and the oppression of women which went 'beyond an acceptable level'. Hence, similarly to the ECHR cases, empirical evidence of its impact upon education or a specific legal basis were not necessary.

The *Land* of Baden-Württemberg, together with a few other *Länder*, subsequently enacted a legislative amendment providing an explicit legal basis for prohibiting religious gear for teachers in public schools, which Fereshta Ludin unsuccessfully challenged. The amendment read:

> 1 Teachers are not allowed … to give external statements [*äussere Bekundungen*] of a political, religious [or] ideological nature which could endanger or disturb the neutrality of the *Land* towards pupils or parents or … the political, religious or ideological peace of the school.
>
> 2 Especially impermissible is an external behaviour which could create the impression, in pupils or parents, that a teacher opposes the equality [principle] according to Article 3 of the Basic Law, basic liberty rights, or the liberal democratic order.
>
> 3 The representation of Christian and occidental values or traditions corresponds to the educational mandate of the [regional] constitution and does not contradict the behaviour required [*Verhaltensgebot*] according to Sentence 1.
>
> (Baden-Württemberg School Act 2004: §38, translated in Joppke 2009: 72)

The second sentence was widely thought to refer specifically to Islamic headscarves and other such Muslim 'symbols', thus inscribing a fixed meaning on veiling as being incompatible with fundamental German values. The wording implies that it is sufficient that an item 'create[s] the impression' of being so anti-modern, without necessarily that impression being grounded in any evidence or objective truth. The exception in the third sentence relating to the 'representation of Christian and occidental values or traditions' (ibid.) is also remarkable. The Federal Administrative Court (2004) reasoned that such 'Christian and occidental' values are divorced from their religious underpinnings and as such fundamentally underlie the German Constitution, including inviolable human dignity (Article 1), equality (Article 3) and religious freedom (Article 4) (*Ludin* 2004: 14). Such candid privileging of the Christian tradition above others is possible in Germany as, unlike France, it never tried to frame itself as an ideologically secular state. Instead, religious education and financing religious institutions are uncontroversially supported through the taxpayer in Germany, and the state relies on its 'Christian occidental' German tradition with pride. To return to the Federal Administrative Court's judgment, demonstrating such Christian and occidental values is not the same as manifesting individual religious faith (ibid.: 10), and thus all public servants ought to be able to agree on them, regardless of their own religious persuasion (ibid.: 14). As the prohibition is 'limited to teachers in public schools', the Islamic community was not considered to be 'excessively affected' (ibid.: 15).

In the United Kingdom, there is no official state discourse of secularism and indeed the Head of State is also the Head of the Church of England. However, secular sensitivities inform the law and judges' logic in more subtle ways. As described in Chapter 2, headscarves have traditionally been accepted in the UK as a benign expression of multiculturalism and thus have rarely been considered incompatible with school uniforms or British values. As mentioned in Chapter 2, a school in Luton briefly prohibited headscarves in 2003, but this policy was soon withdrawn following some significant media coverage and threat of legal action. However, 'stricter' forms of Islamic veiling, such as jilbabs or niqabs, have become the subject matter of legal controversy more recently, in cases such as *Denbigh High School* (2006) and *X* v. *Y School* (2007). It is noteworthy that such 'stricter' Muslims are cast in opposition to their more 'liberal' counterparts in the judgments. Following the Court of Appeal (2005), the House of Lords (2006) in *Denbigh High School* explicitly subdivides Muslims into 'liberal' (those who are content with wearing headscarves and shalwar kameeze) and 'very strict' (those who consider more thorough covering appropriate). The school in question was praised for its inclusive uniform policy, modified in the early 1990s upon consultation with local mosques to allow headscarves. This satisfied 'mainstream Muslim opinion' (para 34), shared by the 'liberal' majority of Muslim students and parents, but not 'very strict Muslims' like Shabina Begum, who brought the case. Thus, it is such 'stricter' garb, rather than mere headscarves, that was considered to symbolise Islamic radicalism.

The media speculated that Shabina herself was under the influence of her older brother, Shuweb Rahman, who was believed to have connections with Hizb ut-Tahrir, a pan-Islamic political organisation aiming to restore the Islamic caliphate in the Muslim world. Hizb ut-Tahrir's ideology and methods are widely believed to be verging on 'extremist', its activities being banned in several countries. Fears of Muslim extremism were widely fuelled in media commentary around the case. The judgment itself is much more nuanced and careful than, for example, that of Conseil d'État in Mme M's case, but constructions of veiling as dangerous religious radicalism are not too far from the surface. A subtle start is the reference in the judgment to Shabina's brother and 'another young man' 'escorting' her to school (Lord Hoffmann: para 46), followed by their 'talk of human rights and legal proceedings', which apparently threatened the assistant headteacher (Lord Bingham: para 10). Lord Scott regretted 'the confrontational nature of the peremptory manner in which the *jilbab* issue was raised with the school' (para 80) – an approach their Lordships considered 'unreasonable' (para 10). This is interesting as the 'peremptory' nature of a religious issue such as veiling is considered unreasonable and possibly indicative of a fundamentalist mentality. So that even their 'talk of human rights and legal proceedings' is seen as a symptom of this confrontational unreasonableness, as opposed to complying with western legal ideology, which one might think would be seen as playing according to the rules of the game.

The House of Lords avoids making a direct pronouncement on the meaning of Shabina's clothes, deferring instead to the expertise of the school, which it believes was 'in the best position to weigh and consider' its 'wish to avoid clothes which were perceived by some Muslims (rightly or wrongly) as signifying adherence to an extremist vision of the Muslim religion and to protect girls against external pressures' (para 65). So, 'liberal Muslims' perceive the jilbab to be extremist and threatening to their more moderate interpretation of Islam, but the Law Lords would not comment on whether such perceptions are *right or wrong*. Yet, the outcome is to uphold the school's decision to ban such clothes, which inevitably gives weight and validation to such perceptions.

The *X* v. *Y School* case, which concerned a niqab, closely follows the reasoning in *Denbigh High School* in most respects. The school's arguments were accepted in full. Here also it was commented that the headteacher thought it was 'regrettable' that the claimant's family had consulted solicitors who stated that 'legal action would ensue if a satisfactory arrangement was not reached' (para 19). The uniform policy was upheld in view of the importance of promoting 'uniformity and an ethos of cohesion', security and 'avoiding applying pressure on girls to wear a niqab' (para 65). The visibility of such 'strict' forms of Islamic veiling was also a significant factor contributing to their perception as an unacceptable expression of radicalism and difference. In the subsequent case of *Watkins-Singh* (2008), an explicit distinction was made between 'visible' items such as jilbabs and niqabs and the more inconspicuous kara, a metal bangle representing one of the five symbols of the Sikh faith, as the latter was considered acceptable. The then leader of the House of Commons, Jack Straw, commented in his controversial column in October 2006 that he saw the veil as 'such a visible sign of separation and of difference'.

The Employment Appeal Tribunal judgment in the case of *Aishah Azmi* (2007), a teaching assistant who had been dismissed for wearing the veil in class, purports to be a measured application of the Employment Equality (Religion and Belief) Regulations 2003 to her claim of indirect discrimination. The judgment records that she did not wear the veil to her job interview following her husband's advice (para 8), which was perceived as undermining her credibility. When asked at a BBC interview why she was unveiled then she apparently replied, after some hesitation, that she had not realised she was going to be interviewed by a male (BBC Online News, 19 October 2006b). As the case attracted a huge amount of media attention, these apparent contradictions were exploited to paint a frightening picture of a woman brainwashed by Islamic fundamentalists. It was reported that she had decided to wear the veil as she was obeying a fatwa from her local cleric, Mufti Yusuf Sacha, who apparently 'follows the teachings of the Tablighi Jamaat, a hardline Muslim group, elements of which are suspected by western intelligence agencies of having links with terrorism' (Taher, 29 October 2009). Obviously, 'obeying a fatwa' scares secular audiences, signifying total compulsion and a lack of rational deliberation on the part of the one obeying. 'Fatwa', of course, simply means a juristic opinion, with its weight varying considerably across the different Islamic traditions and subject matters.

The spectacular coverage of Aishah Azmi's case highlighted some deep-seated anxieties about a figure 'shrouded in veils' being allowed to teach the young generation of British citizens (Marrin, 22 October 2006). According to the *Sunday Times*, 'Mrs Azmi stands for ... what many people fear about Muslims, no matter how tolerant they would like to feel' – that is, 'deliberate cultural separation, voluntary apartheid, a pre-Enlightenment religion' (ibid.). A number of British politicians, including the then Prime Minister, Tony Blair, were recorded to make negative comments on covering the face in general and Aishah Azmi in particular as the case was still *sub judice* – something that is not expected to happen normally. The then Community Cohesion Minister, Phil Woolas, demanded that Aishah Azmi be sacked, accusing her of 'denying the right of children to a full education' and of 'sexual discrimination' against men if they would be barred from working in the same classroom in order to enable her to lift her veil (Herbert, 20 October 2006).

To sum up, it would be unwise to suggest that British decision-makers and judges consciously inscribe an anti-Muslim agenda in the legal decisions they make. Rather, their understated rhetoric, subtly influenced by popular hysteria and anxiety, reveals some deep cultural discomfort about Islamic veiling as a radical religious practice incompatible with modernity and secular ways of doing things. This discomfort, shared throughout the rest of Europe, will be explored in more detail in Part 3 of this chapter.

2 Islamic veiling as a legitimate exercise of freedom of religion

As Part 1 of this chapter showed, constructions of Islamic veiling as dangerous religious extremism are predominant in both judicial and legislative pronouncements and in media coverage and popular commentary around the issue. Yet, as in the previous chapters, here also we have the other side of the coin: those who argue that Islamic veiling is a legitimate and innocuous exercise of freedom of religion, which is an important human right valued in democratic societies and international human rights regimes. Indeed, it is this very argument that enables individual Muslims to bring their cases challenging the veiling restrictions. This argument was made in virtually every case considered in the book, either under national law or the ECHR.

In Germany, Fereshta Ludin as well as applicants in similar cases relied on their right to freedom of religion, protected by Article 4 of the German Constitution. In the '*Verkäuferin mit Kopftuch*' case (10 October 2003), for example, the Federal Labour Court held that a sales assistant wearing a headscarf was *motivated by her religious conviction*, which is a fundamental constitutional right. As we will see later, Article 9 ECHR implies a similar structure of religion, where an act or behaviour stems from a religious belief. In France, Mme M argued before the Conseil d'État that her religious rights were infringed by refusing her French citizenship. According to her, she believed in the fundamental values of the French Republic, above all *laïcité*, which in fact was an opportunity for her to practise her religion. She relied both on the French Constitution and Article 9 ECHR, which is directly applicable in France. The Conseil d'État did not dispute the importance of this right, but denied outright that it was infringed in Mme M's case as 'neither the purpose nor the effect' of the Government's refusal of her citizenship application was 'to target her religious freedom', and thus it 'disregarded neither the constitutional principle of freedom of religious expression nor the provisions of Article 9 of the European Convention…' (27 June 2008). In other words, there is a failure here to deal with the substance of Mme M's religious freedom argument, but the importance of this freedom itself is implicitly confirmed. In the United Kingdom, cases such as *Denbigh High School* and *X* v. *Y School* were decided under the Human Rights Act 1998, which implements the ECHR into UK law and hence Article 9 ECHR was of primary relevance. The aggrieved parties argued that wearing a jilbab, or a niqab, was a legitimate manifestation of their religious belief, while the courts had the task of interpreting and applying Article 9 to the facts. As outlined in Chapter 2, the courts agreed, for the most part, that Islamic veiling did indeed constitute such a manifestation, but it could be legitimately limited according to paragraph 2 of the article.

A similar picture is found in ECHR jurisprudence itself; indeed veiling cases have invariably been brought to Strasbourg authorities under Article 9 ECHR, and UK courts extensively relied on this jurisprudence in their judgments. It is, however, interesting that it is only recently that the European Court of Human Rights accepted that veiling could be a legitimate exercise of freedom of religion. As recounted in the first part of this chapter, in an early case, *Karaduman* v. *Turkey*, it was thought that the headscarf was not covered by freedom of religion as, according to established ECHR jurisprudence:

> [The term 'practice' in Article 9] does not protect every act motivated or inspired by a religion or belief and does not in all cases guarantee the right to behave in the public sphere in a way which is dictated by a belief.
>
> (*Arrowsmith* v. *UK* 1983: para 71)

And thus, Article 9 'does not always guarantee the right to behave in public in a way dictated by this conviction' (*Karaduman*: 100). The next landmark case, *Dahlab* v. *Switzerland*, seems to follow *Karaduman* in not considering the headscarf to be important enough to be protected by Article 9. Like *Karaduman*, *Dahlab* was declared inadmissible for being 'manifestly ill-founded'.

Şahin v. *Turkey*, however, departs from this position by explicitly recognising that wearing a headscarf could amount to a manifestation of religion under Article 9 ECHR. (A similar case was declared admissible under Article 9 in *Tekin* v. *Turkey* (2002); however the applicant soon withdrew her complaint.) The ECtHR did emphasise in *Şahin* that it would not always be so, which presumably indicates sensitivity to context. But it is unlikely that ECHR case-law would significantly depart from the position that veiling *is* a manifestation of religion; indeed, in most subsequent cases involving Islamic veiling, including *Dogru* and *Kervanci*, Article 9 has been the primary legal basis. It can be said with certainty that practising Islamic veiling is now considered to be an exercise of one's freedom of religion under Article 9 ECHR. The reason these later cases have invariably failed before the European Court of Human Rights is that such exercise of freedom of religion was thought to be open to limitations under Article 9(2) ECHR, which provides a list of acceptable grounds.

These decisions have been the subject of heavy academic and lawyerly criticism. As summarised in Part 1 of this chapter, the ECtHR's reasoning is unconvincing as little concrete evidence was induced to prove that the applicants' headscarves were a threat to public order or the rights and freedoms of others, which are the two applicable grounds among those listed in Article 9(2). The existence of such a threat was simply presumed and so the courts' inadequate application of the margin of appreciation doctrine has been criticised (e.g. Davies 2006b; Lewis 2007), taking the critics to the logical conclusion that headscarves ought in fact to be recognised as a legitimate exercise of freedom of religion and not be restricted. This is just the kind of legal reasoning that the applicants would like the courts to adopt. But it is not just the applicants; many legal academics have convincingly written in support of the proposition that restricting veiling is in fact a violation of human rights, and in particular freedom of religion (e.g. Howard 2011; McGoldrick 2006; Ssenyonjo 2007). However, this is not the point of the enquiry pursued in this book. Rather, the task in this chapter is to highlight how such constructions of veiling as an exercise of freedom of religion, sanctioned or restricted by international human rights law, are made possible by the underlying legal and ideological framework. The problematics and limitations of this framework will then be highlighted.

3 How is freedom of religion understood in law?

To understand how veiling gets presented in legal terms as a legitimate exercise of freedom of religion, let us have a closer look at the anatomy of freedom of religion as it is inscribed in Article 9 ECHR. It is worth reproducing the text of Article 9 in full here.

Article 9 – Freedom of thought, conscience and religion

1 Everyone has the right to freedom of thought, conscience and religion; this right includes freedom to change his religion or belief and freedom, either alone or in community with others and in public or private, to manifest his religion or belief, in worship, teaching, practice and observance.

2 Freedom to manifest one's religion or beliefs shall be subject only to such limitations as are prescribed by law and are necessary in a democratic society in the interests of public safety, for the protection of public order, health or morals, or for the protection of the rights and freedoms of others.

Generally speaking, paragraph 1 of Article 9 ECHR protects both the freedom to have a religion and the freedom to manifest it. This distinction is crucial; some commentators even consider these to be two distinct rights (e.g. Pimor 2006). Such a split in the right to freedom of religion is not unique to the European Convention on Human Rights legal framework. In the key American case of *Reynolds* v. *United States* (1878), involving a Mormon convicted of polygamy, it was held that the First Amendment rights were limited to the protection of religious belief, but did not cover *practice*, of which polygamy was an example (see Sandel 1998). A not dissimilar pattern can be found in European domestic frameworks, under which Islamic veiling has been debated and litigated. In every instance, the right to have a religious, or philosophical, belief is considered primary, while the right to *manifest* such belief is secondary and derivative from the former.

In *Şahin* v. *Turkey* itself, it was reiterated that freedom of religion as a whole is 'primarily a matter of individual conscience' (*Kokkinakis* v. *Greece* 1994: para 31), with 'inner belief' being key. Generally speaking, the right to have a religion in Article 9 is absolute and cannot be restricted;[1] this often is referred to as the *forum internum*, indicating an internal, primary and fundamental dimension of freedom of religion. On the other hand, the right to manifest one's religion or belief is known as the *forum externum* – an external, secondary and derivative dimension of freedom of religion, and as such it is less fundamental, being subject to limitations, laid out in paragraph 2. There are four types of 'manifestation' in Article 9, namely 'worship, teaching, practice and observance', but these are not terms of art and tend to be used loosely. Examples of recognised 'manifestations' include proselytising (*Kokkinakis* v. *Greece*), ritual slaughter (*Cha'are Shalom ve Tsedek* v. *France* 2000) and praying for the life of the unborn (*Van Schijndel, Van der Heyden and Leenman* v. *Netherlands* 1998). Islamic veiling is now in this category also.

In addition, a whole range of acts or behaviour is treated as merely 'motivated' by a religion or belief (*Arrowsmith* v. *UK*) but short of a 'manifestation' protected by Article 9. As mentioned earlier, headscarves were previously thought to fall within this category, but were upgraded to a 'manifestation' in *Şahin*. The European Court of Human Rights uses the technique of classifying something as merely 'motivated' by a religion or belief to attrite cases that it considers too far-fetched to merit the protection of Article 9. For example, *Arrowsmith* v. *UK* (1983: para 71) concerned pacifist leaflets calling on soldiers not to serve in Northern Ireland, which was thought to be motivated by a philosophical belief, but below a required level for a 'manifestation' protected by Article 9. Refusing to attend a school parade was considered in the same category of 'merely motivated' in *Valsamis* v. *Greece* (1997) and *Efstratiou* v. *Greece* (1997). In *Kosteski* v. *Macedonia* (2006), leave from work for the purpose of religious holidays was considered to be merely 'motivated' and not a 'manifestation', and hence not protected by Article 9 (para 44). In *Stedman* v. *UK* (1997), refusing to work on Sundays, which was incompatible with the applicant's Christian convictions, was thought to be 'motivated by her religious convictions'. As she was not prevented from 'manifesting' her religion and was free to change employment, the case was 'manifestly ill-founded'. *Ahmad* v. *UK* (1982) was similarly manifestly ill-founded, as it concerned a Muslim teacher who wanted time off work to attend Friday prayers, which, again, was merely motivated by his religion and not a manifestation of it. As referred to in Chapter 3, the 'choice' theme runs through much of the ECHR freedom of religion

1 Similarly, the Human Rights Committee General Comment 22 (para 3) specifies that 'Article 18 distinguishes the freedom of thought, conscience, religion or belief from the freedom to manifest religion or belief. It does not permit any limitations whatsoever on the freedom of thought and conscience or on the freedom to have or adopt a religion or belief of one's choice. These freedoms are protected unconditionally.'

jurisprudence, which has a strong 'expectation of accommodation, compromise and sacrifice' (*Denbigh High School* 2006: para 54) as 'people sometimes have to suffer some inconvenience for their beliefs' (ibid.: para 50). This approach appears to be specific to Article 9. As pointed out by Malcolm Evans (2008: 296), the choice argument would never have been accepted in cases concerning discrimination against homosexuals. Indeed, in *Smith and Grady* v. *UK* (1999), which concerned a policy of no gays in the army, the ECtHR found a violation of the applicants' right to respect for private life, as opposed to stating that they were free to resign like in *Stedman* or *Ahmad*. Arguably, Article 8 rights are considered more fundamental than Article 9 – despite both being subject to similar limitations 'prescribed by law' and 'necessary in a democratic society'.

These limitations are stated in paragraph 2 of Article 9. As mentioned before, it is freedom to manifest one's religion or belief – but not freedom to have it – that can be legitimately limited. As the preceding cases show, public order and the protection of the rights and freedoms of others are the two grounds for limitations that have been thought to apply to headscarves. It is the mechanism of the margin of appreciation, where the state is given a degree of discretion in deciding the balance between the right in question and the proposed limitation of that right, that allows certain 'religious manifestations' to be restricted in view of the presumed fundamentalist danger.

Although the freedom to wear the Islamic headscarf may still be lawfully restricted under Article 9(2), the important point is that it has firmly been recognised as a manifestation of one's religious belief. The UN Human Rights Committee came to that conclusion even earlier, as in its General Comment 22(8) it stated that '[t]he observance and practice of religion or belief may include not only ceremonial acts but also such customs as ... the wearing of distinctive clothing or headcoverings...' (para 4). As said before, a view of Islamic veiling as a manifestation of religion tends to be shared by applicants. Shabina Begum, the claimant in *Denbigh High School*, publicised her case widely outside the courtroom, insisting that she felt very strongly about the jilbab as a freedom of religion issue. In a televised BBC interview, she said that the jilbab was the proper Islamic way to dress, as opposed to shalwar kameeze which she saw as a mere 'Pakistani cultural tradition'. Arguably this way of thinking is encouraged by the structure of the right to freedom of religion itself: an act or a garment is seen as clearly motivated by a religious belief – as opposed to the jilbab itself being part of the 'Arab' cultural tradition, for example.

As to the belief itself, there is an interesting tension in the approach of the European Court of Human Rights, as well as domestic courts. The official line is that Article 9 ECHR 'excludes any discretion on the part of the State to determine whether religious beliefs or the means used to express such beliefs are legitimate' (*Hasan and Chaush* v. *Bulgaria* 2002). However, few Article 9 cases consider evidence of the content of the belief irrelevant. For example, in *Carmuirea Spirituala a Musulmanilor din Republica Moldova* v. *Moldova* (2005), the ECtHR found no violation of Article 9 where the state required 'a document setting out the fundamental principles of their religion' as 'without such a document the State could not determine the authenticity of the organisation seeking recognition as a religion and whether the denomination in question presented any danger for a democratic society'. As a general rule, the belief needs to 'denote a certain level of cogency, seriousness, cohesion and importance' (*Campbell and Cosans* v. *UK* 1982). It must be more than 'mere opinions or deeply held feelings' (*McFeely* v. *UK* 1986), which is understood as holding identifiable spiritual or philosophical convictions. All mainstream religious beliefs would be covered by this definition,[2] with minority or unusual beliefs – such as 'very strict Muslims' – to be subject to more close scrutiny. This contradiction shines through the *Denbigh High School* case, with Scott Baker LJ, on the one hand, saying that 'it is not for school authorities to pick and choose between religious beliefs or shades of religious belief' (Court of Appeal 2005: para 93). On the other hand, both the Court of Appeal and House of Lords went to considerable lengths to cite the 'respectable support' for the jilbab 'among those [Muslim authorities] who were consulted during the course of the dispute' (ibid.: para 48).

There is similar confusion as to the significance of freedom of religion – and religion itself – within the value systems of the state parties to the Convention. The European Court of Human Rights has stated in a leading case that:

> freedom of thought, conscience and religion is one of the foundations of a 'democratic' society within the meaning of the Convention. It is, in its religious dimension, one of the most vital elements that go to make up the identity of believers and their conception of life, but it is a precious asset for atheists, agnostics, sceptics and the unconcerned. The pluralism indissociable from a democratic society, which has been dearly won over the centuries, depends on it.
>
> (*Kokkinakis* v. *Greece* 1993: para 31)

On the other hand, there are ubiquitous indicators that the position is less clear-cut as 'it is not possible to discern throughout Europe a uniform conception of the significance of religion in society' (*Otto-Preminger-Institut* v. *Austria* 1994: para 50). The *Otto-Preminger-Institut* case concerned the legality

2 It also covers non-religious beliefs, including atheism (*Angelini* v. *Sweden* 1986), pacifism (*Arrowsmith* v. *UK* 1983), veganism (*H* v. *UK* 1993) and opposition to abortion (*Knudsen* v. *Norway* 1985).

of a restriction on freedom of expression in order to protect Catholic sensitivities; this was considered acceptable due to the lack of a European consensus on the importance of religion. According to a similar case, *Wingrove* v. *UK* (1997), '[w]here questions concerning the relationship between State and religions are at stake, on which opinion in a democratic society may reasonably differ widely, the role of the national decision-making body must be given special importance' (para 58). And so, when a case came up where a Muslim complained that English blasphemy law only protected Christian, and not Islamic, beliefs, the Strasbourg authorities replied that Article 9 did not include the right to have one's religion protected from ridicule (*Choudhury* v. *UK* 1991). In *Otto-Preminger-Institut* and *Wingrove*, the state decided to restrict artistic expression in order to protect the Christian sensitivities of the majority, while in *Choudhury* it refused to do so when it came to Muslim beliefs. Both outcomes were acceptable under the ECHR.

However, the respondent state's arguments were rejected in *Metropolitan Church of Bessarabia* v. *Moldova* (2001). The Republic of Moldova argued that not recognising the church in question was justified in view of the importance of the mainstream, Moldovan Orthodox Church for Moldovan identity as it 'enabled the entire population to come together within that Church' (para 111). As noted by Carolyn Evans (2008), '[i]t was not so long ago that this claim would have been considered commonplace in many parts of Europe, but today the European Court dismisses its legitimacy in less than a paragraph' (p. 14). As mentioned earlier, there is a strong expectation that people ought to make choices between their religion and other spheres of life, which is not necessarily the case with other rights.

The ECtHR's approach to headscarf and other freedom of religion cases when it comes to determining whether a restriction under Article 9(1) is justified is far less stringent than its approach to Article 8, Article 10 and Article 11 ECHR, which protect the right to respect for private life, freedom of expression and freedom of association, respectively. Under Article 8 ECHR, the margin of appreciation afforded to the states is much narrower, and so mere assertions of risk are not sufficient to justify restrictions on one's right to respect for private life. For example, in *Smith and Grady* v. *UK*, the state party's arguments that homosexuality in the armed forces was endangering national security were rejected as unsubstantiated and based on homophobic prejudice. As far as Article 10 is concerned, it offers much more protection to unpopular views than Article 9. As pointed out by the dissenting Judge Tulkens in *Şahin*:

> the Court has never accepted that interference with the exercise of the right to freedom of expression can be justified by the fact that the ideas or views concerned are not shared by everyone and may even offend some people. Recently, in *Gündüz* v. *Turkey*…, the Court held that there had been a violation of freedom of expression where a

> Muslim religious leader had been convicted for violently criticising the secular regime in Turkey, calling for the introduction of the sharia and referring to children born of marriages celebrated solely before the secular authorities as 'bastards'. Thus, manifesting one's religion by peacefully wearing a headscarf may be prohibited whereas, in the same context, remarks which could be construed as incitement to religious hatred are covered by freedom of expression.
>
> (para 10)

For national restrictions on Articles 10–11 to be upheld, concrete evidence is also usually required that a minority political activity or speech is a threat to democracy (e.g. *Socialist Party* v. *Turkey* 1999; *Freedom and Democratic Party* v. *Turkey* 1999; *Stankov* v. *Bulgaria* 1998). The state's margin of appreciation under those articles is generally much narrower than under Article 9, where a wider range of restrictions tends to be accepted with little scrutiny. Restrictions on expression or association are only acceptable if there is clear evidence that the applicants espouse violent objectives (*Gorzelik* v. *Poland* 2001. See also *Sidiropoulos* v. *Greece* 1998; *EK* v. *Turkey* 2002; *Association Ekin* v. *France* 2001). Under Article 11 ECHR, 'the exceptions to the rule of freedom of association are to be construed strictly ... the States have only a limited margin of appreciation, which goes hand in hand with rigorous European supervision' (*Church of Scientology Moscow* v. *Russia* 2007: para 86). This is a markedly different approach from Article 9.

The contrast between freedom of religion, on the one hand, and freedom of association, on the other, is vivid in cases involving religious organisations that were decided under Article 11, rather than Article 9. *Moscow Branch of the Salvation Army* v. *Russia* (2006), in which a religious organisation was denied registration, is a good example. The respondent state argued that members of the Salvation Army posed a threat to national security as they wore uniforms, which was dismissed by the ECtHR as something that 'could not seriously be maintained' (para 92). As Malcolm Evans (2008) points out, the state's argument here is extremely similar to that in *Şahin*, 'which the court was prepared to accept at face value' (p. 311). In *Salvation Army*, in contrast, '[t]here was no evidence before the domestic courts that in several years of its existence the applicant branch, its members or its founders had contravened any Russian law or pursued objectives other than those listed in its article of association' (para 95). Nothing of the sort was done in any of the ECHR headscarf cases.

On the other hand, the one freedom of association case that clearly stands out from this approach is *Refah Partisi* v. *Turkey* (2003), which concerned the dissolution of a political party advocating a public order based on sharia law. No violation of Article 11 was found as a wider margin of appreciation than normal was afforded to the state. The ECtHR unequivocally stated that 'sharia is incompatible with the fundamental principles of democracy' (para

123). This is in contrast with seeking language rights, or even a federal system or the advocacy of secession, which are not regarded as automatically contrary to the needs of a democratic society (*Sidiropoulos*). Arguably, the outcome in *Refah Partisi* is due to the presumed unacceptability of a political party based on religious ideology – as opposed to the more traditionally 'political' ideologies (e.g. *Socialist Party* v. *Turkey* 1999; *Freedom and Democratic Party* v. *Turkey* 1999). The ECtHR expressed it in the following terms:

> the Court considers that sharia, which faithfully reflects the dogmas and divine rules laid down by religion, is stable and invariable. Principles such as pluralism in the political sphere or the constant evolution of public freedoms have no place in it. ... It is difficult to declare one's respect for democracy and human rights while at the same time supporting a regime based on sharia, which clearly diverges from Convention values, particularly with regard to ... the way it intervenes in all spheres of private and public life in accordance with religious precepts. ... In the Court's view, a political party whose actions seem to be aimed at introducing sharia in a State party to the Convention can hardly be regarded as an association complying with the democratic ideal that underlies the whole of the Convention.
>
> (para 123, quoting Chamber judgment 2001: para 92)

In contrast with religion, the democratic value of secularism is uncontested. According to *Şahin*:

> it is the principle of secularism, as elucidated by the [Turkish] Constitutional Court ... which is the paramount consideration underlying the ban on the wearing of religious symbols in universities. In such a context, where the values of pluralism, respect for the rights of others and, in particular, equality before the law of men and women are being taught and applied in practice, it is understandable that the relevant authorities should wish to preserve the secular nature of the institution concerned and so consider it contrary to such values to allow religious attire, including, as in the present case, the Islamic headscarf, to be worn.
>
> (para 116)

4 What is wrong with the secular view(s) of religion?

To recap, there are two kinds of Islam in operation in the Islamic veiling debate. One is an extreme, irrational radicalism verging on the fundamentalist, which is dangerous for western societies and needs to be managed through legal restriction and prohibition. The other is a tamed, rational version, which is acceptable as long as what it claims is in line with how law in the West understands religion. These two tend to be constructed as each other's opposites, with the 'moderate' version being the only one that secular law is prepared to accept. This situation distorts both Islam and religion more generally. The rest of the chapter argues that this distortion has its roots in the genealogy of western secularism.

It is difficult to provide an overarching definition of secularism as it can be understood in many ways, and its forms vary greatly even within the West (from a very strong official ideology of *laïcité* in France to mild or formally non-existent in Britain). Indeed, 'secular' 'can suggest a condition of being unreligious or antireligious, but also religiously tolerant, humanist, Christian, modern, or simply Western' (Brown 2009: 10). But in general terms, secularism denotes a separation of religion from the state, law and politics, which usually implies a certain relegation of religion to the private sphere. Secularism is a vital discourse in liberal legal orders that prescribe restrictions on Islamic veiling. In contrast with what is often assumed, secularism does not necessarily imply a total banishment of religion from the public sphere (although it may well be the case in France or Turkey). Indeed, religious freedom is a postulate of secularism. However, it is a very particular kind of freedom, as it was outlined in Part 3 of this chapter and will be elaborated on shortly. Mahmood's (2006) study of 'secular hermeneutics' highlights how much of contemporary secularism promotes a 'religious subject who understands religion – its scriptures and its ritual forms – as a congeries of symbols to be flexibly interpreted in a manner consonant with the imperatives of secular political rule' (p. 344).

Although secularism is perhaps necessary in one form or another, its current form does not live up to its claim of being a neutral guarantor of religious freedom. Instead, secularism is thoroughly wrought with its western philosophical and Christian origins. This is perhaps unavoidable as nothing is ever truly neutral, but it is the *pretence* of neutrality that is most disconcerting. By pretending to be unbiased and beyond religion, secularism becomes a powerful ideology and organising discourse, which itself competes with religion when it comes to shaping people's identity allegiances and life choices. As Mme M's case shows, she was expected to believe in, internalise and practise secular values in order to become a French citizen – just as one does when converting to religion. When Nicolas Sarkozy says a Muslim schoolgirl has to take off her headscarf when entering a public school in the same way he would take off his shoes when entering a mosque, the same idea is in operation: submit to secularism as you would to your religion. But let us first have a closer look at what forces are at work in the constructions of 'radical Islam' and its opposite, 'liberal Islam', and why this dichotomy says more about the West than Islam itself.

The two Dutch films, *Submission* and *Fitna*, mentioned in Chapter 2, epitomise western fears about Islam as a palpable threat to everything the West stands for. It is perhaps indicative of the scale of these fears that these films have achieved quite a high profile despite their rather questionable artistic and intellectual value. Islamic veiling codes are an embodiment of this antithesis of Islam and the West as they are 'widely represented as simultaneously *alien* intrusions on Western ground, *premodern* holdovers, and *antimodern* threats to what we have achieved today' (Valenta 2006: 465, original emphasis). Interestingly, this opposition between the modern and the pre/anti-modern, or between the secular and the religious fundamentalist, is also being projected onto Islam itself. In its crudest form, it is the opposition between the 'good' and the 'bad Muslim' (Mamdani 2004) – that is, between 'modernised', 'liberal' Muslims and the fundamentalists. A Muslim woman who veils is illiberal, whereas one who does not is commended for leaving her religion in the private sphere where it rightly belongs. The watershed between 'liberal' and 'fundamentalist' can stand at different points: in France, even a headscarf is unacceptable in the public sphere, whereas in Britain headscarves are, by and large, harmless signs of a successful multiculturalism and so items such as jilbabs and niqabs are seen as 'fundamentalist' (see Part 1 of this chapter). The point is though that there is always some kind of dichotomy between 'liberal' and 'fundamentalist' Muslims.

If some form of veiling is tolerated, it is linked to its ability to be presented as a symbol of Muslim women's liberal transformation, their transition to modernity (see Chapters 3 and 4) – and accordingly its ability to repudiate convincingly the charge of 'traditional', 'fundamentalist' or 'radical' Islam. Liberal commentators openly insist that, for Islamic veiling to become fully acceptable, Islam needs to reinvent itself in a way compatible with the 'fundamental principles of Europe' (Gallala 2006: 593) or to undergo a reformation process like Christianity had (e.g. Joppke 2009). Only some kind of 'modernised' Islam, which can be constructed as compatible with the secular values of the West, can be accepted in the 'civilised world'. As Mahmood (2003) notes, in explorations even by Muslim scholars themselves, 'Islam bears the burden of proving its compatibility with liberal ideals, and the line of question is almost never reversed'.

It is now uncontroversial to demand transformation of Islam from an anachronistic and irrational religion into a democratised one, in which sacred texts are malleable to (re)interpretation. Secularism insists on a particular 'singular relationship' between the subject and a religious text whereby the text is a collection of signs to be interpreted by the subject. Such 'secular hermeneutics' are essential to 'remaking certain kinds of religious subjectivities ... so as to render them compliant with liberal political rule' (Mahmood 2006: 328). Conversely, a traditionalist, 'unquestioning mentality' (ibid.: 333) is threatening for the liberal secular order, and thus religion has to be secularised as a system of signs and symbols not to be taken literally. Indeed, Islam's capability of reinterpretation is central to the efforts of Islamic feminists, described in Chapter 4, as well as the more general efforts to reconcile it with the international human rights doctrine (see e.g. An-Na'im 1990, 1995; Bielefeldt 1995).

For example, An-Na'im's (1990) method is 'to reexamine the scriptural imperatives in the Qur'an to make the dictates of Shari'a consistent with international human rights norms' as he is:

> challenging the failure of contemporary Muslims to appreciate the impact of historical context upon the interpretation and application of ... fundamental sources of Islam. I argue that given the historical contexts of both initial revelation and subsequent interpretations of the texts of the Qur'an and Sunna, some texts are no longer applicable while others need to be interpreted differently. I believe that divine revelation must be understood and applied in historical context because it addresses us in our human condition and circumstances which change over time.
>
> (pp. 13–14)

Such efforts to reconcile Islamic scriptural imperatives with secular values and international human rights norms may well be commendable. However, they may also contribute to the unquestioning embrace of western-type secularism and thus further marginalise other, non-compliant 'religious subjectivities', such as those constructions overviewed in Part 1 of this chapter.

To summarise, there is a dichotomy between two 'Islams': one 'fundamentalist' (as reflected in the constructions of Islamic veiling presented in Part 1), one 'liberal' (Part 2 of this chapter). It is, in essence, a projection of the bigger dichotomy between Islam itself (largely fundamentalist) and the West (liberal and secular). Indeed, according to Huntington, '[t]he underlying problem for the West is not Islamic fundamentalism. It is Islam' (1996: 217). The current situation of Islam as the liberal West's primary ideological foe has much to do with geopolitical shifts after the demise of the Soviet 'Empire of Evil' at the end of the Cold War (see Mamdani 2004). This chapter, however, concentrates on a different aspect, namely on what it is about Islam that could be indicative of the West's discomfort with religion more generally. The analysis that follows is situated within Abrahamic religious and philosophical traditions, although it is possible that much of it applies to other non-Christian paradigms.

Islam had been marginalised in the western civilisation for a very long time, but this marginalisation has become more palpable recently. The rather belated, if tokenistic, inclusion of Jews in the contemporary western civilisational paradigm has inevitably reinforced the exclusion of Muslims. It is interesting that the term 'Judeo-Christian', used so uncontroversially today, is itself a post-Holocaust invention (see Asad 2003). Thus, a new mythology is created: first, that Jews have always been accepted as part of the western tradition and, second, that Muslims have always been, and can only be, its nemesis, unless they drastically reform themselves. There is something shameless about Geert Wilders', the maker of *Fitna*, co-optation of Judaism in his 'solution' to the Islamic 'problem':

> we have to push harder for a kind of *Leitkultur*, a guiding culture. Not a monoculture but a culture that draws on our Christian, Jewish, humanistic traditions and that poses a challenge to the Islamic problem. This is patriotism, not nationalism, this is pride in our own culture.
>
> (*Spiegel*, 31 March 2008)

There is of course a broad 'Judeo-Christian' tradition in the sense that both religions (as well as Islam) have the same Abrahamic roots and Jewish monotheistic ideas have profoundly shaped the moral landscapes of the West. But the claim that the Jewish tradition is truly a part of the West discounts not only centuries of persecution, but also the deep philosophical undercurrents that have constructed Christianity as superior and the only correct way of being religious. It is perhaps the anti-Jewish polemics of the early Church in Late Antiquity that have shaped both Christian theology and, in a mutated form, contemporary secular attitudes to religion.

Saint Paul, who authored much of the New Testament, was instrumental in the establishment of the Christian Church. He referred to Jews as 'Israel according to the flesh' (I Corinthians 10:18), meaning Israel understood literally – that is, ethnic Jews. 'Israel according to the spirit', or 'new Israel', in contrast, denotes Christians who have made a conscious rational decision to accept Jesus Christ as (the Son of) God and universal saviour – a decision which has nothing to do with one's tribal belonging, but everything to do with matters of 'spirit'. As famously expressed by Paul, 'There is neither Jew nor Greek, there is neither slave nor free, there is no female and male, for ye are all one in Christ Jesus' (Galatheans 3:28). This was a revolutionary message; the dichotomy between body and spirit enabled the founders of the Christian Church to universalise the message of the Bible, which had thereto been confined to a particular people. The Jews' refusal to 'move on' and accept this new ideology was resented and gave rise to the authoritative and prolific *adversus Judaeos* tradition in Christian theology, which shaped 'the potent and long-lived hermeneutical idea of the "Jew"' as 'fleshly, hard-hearted, philosophically dim, and violently anti-Christian' (Fredriksen 2007: 37). According to the early influential Fathers of the Church, such as Saint Augustine of Hippo, Jews did 'not understand that there is both a carnal and a spiritual sense to scripture, and by this demonstration, this people condemns itself to remain forever and indisputably carnal and not spiritual' (Boyarin 1993: 1). It is not difficult to see parallels with how ('radical' or 'fundamentalist') Muslims are seen today, as exemplified by accounts in Part 1 of this chapter. By refusing to subject Islam to a Christian-style reformation and sticking to the 'stable and invariable' sharia, they demonstrate their unquestioning mentality and barbaric nature.

In Islam, as well as Judaism, the religious experience is also a lived material experience, embedded in the body and its practices, such as circumcision, regular prayer times, dietary restrictions, fasting and indeed veiling or modest dress. This is in contrast to Christianity, where the material dimension of existence becomes more or less irrelevant as it is the spirit that is all-important – hence the Christian ideas of the original sin, celibacy and mortification of flesh. This Christian thinking is not exclusively a product of its split from its parent creed, Jewish monotheism. Saint Paul's ideas are traceable to classic Greek philosophy and in particular Platonic and Neo-Pythagorean roots, with their clear distinction between body and spirit – wherein the latter enjoys a privileged standpoint in one's quest to understand the world and arrive at truth. Although Hellenistic tropes have also influenced Jewish doctrine, it is accurate to say that they are most salient in Christianity. At its core, Christianity is about the act of accepting Jesus Christ as universal truth, because that is the right and rational thing to do.

Religion as it is known in the West today is itself a Christian invention. Before Christianity, any 'religious' elements of life were embedded in material reality, rather than a 'disembeddable', 'discrete area of human experience' (Schwartz 2001: 179). This process gained ascendance throughout centuries of western thought, eventually loosening its attachment to its anti-Jewish origins. It has been exacerbated by the Protestant Reformation and then the Age of Enlightenment in its reorientation towards a post-Christian, secular society. Mahmood (2009) traces the genealogy of modern interpretative practices of religious texts, such as those employed by Islamic feminists and human rights scholars, as linked to the 'preoccupation ... which agitated Calvin and other Protestant reformers: how best to institute a distinction between the transcendent world of abstract concepts and ideas and the material reality of this world' (p. 844). The Reformation took Saint Paul's contradistinction between body and spirit to another level, utterly rejecting what it saw as Catholicism's pointless preoccupation with ritual and minute details of worship. It is necessary to qualify that other Christian traditions, such as Eastern Orthodoxy or even Catholicism, have not taken the spiritual/material divide quite so far. Bodily practices, such as fasting or modest dress, remain relevant in those branches of Christianity. Nonetheless, the western Protestant Reformation has been most influential in terms of shaping a concept of religion that resonates most with us today, in its detachment from the material and its near-complete relegation of faith to the private sphere of individual conscience.

Via the Enlightenment, the distinction between spiritual and material reality has come to be central to modern secularism, which is, by and large, concerned with remaking, reinterpreting religion, rather than eradicating it altogether. Mahmood (2006) shows how this 'liberalising' agenda is linked to US foreign aid to Muslim countries. Inevitably, this entails a certain devaluing of religion as a source of objective good, while at the same time its province is confined to a somewhat elevated, abstract spiritual world. In other words, contemporary secularism is about knowing the proper place of religion; it is about respecting religion as long as it is not taken (and does not take itself) too seriously. And so, 'moderate' Muslims may be accepted, as long as their veiling practices are not too extreme and comply with how religion is understood in secular law.

As far as the proper place of religion is concerned, *Lautsi* v. *Italy* (2009/2011) is an interesting case. In the first instance, the Chamber of the European Court of Human Rights (2009) found that the Italian state had violated the requirement of neutrality, inherent in freedom of religion under Article 9 ECHR, by displaying the crucifix ('a powerful religious symbol') in the classroom. The Chamber rejected Italy's argument that the Italian tradition sees Catholicism as the source of universal values, such as respect for human rights (not exactly a neutral position, but candid and not devoid of historical truth). In the Chamber judgment, only some kind of abstract secularism appears capable of maintaining a neutral framework enabling young citizens to learn what is right and good for them. The judgment implies that the proper role of secularism is to teach critical distance from religion in order to enable individuals to make the right kind of choices for themselves. Otherwise, they might fall pray to the traditionalist, 'unquestioning mentality' of the religious, just like the Muslim women 'brainwashed' into veiling. As expressed by the applicant in *Lautsi* herself, 'either you think for yourself, or you just believe' (Helsingin Sanomat 2010). It is not just that one is obviously superior to the other, but that the two are seen as mutually exclusive. The Grand Chamber of the ECtHR (2011) eventually overturned the Chamber's judgment, finding in favour of Italy. But unfortunately, the Grand Chamber is also open to criticism for its suspect distinction between 'passive' religious symbols such as crucifixes on classroom walls (neutral and harmless) and headscarves on teachers' and students' heads (fundamentalist and aggressive). Rather than engaging with the complex reality of Christian heritage being at the core of contemporary secularism, the Grand Chamber judgment simply reinforces the privileged position of Christianity.

As to criticism of religion, it has indeed become a 'sign of the modern, of the modern subject's relentless pursuit of truth and freedom, of his or her agency' (Asad 2008: 604). Critique is secular as:

> a constellation of Enlightenment conceits is part of what allows critique to comport so readily with secularism: from Mill to Marx, Diderot to Kant and Hume, we greet the Enlightenment presumption that the true, the objective, the real, the rational, and even the scientific emerge only with the shedding of religious authority or 'prejudice'. This presumption reaches an apex in the Kantian dictum that everything must submit to critique, even reason itself, and also Hegel's attempt to reveal the rational kernel of Christianity through a critical

> history and phenomenology. Hence the conviction that critique displaces religious and other unfounded authority and prejudice with reason, even as it may leave religion itself standing. Hence too, the conviction that critique replaces opinion or faith with truth, and subjectivism with science; that critique is, in short, secular.
>
> (Brown 2009: 11)

But this secular nature of critique is tainted with its Christian origins. As noted earlier, rational truth itself is a major Christian preoccupation – as opposed to more intuitive religious belonging found elsewhere. Asad (2008) highlights how the modern compulsion to dethrone God, to critique religion is 'an act carried out in the knowledge and power of truth' (p. 591) – not unlike a Christian's insistence on the correctness of his faith. Freedom in western societies traditionally is associated with freedom of expression, the latter being instrumental in one's quest for truth – very much in line with the Christian injunction that the 'truth shall set you free' (John 8:32). More recently, Pope Benedict XVI's seminal 2006 lecture reaffirms the identification of reason with (Christian) divinity, while criticising Islam for its perceived lack of reason.

The secular 'critical distance' from religion, promoted in *Lautsi* v. *Italy* as well as Islamic veiling cases, is meant to teach one to approach religion from a (of course ever illusory) neutral standpoint. So that if a religion is adopted, it is done with one's full and informed consent. That is reminiscent of the Christian ritual of baptism, in which one has to perform a symbolic act of acceptance even if one is born to Christian parents. Thus, there is a critical secular notion that 'insomuch as religion is primarily about belief in a set of propositions to which one lends one's assent, it is *fundamentally a matter of choice*' (Mahmood 2009: 844, emphasis added). It is exactly this post-Christian understanding of religion which informs the western bewilderment at the Muslim rage around the controversial 2005 Danish cartoons depicting Prophet Mohammed as a suicide bomber. Hardcore western liberals insist that the offence should not trump freedom of expression as the pictures attack religious concepts (which can be freely chosen and abandoned at will), not immutable characteristics such as race or ethnicity (see further Asad 2008). Offence of religious feelings is thus considered insufficiently 'real' to be regulated by law. As tellingly expressed by Thomas Jefferson (1784/1998) over two centuries ago, 'it does me no injury for my neighbour to say there are twenty gods, or no god. It neither picks my pocket nor breaks my leg' (Query XVII).

The kind of understanding of religion that casts it as 'fundamentally a matter of choice' and a 'set of propositions' (as opposed to an all-encompassing way of life) forms the basis of freedom of religion in law today. As described in Part 3 of this chapter, the freedom to have or change religion is viewed as primary and hence an absolute right, which in no circumstances can be limited or derogated from. The freedom to *manifest* religion is secondary and is subject to a range of limitations, prescribed in paragraph 2 of the same article. Such a split between the innermost spiritual reality as primary and external behaviour as secondary and derivable from the former is inadequate for Islam (or, for that matter, Judaism). To comply with the law, wearing a headscarf has to be formulated as only a manifestation of religion, whereas the wearer in question may see it as the very way of being Muslim. The terminology used in Article 9 cases, such as 'manifestation' or an act merely 'motivated' by religion, implies that these things simply flow from one's rationally chosen beliefs. Perhaps this suits mainstream Protestant Christians whose religious convictions are relatively undemanding on their lifestyles. Yet, as accounts explored in Chapter 3 suggest, in practices such as Islamic veiling the connection between the inner and outer dimensions could well be the other way round. That is, one may start to wear the headscarf and thus the belief is honed. Or the two dimensions could be simply inextricable, if that is how one comes to experience the world.

But it is not just Islamic veiling for which the concept of 'manifestation' of religion is inadequate. A whole range of other practices are covered by this category, as listed in Part 3 of this chapter. For example, ritual slaughter was considered to be a manifestation of the Jewish religious belief, and hence it was easily restricted under Article 9(2) in *Cha'are Shalom ve Tsedek* v. *France*. The purpose of both Jewish and Muslim ritual slaughter is to provide people with meat they consider permissible to eat. It could well be because they believe that it is the correct thing to do, but, contrary to the assumptions of Article 9, *doing* for these religions is not necessarily less important than *believing*. There is of course an inevitable dilemma as any physical act, be it praying, eating or wearing certain clothes, involves interaction with the outside world more readily than belief, which is essentially inside oneself and thus inscrutable. So physical acts are more likely to interfere with the 'rights and freedoms of others'. But the problem is that such acts are automatically presumed to be secondary and derivative from belief, and in many instances are seen as excessive and eccentric, rather than essential to one's sense of identity and connectedness to the world. Such manifestations of religion are demonised as 'barbaric', as, for example, the recent European push to ban Jewish and Muslim ritual slaughter shows (see e.g. Berg, 30 November 2011). These religious methods of slaughter are widely believed to be animal cruelty, whereas the mainstream stunning method tends to be seen as the only humane one, despite the evidence in its favour being shaped by western cultural and aesthetic sensitivities. Rather, the western distaste with ritual slaughter could itself be a symptom of its incomprehension of such 'archaic' religions that believe that the food they eat has spiritual implications.

5 Concluding remarks

This final chapter has looked at the third framework that shapes the Islamic veiling debate in legal discourse and the surrounding public debate. First, it presented an overview of the constructions of Islamic veiling as dangerous Islamic radicalism threatening the secular values of the West. These were gleaned mainly from Islamic veiling cases and popular commentary. It then highlighted the arguments of those on the other side of the debate – mainly, that Islamic veiling is a legitimate manifestation of freedom of religion. Such an argument has been made by those bringing court cases and their lawyers, as well as legal academics criticising the unsatisfactory judicial outcomes. The chapter then made a whistle-stop tour of the right to freedom of religion itself, which is believed to be an important human right in democratic societies. It did so with reference to Article 9 of the European Convention of Human Rights, although a similar structure can be found in other legal frameworks. In brief, freedom of religion presumes a strong split between the right to have a religious belief and the right to manifest it, in other words to act upon it. Hence, Islamic veiling could be defended as a manifestation of religion, but as such it is readily susceptible to legitimate limitations under Article 9(2).

Ultimately, the chapter pursued a critique of such an understanding of freedom of religion, exploring how this came about within a particular secular context. It provided a possible explanation of why Islamic veiling and Islam in general are seen as threatening for the secular West. It showed how Islam is commonly prompted to reform itself according to secular imperatives. These are themselves far from neutral as western secularism is embedded in its Christian origins, but now competes with religion as a thought- and life-governing system. And yet, secularism's objection to Islam can be viewed as symptomatic of something less obvious. It is its more general inability to comprehend forms of religion that do not have a rigid separation between body and spirit like Christianity does. The split in international human rights law and domestic legal systems between the right to have a religion and the right to manifest it is exactly a product of that separation. Freedom of religion thus cannot accommodate forms of religiosity that do not comply with this vision. To be sure, the more encompassing and the more demanding one's religion is, the more likely it is to collide with the issues of others. But in the case of Islamic veiling, the 'rights and freedoms of others' are given automatic precedence, with little genuine enquiry into the nature and weight of competing interests or the practice of veiling itself. It was not the chapter's purpose to advocate dismantling our concepts of freedom of religion and secularism altogether, but it has aimed to expose their limitations. Perhaps a less 'religious' adherence to the primacy of belief over action would at least encourage a different way of resolving Islamic veiling issues; one that is still beyond our grasp at present.

Bibliography

Books and articles

Abu-Lughod, L. (1998) 'The Marriage of Feminism and Islamism in Egypt: Selective Repudiation as a Dynamic of Postcolonial Cultural Politics', in L. Abu-Lughod (ed.), *Remaking Women: Feminism and Modernity in the Middle East*, Princeton, NJ: Princeton University Press, p. 243.

Abu-Odeh, L. (1992) 'Post-colonial Feminism and the Veil: Considering the Differences', *New England Law Review*, 26: 1527.

Afshar, H. (1994) 'Women and the Politics of Fundamentalism in Iran', *Women against Fundamentalism*, 5.

Afshar, H. (1998) *Islam and Feminisms*, Basingstoke: Macmillan.

Afshar, H. and Maynard, M. (2000) 'Gender and Ethnicity at the Millennium: From Margin to Centre', *Ethnic and Racial Studies*, 23: 805.

Ahmad, A. (1992) *In Theory: Classes, Nations, Literature*, London: Verso.

Ahmed, A. (1992) *Postmodernism and Islam: Predicament and Promise*, London: Routledge.

Ahmed, L. (1992) *Women and Gender in Islam: Historical Roots of a Modern Debate*, New Haven, CT: Yale University Press.

Ahmed, L. (2011) *A Quiet Revolution: The Veil's Resurgence from the Middle East to America*, New Haven, CT: Yale University Press.

Ahmed, S. (2000) *Strange Encounters: Embodied Others in Post-Coloniality*, London: Routledge.

Al-Azm, S.J. (1981) 'Orientalism and Orientalism in Reverse', *Khamsin*, 8: 5.

Al-Azmeh, A. (2007) 'Afterword', in A. Al-Azmeh and E. Fokas (eds), *Islam in Europe: Diversity, Identity and Influence*, Cambridge: Cambridge University Press, p. 208.

Alibhai-Brown, J. (2000) *Who Do We Think We Are? Imagining the New Britain*, Harmondsworth: Penguin.

Altschull, E. (1995) *Le Voile contre l'École*, Paris: Seuil.

An-Na'im, A.A. (1990) 'Human Rights in the Muslim World: Socio-Political Conditions and Scriptural Imperatives', *Harvard Human Rights Journal*, 3: 13.

An-Na'im, A.A. (1995) 'Human Rights and Religious Values: An Uneasy Relationship?', in A.A. An-Na'im, J.D. Gort, H. Jansen and H.D. Vroom (eds), *Human Rights and Religious Values*, Grand Rapids, Michigan: William B Eerdmans Publishing, p. 229.

Arda, S. (22 March 2001) 'Geëmancipeerde vrouw kiest niet voor hoofddoek', *De Volkskrant.*

Arnardóttir, O.M. (2009) 'Multidimensional Equality from Within – Themes from the European Convention on Human Rights', in D. Schiek and V. Chege (eds) *European Union Non-discrimination Law: Comparative Perspectives on Multidimensional Equality Law,* London: Routledge, p. 53.

Asad, T. (1968) 'The Idea of an Anthropology of Islam', Occasional Paper Series, Center for Contemporary Arab Studies, Washington, DC: Georgetown University Press.

Asad, T. (2000) 'What Do Human Rights Do? An Anthropological Enquiry', *Theory and Event,* 4: 4.

Asad, T. (2003) *Formations of the Secular: Christianity, Islam, Modernity,* Palo Alto, CA: Stanford University Press.

Asad, T. (2008) 'Reflections on Blasphemy and Secular Criticism', in H. de Vries (ed.), *Religion: Beyond a Concept,* New York: Fordham University Press, p. 580.

Ayotte, K.J. and Hussain, M.E. (2005) 'Securing Afghan Women: Neocolonialism, Epistemic Violence, and the Rhetoric of the Veil', *NSWA Journal,* 17: 112.

Badiou, A. (2006) *Polemics,* London: Verso.

Baer, S. (2004) 'Citizenship in Europe and the Construction of Gender by Law in the European Charter of Fundamental Rights', in K. Knop (ed.), *Gender and Human Rights,* Oxford: Oxford University Press, p. 83.

Balkin, J.M. (1994) 'Being Just with Deconstruction', *Social & Legal Studies,* 3: 393.

Barlow, R. and Akrazadeh, S. (2008) 'Prospects for Feminism in the Islamic Republic of Iran', *Human Rights Quarterly,* 30: 21.

BBC Online News (17 December 2003) 'Chirac's Risky Move'. Available at: http://news.bbc.co.uk/1/hi/world/europe/3329321.stm.

BBC Online News (21 January 2004) 'Dutch Are "Polarised" Says Report'. Available at: http://news.bbc.co.uk/2/hi/europe/3417429.stm.

BBC Online News (2 March 2005) 'Schoolgirl Wins Muslim Gown Case'. Available at: http://news.bbc.co.uk/1/hi/england/beds/bucks/herts/4310545.stm.

BBC Online News (17 October 2005) 'Dutch to Hear Muslim Rights Case'. Available at: http://news.bbc.co.uk/go/pr/fr/-/2/hi/europe/4349584.stm.

BBC Online News (22 March 2006) 'School Wins Muslim Dress Appeal'. Available at: http://news.bbc.co.uk/1/hi/education/4832072.stm.

BBC Online News (19 October 2006a) '"No Discrimination" in Veil Row'. Available at: http://news.bbc.co.uk/1/hi/england/bradford/6066726.stm.

BBC Online News (19 October 2006b) 'The Woman at Centre of Veil Case'. Available at: http://news.bbc.co.uk/1/hi/uk/6068408.stm.

BBC Online News (20 March 2007) 'Schools Allowed to Ban Face Veils'. Available at: http://news.bbc.co.uk/1/hi/6466221.stm.

BBC Online News (16 July 2008) 'French Minister Denounces Burka'. Available at: http://news.bbc.co.uk/1/hi/7509339.stm.

BBC Online News (16 September 2011) 'Paris Ban on Muslim Street Prayers Comes into Effect'. Available at: www.bbc.co.uk/news/world-europe-14945467.

Benhabib, S. (1989) 'On Contemporary Feminist Theory', *Dissent,* 36: 369.

Benhabib, S. (1992) *Situating the Self: Gender, Community and Postmodernism in Contemporary Ethics,* Cambridge: Polity Press.

Benhabib, S. (2002) *The Claims of Culture: Equality and Diversity in the Global Era,* Princeton, NJ: Princeton University Press.

Benhabib, S., Butler, J., Cornell, D. and Fraser, N. (1995) *Feminist Contentions: A Philosophical Exchange,* New York: Routledge.

Benjamin, J. (1988) *The Bonds of Love: Psychoanalysis, Feminism, and the Problem of Domination,* New York: Pantheon Books.

Bennhold, C. (19 July 2008) 'A Veil Closes France's Door to Citizenship', *New York Times.* Online. Available at: www.nytimes.com/2008/07/19/world/europe/19france.html.

Berg, R. (30 November 2011) 'Should Animals Be Stunned Before Slaughter?', BBC Online News. Available at: www.bbc.co.uk/news/magazine-14779271.

Berthou, K. (2005) 'The Issue of the Voile in the Workplace in France: Unveiling Discrimination', *International Journal of Comparative Labour Law and Industrial Relations,* 21: 281.

Bielefeldt, H. (1995) 'Muslim Voices in the Human Rights Debate', *Human Rights Quarterly,* 17: 587.

Blomfield, A. (30 July 2010) 'Israeli Rabbis Clamp Down on Burka', *Daily Telegraph.* Online. Available at: www.telegraph.co.uk/news/worldnews/middleeast/israel/7919501/Israeli-rabbis-clamp-down-on-burka.html.

Bouzar, D. and Kada, S. (2003) *L'une voilée, l'autre pas: Le témoinage de deux musulmanes françaises,* Paris: Albin Michel.

Bowen, J. (2006) *Why the French Don't Like Headscarves? Islam, the State, and the Public Space,* Princeton, NJ: Princeton University Press.

Boyarin, D. (1993) *Carnal Israel: Reading Sex in Talmudic Culture,* Berkeley, University of California Press.

Brown, N.J. and Lombardi, C.B. (2005) 'The Supreme Constitutional Court of Egypt on Islamic Law, Veiling and Civil Rights: An Annotated Translation of Supreme Constitutional Court of Egypt *Case No. 8 of Judicial Year 17* (May 18, 1996)', *American University International Law Review* 21: 43.

Brown, W. (1995) *States of Injury: Power and Freedom in Late Modernity,* Princeton, NJ: Princeton University Press.

Brown, W. (2003) 'Gender in Counterpoint', *Feminist Theory,* 4: 365.

Brown, W. (2005) *Edgework: Critical Essays on Knowledge and Politics,* Princeton, NJ: Princeton University Press.

Brown, W. (2006) *Regulating Aversion: Tolerance in the Age of Identity and Empire,* Princeton, NJ: Princeton University Press.

Brown, W. (2009) 'Introduction', in T. Asad, W. Brown, J. Butler and S. Mahmood, *Is Critique Secular? Blasphemy, Injury and Free Speech,* Berkeley, CA: University of California Press, p. 10.

Brown, W. and Halley, J. (2002) 'Introduction', in W. Brown and J. Halley (eds), *Left Legalism/Left Critique,* Durham, NC: Duke University Press, p. 1.

Browne, A. (13 October 2005) 'Dutch Unveil the Toughest Face in Europe with a Ban on the Burka', *Times.*

Bullock, K. (2007) *Rethinking Muslim Women and the Veil: Challenging Historical and Modern Stereotypes,* London: The International Institute of Islamic Thought.

Butler, J. (1990/1999) *Gender Trouble: Feminism and the Subversion of Identity,* New York: Routledge.

Butler, J. (1993) *Bodies that Matter: On the Discursive Limits of 'Sex',* New York: Routledge.

von Campenhausen, A.F. (2004) 'The German Headscarf Debate', *Brigham Young University Law Review*, 2: 665.
Chafiq, C. and Khosrokhavar, F. (1995) *Femmes sous le voile face à la loi islamique*, Paris: Editions du Félin.
Charlesworth, H. and Chinkin, C. (2000) *The Boundaries of International Law: A Feminist Analysis*, Manchester: Manchester University Press.
CNN Online News (9 February 2008) 'Turkey Moves to Lift Headscarf Ban' (no longer available online).
Conaghan, J. (2000) 'Reassessing the Feminist Theoretical Project in Law', *Journal of Law and Society*, 27: 351.
Cornell, D. (ed.) (2000) *Feminism and Pornography*, Oxford: Oxford University Press.
Cossman, B., Danielsen, D., Halley, J. and Higgins, T. (2003) 'Gender, Sexuality, and Power: Is Feminist Theory Enough?', *Columbia Journal of Gender and Law*, 12: 601.
Craig, R. (2012) 'The Religious Headscarf (Hijab) and Access to Employment under Norwegian Antidiscrimination Laws', in W.C. Durham and T. Lindholm (eds), *Islam in Europe: Emerging Legal Issues*, Leuven: Peeters.
Davies, G. (2005) 'Banning the *Jilbab*: Reflections on Restricting Religious Clothing in the Light of the Court of Appeal in *SB* v. *Denbigh High School*', *European Constitutional Law Review*, 1: 511.
Davies, G. (2006a) 'Thou Shalt Not Discriminate Against Women: Public Subsidies to Religious Parties Condemned in *Clara Wichmann Foundation* v. *The Dutch State*. Court of First Instance, The Hague. Judgment of 7 September 2005', *European Constitutional Law Review*, 2: 152.
Davies, G. (2006b) '(Not Yet) Taking Rights Seriously: The House of Lords in *Begum v. Headteacher and Governors of Denbigh High School*', *Human Rights and Human Welfare Online Working Paper*, No. 37. Available at: www.ssrn.com.
Davies, L. (2 February 2010) 'France Denies Citizenship to Moroccan Man Who Forces Wife to Wear Full Veil', *Guardian*. Online. Available at: www.guardian.co.uk/world/2010/feb/02/france-values-republic-veil-women.
Decker, D.C. and Lloydd, M. (2004) 'Case Comment – *Leyla Sahin* v. *Turkey*', *European Human Rights Law Review*, 6: 672.
Deeb, L. (2006) *An Enchanted Modern: Gender and Public Piety in Shi'i Lebanon*, Princeton, NJ: Princeton University Press.
Dimanche Ouest France (28 December 2003) 'Fadela resiste pour les filles des cités'.
Docherty, S. (2004) 'Legal Threat Over Headscarf Ban', *Sunday Times*, February.
Doi Abdul Rahman, I. (1989) *Woman in Shariah*, London: Ta-Ha Publishers.
Drakopoulou, M. (2000) 'The Ethic of Care, Female Subjectivity and Feminist Legal Scholarship', *Feminist Legal Studies*, 8: 199.
Duits, L. and van Zoonen, L. (2006) 'Headscarves and Porno-Chic: Disciplining Girls' Bodies in the European Multicultural Society', *European Journal of Women's Studies*, 13: 103.
Dworkin, A. and MacKinnon, C.A. (eds) (1994) *In Harm's Way: The Pornography Civil Rights Hearing*, Cambridge, MA: Harvard University Press.
Eberle, E.J. (2005) 'Religion and State in the Classroom: Germany and the United States', *Roger Williams University School of Law Faculty Papers*, Paper 4. Available at: http://lsr.nellco.org/rwu/rwufp/papers/4.
Edelman, O. (19 July 2009) 'Jerusalem Court Convicts "Taliban Mother" of Child

Abuse', *Haaretz*. Online. Available at: www.haaretz.com/news/jerusalem-court-convicts-taliban-mother-of-child-abuse-1.280248.

El Guindi, F. (1999) *Veil: Modesty, Privacy, and Resistance*, Oxford: Berg.

Evans, C. (2006) 'The "Islamic Scarf" in the European Court of Human Rights', *Melbourne Journal of International Law*, 7: 4.

Evans, C. (2008) 'Introduction', in P. Cane, C. Evans and Z. Robinson (eds), *Law and Religion in Theoretical and Historical Context*, Cambridge, Cambridge University Press, p. 1.

Evans, M.D. (2008) 'Freedom of Religion and the European Convention on Human Rights: Approaches, Trends and Tensions', in P. Cane, C. Evans and Z. Robinson (eds), *Law and Religion in Theoretical and Historical Context*, Cambridge: Cambridge University Press, p. 291.

Fassin, E. (2006) 'La démocratie sexuelle et le conflit des civilisations', *Multitudes*, 26: 123.

Favell, A. (2001) *Philosophies of Integration: Immigration and the Idea of Citizenship in France and Britain*, 2nd edition, Basingstoke: Palgrave.

Figaro (8 November 2003) 'Voile islamique: le sondage qui éclaire'.

Foucault, M. (2001) 'What Is Critique?', in D. Ingram (ed.), *The Political*, Oxford: Blackwell, p. 191.

Fourest, C. (2005) *La tentation obscurantiste*, Paris: Grasset.

Fredriksen, P. (2007) 'What "Parting of the Ways"? Jews, Gentiles, and the Ancient Mediterranean City', in A.H. Becker and Reed, A.Y. (eds), *The Ways That Never Parted: Jews and Christians in Late Antiquity and the Early Middle Ages*, Minneapolis: Fortress Press, p. 35.

Freedman, J. (2007) 'Women, Islam and Rights in Europe: Beyond a Universalist/Culturalist Dichotomy', *Review of International Studies*, 33: 29.

Freud, S. (1952) *Totem and Taboo*, New York: Norton.

Freud, S. (1961) *Civilization and Its Discontents*, New York: Norton.

Freud, S. (1975) *Group Psychology and the Analysis of the EGO*, New York: Norton.

Gallala, I. (2006) 'The Islamic Headscarf: An Example of Surmountable Conflict between *Sharî'a* and the Fundamental Principles of Europe', *European Law Journal*, 12: 593.

Garner, R. (23 November 2005) 'Imperial College Bans Students From Wearing Hoodies and Veils', *Independent*.

Gaspard, F. and Khosrokhavar, F. (1995) *Le Foulard et la République*, Paris: La Découverte.

Gerstenberg, O. (2005) 'Germany: Freedom of Conscience in Public Schools', *International Journal of Constitutional Law*, 3: 94.

Gies, L. (2006) 'What Not to Wear: Islamic Dress and School Uniforms. *R (on the application of SB) v. Governors of Denbigh High School* [2006] U.K.H.L. 15', *Feminist Legal Studies*, 14: 377.

Guénif-Souliamas, N. and Macé, E. (2004) *Les féministes et le garçon arabe*, Paris: Editions de l'Aube.

Gunn, T.J. (2005) 'Fearful Symbols: The Islamic Headscarf and the European Court of Human Rights'. Available at: www.strasbourgconsortium.org/document.php?DocumentID=3846.

Halley, J. (2006) *Split Decisions: How and Why to Take a Break from Feminism*, Princeton, NJ: Princeton University Press.

Hammoudi, A. (2006) *A Season in Mecca: Narrative of a Pilgrimage*, New York: Hill & Wang.
Hatem, M. (1994) 'Egyptian Discourses on Gender and Political Liberalization: Do Secularist and Islamist Views Really Differ?', *Middle East Journal*, 48: 661.
Häußler, U. (2001) 'Muslim Dress-Codes in German State Schools', *European Journal of Migration Law*, 3: 45.
Helsingin Sanomat (2010) 'Finnish-born Woman Wins ECHR Verdict over State of Italy in Cruxifix Dispute'. Online. Available at: www.hs.fi/english/print/1135250498097.
Hentsch, T. (1992) *Imagining the Middle East*, Montreal: Black Rose Books.
Herbert, I. (20 October 2006) 'Teaching Assistant "Victimised" for Wearing Veil, Tribunal Rules', *Independent*.
Hirschkind, C. and Mahmood, S. (2002) 'Feminism, the Taliban, and Politics of Counter-Insurgency', *Anthropological Quarterly*, 75: 339.
Hirschmann, N. (1998) 'Western Feminism, Eastern Veiling, and the Question of Agency', *Constellations*, 5: 345.
Ho, C. (2007) 'Muslim Women's New Defenders: Women's Rights, Nationalism and Islamophobia in Contemporary Australia', *Women's Studies International Forum*, 30: 290.
Hoodfar, H. (1993) 'The Veil in Their Minds and on Our Heads: The Persistence of Colonial Images of Muslim Women', *Resources for Feminist Research*, 22: 5.
Howard, E. (2011) *Law and the Wearing of Religious Symbols: European Bans on the Wearing of Religious Symbols in Education*, London: Routledge.
Huntington, S. (1996) *The Clash of Civilizations: And the Remaking of the World Order*, New York: Simon & Schuster.
Jeffay, N. (29 July 2010) 'Ban Jewish Burka, Say Israeli Rabbis', *Jewish Chronicle*. Online. Available at: www.thejc.com/node/36322.
Jefferson, T. (1784/1998) *Notes on the State of Virginia*, Harmondsworth: Penguin.
Johnston, J. (ed.) (1889) *Report of the Centenary Conference on Protestant Missions of the World Held in Exeter Hall, London (June 9–19th)*, 2 vols, New York: F.H. Revell, p. 1.
Joppke, C. (2009) *Veil: Mirror of Identity*, Cambridge: Polity.
Kabbani, R. (1986) *Europe's Myths of Orient: Devise and Rule*, Basingstoke: Macmillan.
Kandiyoti, D. (ed.) (1991) *Women, Islam, and the State*, Basingstoke: Macmillan.
Kandiyoti, D. (1998) 'Some Awkward Questions on Women and Modernity in Turkey', in L. Abu-Lughod (ed.), *Remaking Women: Feminism and Modernity in the Middle East*, Princeton, NJ: Princeton University Press, p. 270.
Kapur, R. (2002) 'Un-veiling Women's Rights in the "War on Terrorism"', *Duke Journal of Gender Law and Policy*, 9: 211.
Kapur, R. (2005) *Erotic Justice: Law and the New Politics of Postcolonialism*, London: Glasshouse.
Kennedy, D. (2002) 'The International Human Rights Movement: Part of the Problem?', *Harvard Human Rights Journal*, 15: 101.
Knights, S. (2005) 'Religious Symbols in the School: Freedom of Religion, Minorities and Education', *European Human Rights Law Review*, 5: 499.
Knop, K. (1999) 'Here and There: International Law in Domestic Courts', *New York University Journal of International Law and Politics*, 32: 511.
The Koran (1861), translated by J.M. Rodwell (2001), London: Phoenix.

Kumm, M. (2006) 'Democratic Constitutionalism Encounters International Law: Terms of Engagement', in S. Choudhry (ed.), *The Migration of Constitutional Ideals*, Cambridge: Cambridge University Press, p. 256.

Lazreg, M. (1994) *The Eloquence of Silence: Algerian Women in Question*, New York: Routledge.

Lewis, T. (2007) 'What Not to Wear: Religious Rights, the European Court, and the Margin of Appreciation', *International and Comparative Law Quarterly*, 56: 395.

Lévy, A. and Lévy, L. (2004) *Des filles comme les autres: Au-delà du foulard*, Paris: La Découverte.

Lim, D. (9 November 2004) 'The Day I Became a Martyr: Islam Protest Brings Fatal Fatwa', *Village Voice*. Available at: www.villagevoice.com/film/0446,lim,58473,20.html.

Lindholm, T. (2005) 'The Strasbourg Court Dealing with Turkey and the Human Right to Freedom of Religion and Belief: A Critical Assessment in the Light of Recent Case Law (*Leyla Sahin* v. *Turkey*, 29 June 2004)'. Available at: www.strasbourgconsortium.org/document.php?DocumentID=3848.

Lyon, D. and Spini, D. (2004) 'Unveiling the Headscarf Debate', *Feminist Legal Studies*, 12: 333.

MacKinnon, C.A. (1987) *Feminism Unmodified: Discourse on Life and Law*, Cambridge, MA: Harvard University Press.

MacKinnon, C.A. (1993) *Only Words*, Cambridge, MA: Harvard University Press.

Mahabir, C. (2004) 'Adjudicating Pluralism: The *Hijab*, Law and Social Change in Post-Colonial Trinidad', *Social & Legal Studies*, 13: 435.

Mahlmann, M. (2003) 'Religious Tolerance, Pluralist Society and the Neutrality of the State: The Federal Constitutional Court's Decision in the Headscarf Case', *German Law Journal: Review of Developments in German, European and International Jurisprudence*, 4: 1099. Available at: www.germanlawjournal.com/article.php?id=331.

Mahmood, S. (2001) 'Feminist Theory, Embodiment, and the Docile Agent: Some Reflections on the Egyptian Islamic Revival', *Cultural Anthropology*, 6: 202.

Mahmood, S. (2003) 'Questioning Liberalism, Too: A Response to "Islam and the Challenge of Democracy"', *Boston Review: A Political and Literary Forum*, April/May. Available at: http://bostonreview.net/BR28.2/mahmood.html.

Mahmood, S. (2005) *Politics of Piety: The Islamic Revival and the Feminist Subject*, Princeton, NJ: Princeton University Press.

Mahmood, S. (2006) 'Secularism, Hermeneutics, and Empire: The Politics of Islamic Reformation', *Public Culture*, 18: 323.

Mahmood, S. (2009) 'Religious Reason and Secular Affect: An Incommensurable Divide?', *Critical Inquiry*, 35: 836.

Mamdani, M. (2004) *Good Muslim, Bad Muslim: America, the Cold War, and the Roots of Terror*, New York: Pantheon Books.

Maris, C. (2007) '*Laïcité* in the Low Countries? On Headscarves in a Neutral State', *Jean Monnet Working Paper*, 14/07. Available at: www.jeanmonnetprogram.org/papers/07/071401.html.

Marrin, M. (22 October 2006) 'UK: How About Secular Schooling?', *Sunday Times*.

Marshall, J. (2006a) 'Feminist Jurisprudence: Keeping the Subject Alive', *Feminist Legal Studies*, 14: 27.

Marshall, J. (2006b) 'Freedom of Religious Expression and Gender Equality: *Sahin* v. *Turkey*', *Modern Law Review*, 69: 452.

Martin, R. (ed.) (2003) *Encyclopedia of Islam and the Muslim World*, New York: Macmillan.

McGoldrick, D. (2006) *Human Rights and Religion: The Islamic Headscarf Debate in Europe*, Oxford: Hart Publishing.

Menon, N. (2005) 'Between the Burqa and the Beauty Parlor? Globalization, Cultural Nationalism, and Feminist Politics', in A. Loomba, S.Kaul, M. Bunzil, A. Burton and J. Esty (eds), *Postcolonial Studies and Beyond*, Durham, NC: Duke University Press, p. 206.

Mernissi, F. (1991) *The Veil and the Male Elite: A Feminist Interpretation of Women's Rights in Islam*, New York: Perseus Books.

Minai, N. (1981) *Women in Islam: Tradition and Transition in the Middle East*, New York: Seaview Books.

Mir-Hosseini, Z. (1999) *Islam and Gender: The Religious Debate in Contemporary Iran*, Princeton, NJ: Princeton University Press.

Mirza, Q. (2000) 'Islamic Feminism and the Exemplary Past', in J. Richardson and R. Sandland (eds), *Feminist Perspectives on Law and Theory*, London: Cavendish Publishing, p. 187.

Mitchell, J. (1974) *Psychoanalysis and Feminism: A Radical Reassessment of Freudian Psychoanalysis*, Harmondsworth: Penguin Books.

Moghissi, H. (1999) *Feminism and Islamic Fundamentalism: The Limits of Postmodern Analysis*, London: Zed Books.

Mohanty, C.T. (1988) 'Under Western Eyes: Feminist Scholarship and Colonial Discourses', *Feminist Review*, 30: 61, reproduced in C.T. Mohanty (2003) *Feminism Without Borders: Decolonizing Theory, Practicing Solidarity*, Durham, NC: Duke University Press, p. 17.

Le Monde (22 September 2011) 'Premières condamnations pour port du voile intégral en France'. Online. Available at: www.lemonde.fr/societe/article/2011/09/22/premieres-condamnations-pour-port-du-voile-integral-en-france_1575819_3224.html.

Montesquieu, C. (1973) *Persian Letters*, Harmondsworth: Penguin Books.

Moran, M. (2004) 'Authority, Influence and Persuasion: *Baker*, Charter Values and the Puzzle of Method', in D. Dyzenhaus (ed.), *The Unity of Public Law*, Oxford: Hart Publishing, p. 389.

Moran, M. (2006) 'Inimical to Constitutional Values: Complex Migrations of Constitutional Rights', in S. Choudhry (ed.), *The Migration of Constitutional Ideals*, Cambridge: Cambridge University Press, p. 233.

Mosher, M.A. (1994) 'The Judgmental Gaze of European Women: Gender, Sexuality, and the Critique of Republican Rule', *Political Theory*, 22: 25.

Motha, S. (2007) 'Veiled Women and the *Affect* of Religion in Democracy', *Journal of Law and Society*, 34: 139.

Mufti, A. (2007) 'Fanatics in Europa', *Boundary 2*, 34: 17.

Munro, V.E. (2007) *Law and Politics at the Perimeter: Re-Evaluating Key Debates in Feminist Theory*, Oxford: Hart Publishing.

Najmabadi, A. (1993) 'Veiled Discourse – Unveiled Bodies', *Feminist Studies*, 19: 487.

Najmabadi, A. (1998) 'Crafting an Educated Housewife in Iran', in L. Abu-Lughod (ed.), *Remaking Women: Feminism and Modernity in the Middle East*, Princeton, NJ: Princeton University Press, p. 91.

Naudé, P.-F. (3 August 2008) 'Moi, Faiza, 32 ans, à qui l'on interdit de devenir française...', *Jeune Afrique.*

Nedelsky, J. (1989) 'Reconceiving Autonomy: Sources, Thoughts and Possibilities', *Yale Journal of Law and Feminism,* 1: 7.

Nietzsche, F. (1969) *On the Genealogy of Morals,* New York: Vintage.

Nussbaum, M.C. (1999) *Sex and Social Justice,* Oxford: Oxford University Press.

Okin, S.M. (1999) *Is Multiculturalism Bad for Women?,* Princeton, NJ: Princeton University Press.

Ong, A. (1990) 'State Versus Islam: Malay Families, Women's Bodies, and the Body Politic in Malaysia', *American Ethnologist,* 17: 258.

Ong, A. (2006) *Neoliberalism as Exception: Mutations in Citizenship and Sovereignty,* Durham, NC: Duke University Press.

Osborne, M.L. (1979) *Women in Western Thought,* New York: Random House.

Otto, D. (1996) 'Holding Up Half the Sky, But For Whose Benefit?: A Critical Analysis of the Fourth World Conference on Women', *Australian Feminist Law Journal,* 6: 7.

Parekh, B. (1997) 'A Varied Moral World: A Response to Susan Okin's "Is Multiculturalism Bad for Women?"', *Boston Review.* Available at: www.bostonreview.net/BR22.5/parekh.html.

Pimor, A. (2006) 'The Interpretation and Protection of Article 9 ECHR: Overview of the Denbigh High School (UK) Case', *Journal of Social Welfare & Family Law,* 28: 323.

Poole, T. (2005) 'Of Headscarves and Heresies: The *Denbigh High School* Case and Public Authority Decision Making under the Human Rights Act', *Public Law,* Winter: 685.

Poulter, S. (1997) 'Muslim Headscarves in School: Contrasting Legal Approaches in England and France', *Oxford Journal of Legal Studies,* 17: 43.

Pourzand, N. (1999) 'Female Education and Citizenship in Afghanistan: A Turbulent Relationship', in N. Yuval-Davis and P. Werbner (eds), *Women, Citizenship and Difference,* London: Zed Books.

Raday, F. (2003) 'Culture, Religion and Gender', *International Journal of Constitutional Law,* 1: 663.

Rajagopal, B. (2007) 'Introduction: Encountering Ambivalence', in M. Goodale and S.E. Merry (eds), *The Practice of Human Rights: Tracking Law between the Global and the Local,* Cambridge: Cambridge University Press, p. 273.

Ramazani, N. (1993) 'Women in Iran: The Revolutionary Ebb and Flow', *Middle East Journal,* 47: 409.

Razack, S.H. (2004) *Dark Threats and White Knights: The Somalia Affair, Peacekeeping, and the New Imperialism,* Toronto: University of Toronto Press.

Rennie, D. (30 August 2005) 'Woman Defies Law Banning the Burqa', *Telegraph.*

Riles, A. (2002) 'The Virtual Sociality of Rights: The Case of "Women's Rights Are Human Rights"', in M. Likosky (ed.), *Transnational Legal Process,* London: Butterworths, p. 420.

Riley, D. (2003) *'Am I That Name?' Feminism and the Category of Women in History,* 2nd edition, Minnesota, MN: University of Minnesota Press.

Sabbah, F. (1988) *Women in the Muslim Unconscious,* Oxford: Pergamon Press.

Sadiqi, F. (2006) 'The Impact of Islamization on Moroccan Feminisms', *Signs: Journal of Women in Culture and Society,* 32: 32.

Said, E.W. (1978) *Orientalism: Western Conceptions of the Orient*, Harmondsworth: Penguin.

Samuel, H. (15 September 2011) 'Praying in Paris Streets Outlawed', *Daily Telegraph*. Online. Available at: www.telegraph.co.uk/news/worldnews/europe/france/8766169/Praying-in-Paris-streets-outlawed.html.

Sandel, M.J. (1998) 'Religious Liberty: Freedom of Choice or Freedom of Conscience', in R. Bhargava (ed.), *Secularism and Its Critics*, New Delhi: Oxford University Press, p. 73.

Schiek, D. (2004) 'Just a Piece of Clothing? German Courts and Employees with Headscarves', *Industrial Law Journal*, 33: 68.

Schiek, D. (2007) 'Indirect Discrimination', in D. Schiek, L. Waddington and M. Bell (eds), *Cases, Materials and Text on National, Supranational and International Non-discrimination Law*, Oxford: Hart Publishing, p. 323.

Schwartz, S. (2001) *Imperialism and Jewish Society from 200 B.C.E. to 640 C.E.*, Princeton: Princeton University Press.

Scolnicov, A. (2005) 'A Dedicated Follower of (Religious) Fashion?', *Cambridge Law Journal*, 64: 527.

Scott, J.W. (2005) *Parité: Sexual Equality and the Crisis of French Universalism*, Chicago, IL: University of Chicago Press.

Scott, J.W. (2007) *The Politics of the Veil*, Princeton, NJ: Princeton University Press.

Seifert, A. (2003) 'Federal Labor Court Strengthens Religious Freedom at the Workplace', *German Law Journal*, 4(6): 559.

Seth Fogel, R. (2007) 'Headscarves in German Public Schools: Religious Minorities are Welcome in Germany, Unless – God Forbid – They are Religious', *New York Law School Law Review*, 51: 619.

Shaditalab, J. (2006) 'Islamization and Gender in Iran: Is the Glass Half Full or Half Empty?', *Signs: Journal of Women in Culture and Society*, 32: 14.

Shaikh, N. (20 March 2002) Interview with Lila Abu-Lughod (no longer available online).

Shakry, O. (1998) 'Schooled Mothers and Structured Pay: Child Rearing in Turn-of-the-Century Egypt', in L. Abu-Lughod (ed.), *Remaking Women: Feminism and Modernity in the Middle East*, Princeton, NJ: Princeton University Press, p. 126.

Shaviv, M. (18 April 2011) 'France's Ban, and Israel's Burka Problem', *Forward*. Online. Available at: www.forward.com/articles/137102.

Skach, C. (2006) 'Sahin v. Turkey. App. No. 44774/98; "Teacher Headscarf." Case no. 2BvR 1436/02', *American Journal of International Law*, 100: 186.

Skjeie, H. (2007) 'Headscarves in Schools: European Comparisons', in M.L.P. Loenen and J.E. Goldschmidt (eds), *Religious Pluralism and Human Rights in Europe: Where to Draw the Line?*, Antwerp-Oxford: Intersentia, p. 129.

Skjeie, H. (2009) 'Multiple Equality Claims in the Practice of the Norwegian Anti-Discrimination Agencies', in D. Schiek and V. Chege (eds), *European Union Non-discrimination Law: Comparative Perspectives on Multidimensional Equality Law*, London: Routledge, p. 295.

Smith, A.D. (1 February 2004) 'France Divided as Headscarf Ban is Set to Become Law', *Observer*.

Spelman, E.V. (1988) *Inessential Woman: Problems of Exclusion in Feminist Thought*, Boston, MA: Beacon Press.

Spiegel (31 March 2008) 'Moderate Islam Is a Contradiction: *Spiegel* Interview with Dutch Populist Geert Wilders'. Available at: www.spiegel.de/international/europe/0,1518,544347,00.html.

Spivak, G.C. (1985) 'Can the Subaltern Speak? Speculations on Widow-Sacrifice', *Wedge*, 7/8: 120.

Ssenyonjo, M. (2007) 'The Islamic Veil and Freedom of Religion, the Rights to Education and Work: a Survey of Recent International and National Cases', *Chinese Journal of International Law*, 6: 653.

Stokes, P. (20 October 2006) 'Teacher Who Refused to Remove Veil Wins £1,100 for Hurt Feelings', *Daily Telegraph*.

Straw, J. (2006) 'I Felt Uneasy Speaking To Someone I Couldn't See', originally published in *Lancashire Telegraph*. Available at: http://politics.guardian.co.uk/homeaffairs/story/0,,1889231,00.html.

Stychin, C.F. (2003) *Governing Sexuality: The Changing Politics of Citizenship and Law Reform*, Oxford: Hart Publishing.

Stychin, C.F. (2004) 'Same-Sex Sexualities and the Globalization of Human Rights Discourse', *McGill Law Journal*, 49: 951.

Sugden, J. (1 July 2004) 'Commentary: A Certain Lack of Empathy', *Zaman Daily Newspaper*. Available at: http://hrw.org/english/docs/2004/07/01/turkey8985.htm.

Sullivan, Z.T. (1998) 'Eluding the Feminist, Overthrowing the Modern? Transformations in Twentieth-Century Iran', in L. Abu-Lughod (ed.), *Remaking Women: Feminism and Modernity in the Middle East*, Princeton, NJ: Princeton University Press, p. 215

Sztokman, E. (7 April 2010) 'Why Jewish Women Are Wearing Burkas', *Forward*. Online. Available at: http://blogs.forward.com/sisterhood-blog/127114/.

Taher, A. (29 October 2006) 'Veil Teacher Was Obeying a Fatwa', *Sunday Times*. Available at: www.timesonline.co.uk/tol/news/uk/article616692.ece.

Tarlo, E. (2005) 'Reconsidering Stereotypes: Anthropological Reflections on the *Jilbab* Controversy', *Anthropology Today*, 21(6): 13.

Tarlo, E. (2010) *Visibly Muslim: Bodies of Faith*, Oxford: Berg.

Tohidi, N. (1994) 'Modernity, Islamization, and Women in Iran', in V. Moghadam (ed.), *Gender and National Identity: Women and Politics in Muslim Societies*, London: Zed Books.

Travis, A. (22 September 2005) 'Clarke Sets Up Commission to Overcome Barriers to Integration', *Guardian*.

Vakulenko, A. (2007) '"Islamic Headscarves" and the European Convention on Human Rights: An Intersectional Perspective', *Social & Legal Studies*, 16: 183.

Valenta, M.G. (2006) 'How to Recognize a Muslim When You See One: Western Secularism and the Politics of Conversion', in H. de Vries and L.E. Sullivan (eds), *Political Theologies: Public Religions in a Post-Secular World*, New York: Fordham University Press, p. 444.

Vance, C.S. (ed.) (1984) *Pleasure and Danger: Exploring Female Sexuality*, Boston: Routledge.

Weil, P. (25 March 2004) 'A Nation in Diversity: France, Muslims and the Headscarf', *Open Democracy*. Online. Available at: www.opendemocracy.net/faith-europe_islam/article_1811.jsp.

Werbner, P. (2007) 'Veiled Interventions in Pure Space: Honour, Shame and Embodied Struggles among Muslims in Britain and France', *Theory, Culture & Society*, 24: 161.

Werdmölder, H. (2007) 'Headscarves at Public Schools: The Issue of Open Neutrality Reconsidered', in M.L.P. Loenen and J.E. Goldschmidt (eds), *Religious Pluralism and Human Rights in Europe: Where to Draw the Line?*, Antwerp-Oxford: Intersentia, p. 155.

Wing, A.K. and Smith, M.N. (2006) 'Critical Race Feminism Lifts the Veil?: Muslim Women, France, and the Headscarf Ban', *University of California Davis Law Review*, 39: 743.

Wollstonecraft, M. (1996) 'Vindication of the Rights of Women', in A.K. Mellor and R.E. Matlak (eds), *British Literature: 1780–1830*, Fort Worth: Harcourt College.

Yuval-Davis, N. (1992) 'Fundamentalism, Multiculturalism and Women in Britain', in J. Donald and A. Rattansi (eds), *'Race', Culture and Difference*, London: Sage, p. 278.

Zia, H. (1997) 'Where Race and Gender Meet: Racism, Hate Crime and Pornography', in E. Disch (ed.), *Reconstructing Gender: A Multicultural Ontology*, Mountain View, CA: Mayfield, p. 504.

Reports and speeches

Bush, G.W. (29 January 2002) 'State of the Union Address' (no longer available online).

Bush, L. (2001) Radio address by Mrs Bush (no longer available online).

Debré, J.-L. (2003) *La laïcité à l'école: Un principe républican à réaffirmer*, Rapport n° 1275, 2 vols, Paris: Assemblée Nationale.

European Union Monitoring Centre on Racism and Xenophobia (EUMC) (now the European Agency for Fundamental Rights) (2006) 'Muslims in the European Union: Discrimination and Islamophobia', p. 41. Available at: http://fra.europa.eu/fraWebsite/attachments/Manifestations_EN.pdf.

The Governance of Britain (2007) Green Paper presented to Parliament by the Secretary of State for Justice and Lord Chancellor by command of Her Majesty, July. Available at: www.official-documents.gov.uk/document/cm71/7170/7170.pdf.

Home Office (2005) *Improving Opportunity, Strengthening Society*. Available at: http://resources.cohesioninstitute.org.uk/Publications/Documents/Document/DownloadDocumentsFile.aspx?recordId=83&file=PDFversion.

Human Rights Watch (27 February 2004) 'France: Headscarf Ban Violates Religious Freedom', 27 February. Available at: www.hrw.org/news/2004/02/26/france-headscarf-ban-violates-religious-freedom.

Human Rights Watch (24 June 2004) 'Memorandum to the Turkish Government on Human Rights Watch's Concerns with Regard to Academic Freedom in Higher Education, and Access to Higher Education for Women Who Wear the Headscarf', HRW Briefing Paper, 24 June, 26–32.

Human Rights Watch (16 November 2006) 'Turkey: Headscarf Ruling Denies Women Education and Career', 16 November, HRW New York. Available at: www.hrw.org/english/docs/2005/11/16/turkey12038_txt.htm.

Human Rights Watch (1999) 'Uzbekistan Class Dismissed: Discriminatory Expulsions of Muslim Students', October. Available at: www.hrw.org/reports/1999/uzbekistan/index.htm#42_754.

Human Rights Without Frontiers International (17 December 2003) 'A Ban on Religious Symbols Violate International Protections of Freedom of Religion'. Available at: www.hrwf.org.

Institut für europäisches Verfassungsrecht (IEVR), Arbeitsmaterialen zum Staatskirchenrecht: Kopftuchverbot für Lehrkräfte in Deutschland, available at: www.uni-trier.de/index.php?id=7524&L=0 (German) and www.uni-trier.de/index.php?id=7524&L=2 (English).

International Religious Liberty Association (IRLA) Board of Experts (2005) *Guiding Principles Regarding Student Rights to Wear or Display Religious Symbols*, Sigüenza, 15 November. Available at: http://irla.org/symbols.htm.

Islamic Human Rights Commission (IHRC) (19 October 2006) 'Press release: IHRC response to Aisha Azmi verdict'. Available at: www.ihrc.org.uk/show.php?id=2197.

Minority Rights Group (28 January 2004) 'French Ban on Faith Symbols Would Contravene International Human Rights Law'. Available at: http://groups.yahoo.com/group/balkanhr/message/6430.

Phillips, T. (22 September 2005) 'After 7/7: Sleepwalking to Segregation', speech at the Manchester Council for Community Relations. Available at: www.cre.gov.uk.

Sarkozy, N. (9 June 2005) 'Convention sur l'immigration – Une immigration choisie, une intégration réussie'. Available at: www.sarkozyblog.com/2005/immigration-une-immigration-choisie/.

Sauer, B. and Rosenberger, S. (2005) *VEIL – Values, Equality and Difference in Liberal Democracies: Debates about Muslim Headscarves in Europe*, Proposal, EU research arena 7.2.1.

Stasi, B. (2004) *Laïcité et République: Rapport de la commission de réflexion sur l'application du principe de laïcité dans la République remis au Président de la République le 11 décembre 2003*, Paris: La Documentation française.

United Nations (30 September 2005) 'Special Rapporteur on Freedom of Religion Ends Visit to France', Press Release. Available at www.un.org.

United Nations Committee on the Elimination of Racial Discrimination (18 April 2005) Concluding Observations: France, CERD/C/FRA/CO/16.

United Nations Committee on the Rights of the Child (30 June 2004) Concluding Observations: France, CRC/C/15/Add.240.

United Nations Economic and Social Council (1997) Report of the Economic and Social Council for 1997, A/52/3.18, September.

United Nations High Commissioner for Refugees Regional Office for the Baltic and Nordic Countries (3 February 2004) 'Nordic Headlines 3 February 2004' (no longer available online).

United Nations Human Rights Committee (4 August 1997) Concluding Observations on the French Report of 1997, UN Doc CCPR/C/79/Add 80.

Table of legislation and international instruments

United Nations

International Covenant on Civil and Political Rights, adopted and opened for signature, ratification and accession by General Assembly resolution 2200A (XXI) of 16 December 1966 17
Convention on the Elimination of All Forms of Discrimination Against Women, adopted and opened for signature, ratification and accession by General Assembly resolution 34/180 of 18 December 1979 110
Human Rights Committee, General Comment 22, The right to freedom of thought, conscience and religion (Article 18), 30 July 1993, UN Doc CCPR/C/21/Rev/1/Add.4 52
Human Rights Committee, General Comment 23, The Rights of Minorities, 8 April 1994, UN Doc CCPR/C/21/Rev/1/Add.5 17

Council of Europe

European Convention for the Protection of Human Rights and Fundamental Freedoms as amended by Protocol No 11, Rome, 4.XI. 1950, European Treaty Series – No 5 .... 12, 15–16, 92, 117, 126
Council of Europe Parliamentary Assembly Resolution on Women and Religion in Europe, Resolution 1464 (2005), 4 October 2005 82

European Union

Council Directive 2000/78 EC of 27 November 2000 establishing a general framework for equal treatment in employment and occupation, OJ L 303, 2.12.2000 at 16–22 31

United Kingdom

Race Relations Act 1976, Ch 74 .... 24, 31
School Standards and Framework Act 1998, Ch 31 25
Human Rights Act 1998, Ch 42 .... 25, 28, 124

Education Act 2002, Ch 32 25
Employment Equality (Religion and Belief) Regulations 2003, implementing EU Framework Directive 2000/78/EC of 27 November 2000, SI 2003/1660 . . . . . 31, 127
Equality Act 2006, Ch 3 . . . . . 24n5, 31
Equality Act 2010, Ch 15 . . . . . 24n5

France

La Constitution de la Cinquième République du 4 octobre 1958 . . . . . 16n1
Loi concernant la séparation des Eglises et de l'État du 9 décembre 1905, Journal Officiel de la République Française, 11 décembre 1905, 7205 16
Loi n° 2004–228 du 18 mars 2004 encadrant, en application du principe de laïcité, le port de signes ou de tenues manifestant une appartenance religieuse dans les écoles, collèges et lycées publics 18n2
Loi n° 2010–1192 du 11 octobre 2010 interdisant la dissimulation du visage dans l'espace public 21

Germany

Grundgesetz für die Bundesrepublik Deutschland vom 8. Mai 1949 . . . . . 33, 33n12
Gesetz zur Änderung des Schulgesetzes vom 01. April 2004, GBI. S.178, Nr 6 (Baden-Württemberg) 36n16, 120

The Netherlands

General Equal Treatment Act (Algemeen Wet Gelijke Behandeling) 1994 39

Norway

Gender Equality Act 1978/2003 41
Act relating to prohibition of discrimination on the basis of ethnicity, national origin, ancestry, skin colour, language, religious and ethical orientation (Discrimination Act) 2006 . . . . . 41n20

Turkey

Constitution of 7 November 1982 42
Dress Regulations Act of 3 December 1934, Law No 2596 . . . . . 43n23
Higher Education Act 1988/1990, Law No 2547 43

Uzbekistan

Law on the Freedom of Consciousness and Religious Organisations 1998 52

Table of cases

United Nations Human Rights Committee

Hertzberg and Others v. *Finland*, UN Doc CCPR/C/OP/1, views of 2 April 1982 . . . . 53n34
Hudoyberganova v. *Uzbekistan*, UN Doc CCPR/C/82/D/931/2000, views of 18 January 2005 51
TK v. *France*, Annual Report of the Human Rights Committee, UN Doc A/45/40, 118 17
Toonen v. *Australia*, UN Doc CCPR/C/50/D/488/1992, views of 4 April 1994 . . . . 53n34
SG v. *France*, Annual Report of the Human Rights Committee, UN Doc A/47/40, 346 17

United Nations Committee on the elimination of discrimination against women

AT v. *Hungary*, communication no. 2/03, views adopted on 26 January 2005 . . . . 54n37
Goekce v. *Austria*, communication no. 5/05, views adopted on 6 August 2007 . . . . 54n37
Kayhan v. *Turkey*, communication no. 8/05, CEDAW/C/34/D/8/2005 (2006) 53, 54, 78
Yildirim v. *Austria*, communication no. 6/05, views adopted on 6 August 2007 . . . . 54n37

European Court of Human Rights and European Commission on Human Rights

Abdulaziz, Cabales and Balkandali v. *United Kingdom* (1985) 7 EHRR 471 82
Ahmad v. *UK* (1982) 4 EHRR 126 . . . . 58, 127
Angelini v. *Sweden* (1986) 51 DR 41 . . . . 129n2
Arrowsmith v. *UK* (1983), application no. 7050/75, DR 19 . . . . 125, 127, 129n2

Association Ekin v. *France*, application no. 39288/98, judgment of 17 July 2001 131
Baspinar v. *Turkey*, application no. 45631/99, admissibility decision of 3 October 2002 48
The Belgian Linguistic Case (No 2) (1968) 1 EHRR 252 84
Bulut v. *Turkey*, application no. 18371/91, admissibility decision of 3 May 1993 . . . . . 43, 44n29
Campbell and Cosans v. *United Kingdom* (1982) 4 EHRR 293 129
Carmuirea Spirituala a Musulmanilor din Republica Moldova v. *Moldova*, application no. 12282/02, judgment of 14 June 2005 129
Çevik v. *Turkey*, application no. 39443/98, admissibility decision of 9 July 2002 48
Choudhury v. *UK* (1991), application no. 17349/90 . . . . . 23, 130
Church of Scientology Moscow v. *Russia*, application no. 18147/02, judgment of 5 April 2007 131
Dahlab v. *Switzerland* (2001) 2001-V 447 . . . . . 45, 48, 77, 83, 90, 113, 125
Dal and Özen v. *Turkey*, application no. 45378/99, admissibility decision of 3 October 2002 48
Dogru v. *France*, application no. 27058/05, judgment of 4 December 2008 . . . . . 50, 58, 115
Efstratiou v. *Greece* [1997] 24 EHRR 294 127
EK v. *Turkey*, application no. 28496/95, judgment of 7 February 2002 131
El Morsli v. *France*, application no. 15585/06, admissibility decision of 4 March 2008 . . . . . 49, 58
Freedom and Democratic Party v. *Turkey*, Reports of Judgments and Decisions 1999–VIII 131, 132
Goodwin v. *United Kingdom*, application no. 28957/95, judgment of 11 July 2002 . . . . . 48, 67
Gorzelik and Others v. *Poland*, application no. 44158/98, judgment of 20 December 2001 131
H v. *UK* (1993) 16 EHRR CD 44 . . . . . 129n2
Hasan and Chaush v. *Bulgaria* 2000-XI 117; (2002) 34 EHRR 55 129
Ilicak v. *Turkey*, application no. 15394/02, admissibility decision of 6 April 2004, judgment of 5 April 2007 49
Jewish Liturgical Association Cha'are Shalom ve Tsedek v. *France* (2000) 9 BHRC 27 . . . . . 30n9
Kalaç v. *Turkey* (1997) 27 EHRR 552 . . . . . 48, 58
Karaduman v. *Turkey* (1993) 74 DR 93 . . . . . 43, 58, 82, 113, 124
Keenan v. *United Kingdom* (2001) 33 EHRR 913 . . . . . 48, 67
Kervanci v. *France*, application no. 31645/04, judgment of 4 December 2008 . . . . . 50, 58, 115
Knudsen v. *Norway* (1985) 42 DR 247 . . . . . 129n2
Kokkinakis v. *Greece* 260 A (1993); (1994) 17 EHRR 397 . . . . . 126, 127, 129

Konttinen v. *Finland* (1996) 87-A DR 68 .... 30n9, 58
Kosteski v. *Macedonia*, application no. 55170/00, judgment of 13 April 2006.. 127
Lautsi v. *Italy*, application no. 30814/06, judgments of 9 November 2009 and 18 March 2011 .... 138, 139
McFeely v. *UK* (1986) 3 EHRR 293 129
Metropolitan Church of Bessarabia v. *Moldova*, 2001-XII, 35 EHRR 3 130
Moscow Branch of the Salvation Army v. *Russia*, application no. 72881/01, judgment of 5 October 2006 131
Otto-Preminger-Institut v. *Austria* (1994) ECHR 26 .... 23, 129, 130
Phull v. *France*, application no. 35753/03, decision of 11 January 2005 49
Pretty v. *United Kingdom*, application no. 2346/02, judgment of 29 April 2002 .... 48, 67
Refah Partisi (The Welfare Party) and Others v. *Turkey*, applications nos 41340/98, 41342/98, 41343/98 and 41344/98, Grand Chamber judgment of 13 February 2003; chamber judgment of 31 July 2001 131
Sidiropoulos and Others v. *Greece*, application no. 26695/95, judgment of 10 July 1998 131
Smith and Grady v. *UK* (1999) 29 EHRR 493......................... 128, 130
Socialist Party and Others v. *Turkey* (1999) 25 EHRR 51................. 131, 132
Stankov and the United Macedonian Organisation Ilinden v. *Bulgaria* (1998) 26 EHRR CD 10.. 131
Stedman v. *United Kingdom* (1997) 23 EHRR CD168 .... 30n9, 58, 127
Şahin v. *Turkey* (2007) 44 EHRR 5......... 38, 46, 64, 66, 67, 84, 114, 125, 126
Şen and Others v. *Turkey*, application no. 45824/99, admissibility decision of 8 July 2003 48
Tekin v. *Turkey*, application no. 41556/98, admissibility decision of 2 July 2002; judgment of 29 June 2004 .... 46n32, 125
Valsamis v. *Greece* 1996-VI 2312; (1997) 24 EHRR 294............... 30n9, 127
Van Schijndel, Van der Heyden and Leenman v. *Netherlands*, application no. 30936/96, admissibility decision of 20 May 1998...................... 127
Wingrove v. *UK* (1997) 24 EHRR 1 .... 23, 130

United Kingdom

Azmi v. *Headfield School and Kirklees Metropolitan Borough Council*, Employment Tribunal, case no. 1801450/2006, 6 October 2006........... 3 1
Azmi v. *Headfield School and Kirklees Metropolitan Borough Council*, Employment Appeals Tribunal, appeal no. UKEAT/0009/07/MAA, judgment of 30 March 2007. Available at: www.employmentappeals.gov.uk/Public/Upload/07_0009 resfhAMMAA.doc 32
Mandla v. *Dowell Lee* [1983] 2 AC 548 .... 24n6
R v. *Bow Street Magistrates' Court, ex parte Choudhury* [1991] 1 QB 429; [1991] 1 All ER 306.. 23

R (on the application of Begum (Shabina)) v. *The Headteacher and Governors of Denbigh High School* [2004] EWHC 1389 (Admin); [2004] Education Law Reports 274, QBD 25, 57, 89
R (SB) v. *Headteacher and Governors of Denbigh High School* [2005] EWCA Civ 199; [2005] Education Law Reports 198.......... 25, 57, 64, 89
R (on the application of Begum (by her litigation friend, Rahman)) (Respondent) v. *Headteacher and Governors of Denbigh High School (Appellants)* [2006] UKHL 15; [2007] 1 AC 100.......... 25–26, 28–30, 57–58, 64, 89
R (on the application of Sarika Angel Watkins-Singh (A child acting by Sanita Kumari Singh, Her Mother and Litigation Friend)) v. *The Governing Body of Aberdare Girls' High School* [2008] EWHC 1865 (Admin).......... 30
R (on the application of X (by her father and litigation friend)) v. *The Headteachers of Y School, The Governors of Y School* [2007] EWCH 298 (Admin).......... 29–30, 58, 63–65, 121–123

France

Opinion of the Conseil d'État no. 346.893, session of 27 November 1989 17
Decision of the Conseil d'État no. 130.394 of 2 November 1992.......... 17
Mme M, No. 286798, Conseil d'État, séance du 26 mai 2008, lecture du 27 juin 2008.......... 20–21

Germany

'Verkäuferin mit Kopftuch', BVerfG, I BvR 792/03, of 30 July 2003.......... 34
'Verkäuferin mit Kopftuch', BAG, 2 AZR 472/01, NJW 2003, 1685, of 10 October 2003 .... 34, 124
Ludin v. *Land Baden-Württemberg* ('Lehrerin mit Kopftuch'), 2 BvR 1436/02, of 24 September 2003.......... 34, 84, 90, 119
Ludin v. *Land Baden-Württemberg* ('Lehrerin mit Kopftuch'), BVerwG, 2 C 45.03, of 24 June 2004 .... 36, 43

The Netherlands

Clara Wichmann Foundation v. *The Dutch State*, Court of First Instance, The Hague, judgment of 7 September 2005 110
Commissie Gelijke Behandeling, Opinion 1996–109 39
Commissie Gelijke Behandeling, Opinion 1999–18 39
Commissie Gelijke Behandeling, Opinion 2003–40 39

United States of America

Reynolds v. *United States*, 98 US 145 (1878) (US Supreme Court) 126

Index

A-møbler 41
abaya 4
Abrahamic religious traditions 74, 135–6
Abu-Lughod, L. 68, 94, 97
Abu-Odeh, L. 67, 90, 93, 102
Afshar, H. 92, 93, 101
Ahmed, L. 93, 94, 96
Ahmed, S. 70, 97
Akrazadeh, S. 92
Al-Azmeh, A. 89
Alibhai-Brown, J. 65
alternative schooling, availability of 20, 29, 30, 58–9
Altschull, E. 85
Amara, Fadela 85–6
Amin, Qasim 97
An-Na'im, A.A. 135
anti-pornography campaign 109–10
Arnardóttir, O.M. 84
Asad, T. 11, 74–5, 135, 138–9
assimilation 21, 87, 88, 116–17
autonomy: problems with 69–73; protection of 66–7; research questions 6–7; veiling as lack of 56–64; veiling as positive choice 64–8; towards a different view of religious agency 73–8

Badinter, Elisabeth 85
Badiou, A. 98–100
Baer, S. 82
Balkin, J.M. 9
Barlow, R. 92
Basic Law, Germany 120
Begum, Shabina 25–9, 57–8, 64–5, 89–90, 121, 128
Belgian Linguistic case (1968) 84
Belgium, veiling restrictions 40
Benhabib, S. 66, 75, 106
Berg, R. 140
Berthou, K. 17
Bible 136–7, 139
Bielefeldt, H. 135
Blair, Tony 33, 123
blasphemy 23, 130
Bouzar, D. 19, 77
Bowen, J. 5
Boyarin, D. 136
Brown, N.J. 15
Brown W. 7, 8, 9, 10–11, 60, 69, 71, 72, 89, 98, 100, 106, 108, 133, 139
Bullock, K. 5, 95
burka (burqa) 4
Bush, Laura 100
Butler, J. 75–6, 109

Catholic Church 16, 22, 103, 118–19, 130, 137–8
celibacy 103
chador 4
Chafiq, C. 66
childcare 71
choice: degrees of 71–2; problems with 69–73; research questions 6–7; towards a different view of religious agency 73–8; veiling as lack of 56–64; veiling as positive choice 64–8
Christianity: privileging of 118–19, 120–1; and sexuality 103; as superior religion 136–40
Church of England 23, 121
citizenship, refusal of 21, 101
Civil Code, France 21
Civil Service Law, Baden-Würtemberg 35

coercion 18, 52, 60–4, 68, 104, 123
Collective of Muslims in France 18
colonial feminism 72, 97–8, 102–3, 107
colonial unveiling campaign 67, 96–7
Commission for Racial Equality, UK 23, 24
Commission on Integration and Cohesion, UK 23–4
Conaghan, J. 109
confrontational unreasonableness 57, 121–2
Conseil d'Etat, France 17, 20–1, 22–3, 49, 58, 62–3, 86–9, 116–17, 124
Constitution: France 17, 117, 124; Germany 33–4, 36, 119–20, 124; Switzerland 45; Turkey 42–3
Constitutional Court: Germany 90; Turkey 43, 131–2
Cornell, D. 110
Cossman, B. 106
Council of Europe 106; Resolution on Women and Religion in Europe 82
Council of the Muslim Faith (CFCM), France 18
counterpoint 7–8
Craig, R. 41
critical analysis 7–10
Cromer, Lord 96
cultural chauvinism 60, 71
cultural diversity 22, 28, 29, 59, 89
culture, subsumed by autonomy 69–70

Davies, G. 28, 110, 125
Declaration of the Rights of Man and Citizen (1789), France 17
Deeb, L. 15
democratic value of religion 129–32
democratic value of secularism 132
denominational neutrality 36, 45, 83, 113, 138; pretence of 133–4
Department for Education and Skills (DfES), UK 27–8
Docherty, S. 24
Doi Abdul Rahman, I. 103
domestic human rights law 11–12
domestic remedies, non-exhaustion of 44, 50, 55, 78
Drakopoulou, M. 106
Duits, L. 39
dupatta 4
Dworkin, A. 109, 110

Eberle, E.J. 33
Edah Haredit Beth Din 1–2, 56–7, 72–3
Education Act (2002), UK 25
education, denial of access to 19, 25–6, 46–7, 50, 52
Egypt, women's mosque movement 75, 109
El Guindi, F. 91, 97
emancipation, veiling as 67–8, 90–4
emancipatory model of agency 75–6
Employment Appeal Tribunal (EAT), UK 31–2, 60–1, 122–3
Employment Equality (Religion and Belief) Regulations (2003), UK 31, 122–3
'encumbered' personhood 74
Enlightenment 95, 100, 137–9
Equal Treatment Commission, Netherlands 38–40
Equality Act (2006), UK 31
Equality and Anti-Discrimination Ombud, Norway 41–2, 77, 101
European Commission on Human Rights (ECmHR) 16, 43–4, 58, 113, 115
European Convention of Human Rights (ECHR): Article 2 25, 46, 49, 50; Article 3 49; Article 8 46, 48, 49, 50, 67, 128, 130–1; Article 9 23, 26–7, 28, 29, 30, 43–4, 46, 47, 49–50, 52, 57, 58, 63, 82, 113, 114, 115, 124–9, 130–1, 138, 140, 141; Article 10 23, 45, 46, 130–1; Article 11 130–2; Article 14 23, 43, 46, 49, 83–4, 115; Article 26 44; Article 27 44; Article 35 44
European Council, Directive 2000/78/EC 31
European Court of Human Rights (ECtHR) 16, 19, 58, 77, 82–3, 113–16, 124–6, 128–9, 130–4, 138–9; veiling restrictions 42–51
Evans, C. 84, 130
Evans, M. 128, 131

false consciousness 2, 46, 49, 52, 60, 61, 66, 73, 75, 90, 105
family life, right to respect for 48, 49, 67
family pressure 61–3, 67, 71–2, 88, 101
Fassin, E. 86

Federal Administrative Court, Germany 36, 120–1
Federal Constitutional Court, Germany 34–5, 36, 62, 84, 119–21
Federal Court, Switzerland 45, 77, 113–14
Federal Labour Court, Germany 34, 124
fegh-e pouya (dynamic jurisprudence) 104
feminist foundationalism 106, 108, 109
festivities, clothes worn in context of 22, 118–19
Fitna (film) 38, 86, 119, 133–4, 136
Fortuyn, Pim 36
Foucault, M. 75
Fourest, C. 5, 20, 116
France, veiling restrictions 16–22
Fredriksen, P. 136
Freedman, J. 85
freedom of association 130–2
freedom of expression 46, 49, 52, 66–7, 130–1, 139
freedom of religion; limitations 'prescribed by law' 26–7, 30, 47, 52, 114, 128; right of 57–9; understandings of 126–32; veiling as legitimate exercise of 123–6
Freedom Party, Netherlands 40, 119
French Muslim Women in Action 19
Freud, S. 69, 70

Gallala, I. 66, 134
Gaspard, F. 66
Gender Equality Act (1978), Norway 41
gender equality: need for justification 105–11; problems with 95–105; research questions 6–7; teaching of 59; veiling as emancipation 90–4; veiling as subordination 81–90
gender mainstreaming 105–6
General Equal Treatment Act (1994), Netherlands 39
Germany, veiling restrictions 33–6
Gies, L. 59, 60
global norm diffusion 11–12
governance feminism 106, 107–8, 110
group sociology 69–70
Guénif-Souliamas, N. 86, 110

habituated learning 75
Hadith 4
Halimi, Gisèle 85
Halley, J. 8, 9, 106, 107, 108, 110
Hammoudi, A. 76
Hatem, M. 97
headscarf 4
Higher Education Act , Turkey 43
higher education restrictions: Turkey 43–4, 46–8; Uzbekistan 51–3
hijab 3–5
Hirschmann, N. 59–60
Hirsi Ali, Ayaan 37–8, 107, 119
Hizb ut-Tahrir 121
House of Lords, UK 28–9, 38, 57–9, 64–5, 121–2, 129
Howard, E. 5, 126
human rights 10–12
Human Rights Act (HRA) (1998), UK 25–7, 28, 124
Human Rights Watch (HRW) 43, 51
Huntington, S. 135

inconvenience for beliefs 28, 57–8, 128
individualism 17, 22, 66, 94, 118
international human rights bodies, reaction to French laws 19–20
international human rights law 11–12
International Network of Women from Turkey 61
International Religious Liberty Association (IRLA) 17
Islam: reinterpretation of 66, 73, 92–3, 134–5; as west's ideological enemy 135–40
Islamic Council of Norway 42
Islamic feminism 65–6, 81, 91–3, 101–3, 104, 111, 135
Islamic radicalism, veiling as 113–23
Islamic Revolution, Iran 92
Islamic veiling 2–5

Jefferson, Thomas 139
'Jewish Burka' 1–2, 56–7, 72–3
jilbäb 4
Johnston, J. 96
Joppke, C. 5, 105, 118, 120, 134
Judaism 1–2, 56–7, 72–3, 104; western acceptance of 135–7

Kabbani, R. 96
Kada, S. 19, 77
Kandiyoti, D. 68, 94
Kantianism 69, 138–9

Kapur, R. 70–1, 97
kara 30–1, 122
khimär (khumür) 4
Khosrokhavar, F. 66
Knop, K. 11
Koran 3–4, 103, 104, 135
Kumm, M. 11

laïcité 16, 17–18, 20, 21, 86, 115–19, 124
Law of 10 February 2004, France 18, 116
Law of 11 October 2010, France 21–2, 61, 118
Law of Separation (1905), France 16
Law on the Freedom of Consciousness and Religious Organisations (1998), Uzbekistan 52
Lazreg, M. 97
Lévy, A. & L. 19, 65, 76–7
Lewis, T. 125
Leyla ahin v. Turkey (2007) 38, 46–8, 53; autonomy and choice in 64, 66, 67; gender and equality in 83, 84–5, 107; religion and secularism in 114–15, 125, 126–7, 130–1, 132
Lijst Pim Fortuyn 36
literature 5
Lombardi, C.B. 15
Lyon, D. 65, 91

Macé, E. 86, 110
McGoldrick, D. 5, 16, 18, 19, 20, 23, 24, 27, 33, 40, 52, 126
McKinnon, C.A. 109, 110
Mahabir, C. 15
Mahlmann, M. 33
Mahmood, S. 73, 74, 75, 76, 77, 104, 109, 133, 134, 135, 137, 138, 139
mainstream feminism 60, 65, 98, 100, 105, 107
Mamdani, M. 70, 134, 135
Maris, C. 38, 61
Marshall, J. 9
Martin, R. 3
Marx, Karl 9
Maynard, M. 92, 93, 101
Menon, N. 72
Mernissi, F. 5, 93
Minai, N. 102
Mir-Hosseini, Z. 92, 105
Mirza, Q. 102, 104
Mme M. case (2008) 20–1, 62–3, 86–9, 98, 101, 107, 108, 116–18, 121, 124, 133–4
modernity, transition to 66, 73, 134–5
modesty 1–3, 25, 57, 73, 75–6
Moghissi, H. 68, 102, 103, 104, 105
Mohanty, C.T. 70, 71, 97
Montesquieu, C. 95
Moran, M. 11
Mosher, M.A. 95
Motha, S. 28, 59, 73
'mother and whore' binary 99–100
Mufti, A. 89
multiculturalism 22, 23, 25, 28, 29, 36, 37, 59, 65, 89, 100, 121, 134
Muslim Board of Uzbekistan 51
Muslim population: France 16; Germany 33; Netherlands 36; Norway 40; Turkey 43; UK 23–5

Najmabadi, A. 68, 94
Naudé, P.-F. 63
Nedelsky, J. 69
Netherlands, veiling restrictions 36–40
Ni Putes Ni Soumises (Neither Whores Nor Submissives) 19, 21, 85–6
Nietzsche, F. 10–11, 108
niqab (nikaab) 4
Norway, veiling restrictions 40–2
Nussbaum, M.C. 71–2

'objective understanding' 35, 119–20
Okin, S.M. 60, 65
One veiled, the other not (Bouzar/Kada) 18–19, 77
Ong, A. 15
Ordinary girls (Lévy/ Lévy) 19, 76–7
Orientalism 68, 95–6
Orthodox Christianity 103
Osborne, M.L. 95
Otto, D. 106

Parekh, B. 65
paternalism 59, 71, 85, 98
patriarchy 29, 60, 65–6, 67, 75, 80, 89, 90, 91, 100, 100–2
Paul, Saint 136–7
performativity of gender 75–6
Phillips, Trevor 23
Pimor, A. 126
political context, Netherlands 36–8
political defiance 65
political Islam 35, 102, 117, 120

Poole, T. 28
'portable seclusion' 67
positive choice, veiling as 64–8
postcolonial feminism 67–8, 71, 90, 95–6, 107
Poulter, S. 24
private life, right to respect for 46, 67, 128, 130–1
Protestant Reformation 137–8
public opinion: France 18–19; UK 23–4
public order 16, 18, 47, 49, 114, 125, 126, 128, 131–2
public safety 47, 52, 114, 115, 126
public space restrictions: France 21–2, 118–19; Netherlands 40

Qur'an 135

R v. The Headteacher and Governors of Denbigh High School (2005) 25–9, 30; autonomy and choice in 57–9, 63, 64–5, 66–7, 73–4; gender equality in 81–2, 89–90; religion and secularism in 121–2, 124, 128, 129
rabbinical court 1–2, 56–7, 72–3
Race Relations Act (1976), UK 24, 31
Raday, F. 29, 59, 60, 81, 82–3, 89
Rajagopal, B. 11
Razack, S.H. 70
refusal to comply with rules 51, 58, 116
religion: critical distance from 138–9; democratic value of 129–32; problems with secular views of 132–40
religious agency, towards a different view of 73–8
religious context: France 16; Germany 33–4; Netherlands 36; UK 23
religious manifestation 14, 18, 25–6, 27, 30, 35, 39, 47, 50, 52, 114, 124, 125, 126–7, 140
religious proselytism 16, 17, 18, 45, 114, 116, 127
rights and freedoms of others 26, 44, 45, 47, 52, 64, 113–15, 125, 126, 128, 140, 141
Riles, A. 106
Riley, D. 108
ritual 76
ritual slaughter, cruelty of 140
Rosenberger, S. 15
Roudinesco, Elisabeth 86
Rushdie, Salman 23

Sabbah, F. 103
Sadiqi, F. 92, 105
Said, E.W. 95–6
Salafism 117
Sandel, M.J. 74, 126
Sarkozy, Nicolas 22, 86, 118, 133–4
Sauer, B. 15
Schiek, D. 39
school restrictions: France 17–19; Netherlands 39; Norway 42; Turkey 50–1; UK 24–33
School Standards and Framework Act (1998), UK 25
Schwartz, S. 137
Scott, J.W. 20, 61, 62, 64, 66, 67, 76, 98, 99
secularism: democratic value of 132; problems with secular view of religion 132–40; research questions 6–7; veiling as Islamic radicalism 113–23; veiling as legitimate exercise of freedom of religion 123–6; understandings of freedom of religion 126–32
segregation 23, 37, 102
Seifert, A. 34
self-regulation 69, 70, 73, 74–5, 77
sexual accessibility 98–9
sexual harassment 67, 93, 102
sexuality 93–4, 103–4
Shaditalab, J. 92, 93, 104
Shaikh, N. 67, 68, 96
Shakry, O. 94
shalwar kameeze 25, 26, 57, 121, 128
shari'a 135
shayla 4
Skjeie, H. 15, 40–1, 42
slave morality 10–11, 108
Smith, M.N. 86
social recognition 66, 67
SOS Racisme 85
Spini, D. 65, 91
spiritual/material divide 137–8
Spivak, C.C. 70, 71, 97
Ssenyonjo, M. 5, 15, 17, 20, 24, 33, 126
Staatkundig Gereformeerde Partij (SGP) 110
Stasi Commission 17–18, 19, 61–2, 85, 97, 110, 116
Straw, Jack 31, 122

street prayers 22, 119
Stychin, C.F. 11
Submission (film) 37–8, 86, 107, 119, 133
subordination, veiling as 81–90
Sullivan, Z.T. 94
Sura 3–4, 103, 104
Switzerland, ECHR cases 45–6

Tablighi Jamaat 32, 60–1, 123
Tarlo, E. 5, 9
terrorism 14, 32, 37, 38, 40, 61, 100–1, 123
Turkey, ECHR cases 42–5, 46–9, 53–5

UK, veiling restrictions 22–33
Union of the Islamic Organisations of France (UOIF) 18
United Nations: Committee on the Elimination of Racial Discrimination (CERD) 19–20; Committee on the Rights of the Child (CRC) 19; Convention on the Elimination of All Forms of Discrimination Against Women (CEDAW) 53–5, 110; Fourth World Conference on Women (1995) 105–6; Human Rights Committee 17, 128; International Covenant on Civil and Political Rights (ICCPR) 17, 51–3; Special Rapporteur on Freedom of Religion 20, 61; veiling restrictions 51–5
'untimely' critique problem 9–10
US, Antipornography Civil Rights Ordinance 110
Uzbekistan, UN cases 51–3

Valenta, M.G. 96, 134
van Gogh, Theo 37, 38, 40, 119
van Zoonen, L. 39
Vance, C.S. 110
veiled sexuality 93–4
veiling restrictions: European Court of Human Rights 42–51; France 16–22; Germany 33–6; Netherlands 36–40; Norway 40–2; UK 22–33; United Nations 51–5
veiling types 4–5
Verkäuferin mit Kopfluch case (2003) 124
visas, refusal of 49–50, 58

Watkins-Singh (2008) 30–1, 122
Werbner, P. 66
Werdmölder, H. 39
western dress codes, compared to Islamic 71–2
western feminism 13, 66–7, 91–2, 93–4, 97–8, 101–2
western understandings of secularism 132–40
Wilders, Geert 38, 40, 119, 136
willing self 76–8
Wing, A.K. 86
Wollstonecraft, Mary 95
women's mosque movement, Egypt 75, 109
Woolas, Phil 32, 123
workplace restrictions: Germany 34–6; Netherlands 39–40; Norway 40–2; Switzerland 45–6; Turkey 53–5; UK 31–3

For Product Safety Concerns and Information please contact our EU representative GPSR@taylorandfrancis.com Taylor & Francis Verlag GmbH, Kaufingerstraße 24, 80331 München, Germany

Batch number: 10725973

Printed by Printforce, the Netherlands